"Ari Kohen's book is a beautiful example of cutting-edge contemporary political theory. Kohen explores heroism as a procedurally determined category of concepts for personal identification that emerges as a timeless and universal social fact. He persuasively argues for a richer understanding of Socrates as the common man's hero par excellence and for Plato as the principle educator of the Greeks. *Untangling Heroism* links contemporary examples (Kerry, McCain, Korczak, and Munyeshyaka) to classical heroic archetypes in a way that celebrates both their heroic acts and their humanity. This book succeeds superbly as a work in cross-temporal political philosophy by illuminating not what heroism is and has been, but what a hero does and why."

—Robert L. Oprisko, *Butler University*

"Professor Kohen's exploration of heroism, its meaning and purpose, effectively reconsiders those virtues requisite to the heroic life. By looking at heroism first within the conceptual framework of the ancient Greeks and then moving the discussion forward into more recent cases and situations, the author has successfully provided a relevant, working framework for further explorations of the enduring qualities of heroism. This book will help to reinvigorate our discussion of heroism and what heroic acts mean to us and provide for us, and what kind of commitment is still needed for our own heroes to emerge in our time."

—Scott Hammond, *James Madison University*

Untangling Heroism

The idea of heroism has become thoroughly muddled today. In contemporary society, any behavior that seems distinctly difficult or unusually impressive is classified as heroic: everyone from firefighters to foster fathers to freedom fighters are our heroes. But what motivates these people to act heroically and what prevents other people from being heroes? In our culture today, what makes one sort of hero appear more heroic than another sort?

In order to answer these questions, Ari Kohen turns to classical conceptions of the hero to explain the confusion and to highlight the ways in which distinct heroic categories can be useful at different times. *Untangling Heroism* argues for the existence of three categories of heroism that can be traced back to the earliest Western literature—the epic poetry of Homer and the dialogues of Plato—and that are complex enough to resonate with us and assist us in thinking about heroism today. Kohen carefully examines the Homeric heroes Achilles and Odysseus and Plato's Socrates, and then compares the three to each other. He makes clear how and why it is that the other-regarding hero, Socrates, supplanted the battlefield hero, Achilles, and the suffering hero, Odysseus. Finally, he explores in detail four cases of contemporary heroism that highlight Plato's success.

Kohen states that in a post-Socratic world, we have chosen to place a premium on heroes who make other-regarding choices over self-interested ones. He argues that when humans face the fact of their mortality, they are able to think most clearly about the sort of life they want to have lived, and only in doing that does heroic action become a possibility. Kohen's careful analysis and rethinking of the heroism concept will be relevant to scholars across the disciplines of political science, philosophy, literature, and classics.

Ari Kohen is the Schlesinger Associate Professor of Political Science and Director of the Forsythe Family Program on Human Rights and Humanitarian Affairs at the University of Nebraska–Lincoln. His first book, *In Defense of Human Rights*, was published by Routledge in 2007.

Routledge Innovations in Political Theory

For a full list of titles in this series, please visit www.routledge.com

Untangling Heroism

Classical Philosophy and the
Concept of the Hero

Ari Kohen

NEW YORK AND LONDON

First published 2014
by Routledge
711 Third Avenue, New York, NY 10017

Simultaneously published in the UK
by Routledge
2 Park Square, Milton Park, Abingdon, Oxfordshire OX14 4RN

First issued in paperback 2015

*Routledge is an imprint of the Taylor & Francis Group,
an informa business*

Library of Congress Cataloging-in-Publication Data

Kohen, Ariel, 1977–
Untangling heroism : classical philosophy and the concept of the hero / Ari
Kohen.
    pages cm. — (Routledge innovations in political theory)
1. Heroes.   2. Heroes—Political aspects.   3. Philosophy, Ancient.
I. Title.
BJ1533.H47K65 2013
302.5′4—dc23
2013019874

ISBN 13: 978-1-138-94472-5 (pbk)
ISBN 13: 978-0-415-71899-8 (hbk)

Typeset in Sabon
by Apex CoVantage, LLC

For Sara, Judah, and Talia:
Thanks to you I understand why Odysseus
risked everything to get back home.

Contents

Acknowledgments

This book began during a meeting with Peter Euben, my dissertation advisor, who casually mentioned that the conversation between Achilles and Priam at the end of the *Iliad* might be a good example of Richard Rorty's offhand comment that personal identification with those who are suffering is the likeliest explanation for helping behavior. At the time, having just finished a book on human rights, it seemed clear to me that risking one's life for others was both heroic and very much related to the idea of human rights, but I had no idea that one comment would lead me quite so far down the rabbit hole of heroism.

In the time since that comment, I've amassed a wonderful group of friends and colleagues to whom thanks is owed. In one way or another they have all participated in the generation of this book, either by engaging me on the ideas or providing support and encouragement about the project. Thank you to Shira and Steven Abraham, Melinda Adams, Richard Avramenko, Chris Blake, Jean and David Cahan, Miguel Centellas, Liz and Dave Ciavarella, Michael Combs, Andrew Cohen, Lane Crothers, Phil Demske, Gerry DiGiusto, Anel Du Plessis, Mike Ensley, Dan Eschtruth, PJ and Jordan Feinstein, Becca and David Finkelstein, Dave Forsythe, Ted Goodman, Dana Griffin, John Gruhl, Scott Hammond, John Hibbing, Courtney Hillebrecht, Drew Jacob, Seth Jolly, Alice Kang, Heather and Mark Kelln, Elizabeth Kiss, Jonathan Knoll, Matt Langdon, Dave LaRoy, Howard Lubert, Patrice McMahon, Sarah Michaels, Megan Mikolajczyk, Ross Miller, Dona-Gene Mitchell, Mark Moon, Robert Oprisko, Jon Pedersen, Marcus Sanborn, Michael Schechter, John Scherpereel, Tom Scotto, Kevin Smith, Gerald Steinacher, Kerstin Steiner, Michael Strausz, Drew Taub, Beth Theiss-Morse, Michael Tofias, Michael Wagner, Alice Pinheiro Walla, Sergio Wals, Margie Williams, Anicee Van Engeland, and Dick Zinman. A special word of gratitude is owed to Bill Curtis and Dennis Rasmussen for reading drafts of each chapter and offering a great many helpful suggestions.

Thank you also to my graduate and undergraduate students, especially those undergraduates in my "Justice and the Good Life" course at the University of Nebraska; their thoughtful discussions of Homer and Plato have encouraged me in my belief that these ancient texts have a great deal to say to a contemporary audience and have helped me to clarify my thinking about heroism. Thank you, in particular, to Adam Azzam, Cassi Baumgardner, Jacob Colling, Joe Destache, Marty Nader, and Robie Sprouse for extremely helpful research assistance, and to the Department of Political Science and the University of Nebraska's Undergraduate Creative Activities and Research Experiences program that funded their work.

I began writing this book while on a three-month research fellowship at the Wissenschaftszentrum Berlin für Sozialforschung, for which I owe a debt of gratitude to the Irmgard Coninx Stiftung and, specifically, to Sabine and Ingo Richter, Sabine Berking, Ralf Müller-Schmid, and Leo von Carlowitz.

One chapter of this book previously appeared in slightly different form in *Polis* (vol. 28, no. 1: 45–73). Thank you to the anonymous reviewers for their helpful comments and to the editor, Kyriakos Demetriou, for his assistance, comments, and permission to reprint the article here with changes. My editors at Routledge, Natalja Mortensen and Darcy Bullock, deserve special thanks for taking on this project and for answering my steady stream of questions; thanks also to the anonymous reviewers who read the manuscript, offered constructive criticism, and suggested that it ought to be published.

Finally, special thanks to my sister and brother-in-law, Ilana and Zachary Liss; my sister-in-law, Ann Lunsford; my mother- and father-in-law, Lyn and Jon Lunsford; my grandparents, Frances and Leonard Fink and Sheri and Zoli Kohen; and my parents, Belle and Jerry Kohen, for their unwavering love, good counsel, and encouragement. And, of course, my amazing wife and children, to whom this book is dedicated. I wouldn't have written this book and I certainly wouldn't be the person I am without all of you.

1 Introduction
The Tangled Web of Heroism

The heroic ideal pervades popular culture in the United States. While other countries undoubtedly celebrate their heroes—think, for example, of Latin American revolutionary heroes like Bolívar or even Che—no one does it quite like the United States. Whether we are talking about the citizen-soldier, the Wild West lawman, or even the comic book superhero, Americans are either consciously or unconsciously the greatest lovers of the greatest number and variety of heroes. The superhero genre, for example, has generated billions of dollars in comic book revenue alone, without even considering the impact of the myriad television shows and films based on the same characters. Americans are partial to stories about outsized personalities—no matter if they rely on radioactive spiders or focus on a masked vigilante— and they reward their storytellers handsomely. But the attention paid to heroes is not limited to the superhuman in fiction and film; indeed, throughout the country's history, Americans have rewarded the real-life, everyday heroes who emerge from their midst by honoring them at gala events or with medals, writing books and articles about their deeds, and plastering their photos everywhere.

At the heart of this reverence for the heroic man or woman is almost certainly the egalitarian and populist sentiment that defines the American democratic experiment for the vast majority of Americans. As Alexis de Tocqueville (2002: ch. 3, pt. 1) noted in *Democracy in America*, "There is in fact a manly and legitimate passion for equality that spurs all men to wish to be strong and esteemed. This passion tends to elevate the lesser to the rank of the greater." While this might initially seem contradictory or at least confusing, the explanation is quite straightforward: Americans consider their ordinariness a virtue, especially when it comes to self-government, but because they recognize the ways in which they are very much alike, they are also drawn to anyone who falls outside the normal parameters.

The American fascination with the heroic often raises the status of an otherwise average citizen to that of a celebrity, at least for a bounded period of time. Consider the recent examples of Wesley Autrey and Chesley Sullenberger, whose respective actions in 2007 and 2009 saved lives and earned them well-deserved plaudits from their fellow citizens, the media, and even

Presidents Bush and Obama.[1] With the passage of time, their names are most likely no longer as immediately recognizable to as wide an audience as was once the case, and the fame that still attends them will likely continue to diminish. After all, the amount of time and attention paid to these heroes is far surpassed by that given to entertainers like Britney Spears and Michael Jackson—or to someone like Kim Kardashian, who seems to be famous for no particular reason at all. But it is also important to note that Americans' fascination with everyday heroes is seldom prurient in the way it often is with other celebrities; it is not at all the case that Americans want their heroes to fail in the way that they seem to relish when it happens to singers, models, actors, or athletes. In a certain sense, these heroes are rewarded with a small measure of fame but are then allowed to fade back into the broader American tableau before anything untoward might be revealed about them (if any such thing, in fact, exists). For the time that they capture our attention, their ordinariness is what shines through for us; they encourage us to think about what we might have done in a similar situation—and to hope that we would be able to take the heroic course that they took.

Of course, this distinctly American fascination with heroism is not free from problems. While we are happy to separate our heroes from our celebrities, and to assign a different sort of fame to them, we have some difficulty separating one sort of hero from another, and this leads to confusion about what to expect from our heroes. Perhaps the best way to think about this problem is to reflect very briefly on contemporary American politics and, in particular, claims about heroism that arose in two recent presidential elections. The first was an effort to discredit the heroic record of Senator John Kerry—a Vietnam veteran who received a Bronze Star, a Silver Star, and three Purple Hearts—during his 2004 campaign against President George W. Bush. While there have always been people who took a negative view of the fact that Kerry became an outspoken critic of America's entanglement in Vietnam after he returned home, at the heart of these recent attacks were the so-called Swift Boat Veterans for Truth, who alleged that Kerry's actions were not really so heroic and that his wounds were not at all serious. A great deal of the effort seemed to be aimed at leveling out Kerry's military record with that of Bush, who was a member of the Texas Air National Guard while Kerry was serving overseas (cf. Ignatius 2004).

Such leveling, however, proves quite difficult once the service records of Kerry and Bush are examined side by side. In the heat of combat and at risk of grave personal harm, Kerry performed his task with admirable skill; neither his opposition to the war nor his ability to avoid more serious injury should be thought of as somehow detracting from his battlefield heroics. As Jacob Weisberg points out, in a dialogue with William Saletan (2004), the attack ad against Kerry

"planted doubts in the minds of 27 percent of independent voters who planned to vote for Kerry or leaned pro-Kerry. After seeing it, they were no longer sure they'd back him, the study found." The reason the ad really might be so effective, despite its fraudulence, is that it undermines the heroic part of Kerry's biography, which forms the basis of a big, positive personal contrast with Bush, while at the same time bolstering the GOP theme that Kerry is "untrustworthy."

At bottom, Kerry should be considered a war hero, based solely on his actions on the battlefield;[2] his public stance in opposition to the war does not change the fact of his heroism. By contrast, Bush did nothing that can be considered comparable during his time as a member of the Texas Air National Guard; indeed, many have argued that he joined the Guard to avoid far more dangerous service overseas and that he did not even fulfill his minimal obligations to the Guard (cf. Robinson 2004). Their service records could not be any more different, but voters were encouraged to think of them as similar and many did—in no small part because of a general lack of clarity about what it means to be a war hero.

Even more to the point about Americans' confusion when it comes to heroic behavior is the second example, the wide-ranging discussion of the war record of Senator John McCain—also a Vietnam veteran—throughout his 2008 campaign against a series of challengers for the Republican nomination and, eventually, against then-Senator Barack Obama. The prevailing sentiment among the electorate was that John McCain was a war hero, but the truth of the matter is that he was a very different sort of hero from John Kerry. Whereas Kerry's heroic stature is derived from actions he undertook in the midst of battle, McCain's heroism arose as a result of his imprisonment in Hanoi. To put a finer point on it, McCain was not particularly successful as a warrior: though he was injured in the line of duty, like Kerry, he did not successfully complete his mission as Kerry did. Instead, his plane was shot down, and he was captured and tortured, suffering a great deal at the hands of his Vietnamese captors over several years. Rather than accomplishing particularly impressive deeds on the battlefield, McCain's heroism is that of a survivor, one who has the ability to endure terribly difficult conditions or challenges.[3]

Interestingly, McCain's image has been tarnished a great deal in the years that followed his twice-unsuccessful presidential campaigns, in large part because of mistaken assumptions about his heroism. A recent article in *Vanity Fair*, for example, makes the argument that he stands for no principle in particular but simply shifts with the prevailing political winds. Implicit in this argument is that there is nothing heroic about the way that McCain has always conducted himself:

It's quite possible that nothing at all has changed about John McCain, a ruthless and self-centered survivor who endured five and a half years in captivity in North Vietnam, and who once told Torie Clarke that his favorite animal was the rat, because it is cunning and eats well. It's possible to see McCain's entire career as the story of a man who has lived in the moment, who has never stood for any overriding philosophy in any consistent way, and who has been willing to do all that it takes to get whatever it is he wants. (Purdum 2010)

But why is it problematic that someone should be "willing to do all that it takes to get whatever it is he wants"? What exactly is the problem with being "self-centered," especially if that quality contributed directly to McCain's survival? And why *not* choose the rat as one's favorite animal— what's wrong with being cunning and eating well? These are precisely the attributes that allowed McCain to accomplish his heroic feats of endurance in Vietnam. What's more, it is a mistake to assume that McCain's endurance would somehow *not* be connected to the way he conducts himself even now. That is not to say that we ought not to criticize John McCain, the politician, because he is related to John McCain, the hero who suffered and survived. It is, instead, to say that we ought to realize that those things that allowed for his heroism might not make him the noblest politician in all of our eyes. We ought not to be surprised—or to assume that it would somehow be an obvious critique—that McCain continues to privilege the experience of the rat, who endures whatever life throws at him and who attempts to take care of himself at any cost.

Both of these examples ultimately highlight a problem for Americans' views of heroism: the traditional heroic categories have become muddled, resulting in the diminution of one sort of hero when judged by the standards of another, very different sort of hero. No one ought to confuse the actions of John Kerry with those of George W. Bush, just as no one ought to expect Kerry or McCain to behave like Nelson Mandela, who "reached out to his former enemies and did whatever he could to assure them that they would suffer no evil at his hands" (Govier 2002: 71). Of course, to argue that traditional categories have become confused, it will be necessary to present a detailed case regarding those categories. In what follows, then, I will make an argument for three distinct categories of heroism that can be traced back to the earliest Western literature—the epic poetry of Homer and the dialogues of Plato—and that are complex enough to resonate with us and to assist us in thinking about heroism today.

In making the case for the relevance of classical categories of heroic behavior, this book proceeds under the assumption that not all heroes are created equal. Though obvious to the Greeks both of Homer's day and Plato's, this might be something of a surprising statement today. In contemporary society, all behavior that is seen as distinctly difficult or unusually impressive is classified as heroic: everyone from firefighters to foster fathers and from quadriplegics to freedom fighters are our heroes. But what motivates these people to act heroically and what prevents other people from being heroes? And, in our culture today, what makes one sort of hero appear more heroic than another sort? In order to begin answering these questions, we must untangle one kind of heroic behavior from another, examine the motivations of the particular heroes, and compare some very different heroic behaviors and motivations.

In chapter 2, "Heroism in Homer's *Iliad*: Violence, Mortality, and Difficult Choices," I explore the first of three classical archetypes, that of the Homeric battlefield hero. Central to that exploration is a detailed look at the connection between an appreciation of the necessity of death and the decision to take heroic action. While it might seem counterintuitive that recognizing one's mortality could lead to actions that result more immediately in death, I argue that it is only in recognizing the limits of our existence that we can open up a space for heroic behavior. The most striking classical example, of course, is the character of Achilles in Homer's *Iliad*, as Achilles' understanding of the limits of his existence leads to the question of the kind of life he will choose to live. In the end, Achilles chooses *kléos* [κλέος], the glory of heroic deeds, despite the recognition that doing so will lead to his untimely death. That said, it is important to think carefully about the fact that many of Achilles' heroic deeds—including the most famous, his victory over Hector—would likely be considered infamous today: both his desire for vengeance and the violence that he exhibits in attaining it are overwhelming. But this is not the end of the story, for Achilles experiences a noteworthy rehabilitation later in the *Iliad*. This shift away from being simply a murderous warrior is most apparent when he meets with Priam to negotiate the return of Hector's body. In particular, I consider here the role played by Achilles' reintegration into the community of human beings like himself, and I argue that his ultimate acceptance of the norms of his day is of fundamental importance to the enduring glory that he achieves through the poets' chronicling his great deeds.[4] Finally, in comparing Achilles with Coriolanus, one of the most infamous warriors of Rome's republican era, I demonstrate the priority of embracing societal norms to the classical understanding of battlefield heroism. Achilles, the battlefield hero *par excellence*, experiences a transformation that Coriolanus does not, and this allows for his extremely brutal deeds—which hearken back to an earlier, more violent age—to be seen in a more positive light.

Chapter 3, "The Polytropic Hero: Suffering, Endurance, and Homecoming in Homer's *Odyssey*," is built around the unusual epithet by which Homer refers to Odysseus—*polytropos* [πολύτροπος]—and I argue that it provides insight into the distinct type of heroism that Odysseus embodies. By introducing Odysseus as a "man of many ways," Homer (1999: I.1) identifies him as one who is well known and lauded for possessing some classically heroic trait even though it is never clear that he embodies that trait. Thus, Odysseus is often referred to as a "master mariner" and a "great tactician," but nothing that he does in the *Odyssey* suggests that he is particularly deserving of these epithets. Indeed, the *Odyssey* is a story about his inability to sail home, and, during the course of his difficult journey, every single member of his crew dies a distinctly unpleasant death: either eaten by monsters, crushed by giants, or drowned by the gods. Further, the best examples of his tactical brilliance—his blinding of Polyphemos and his elaborate vengeance against Penelope's suitors—allow him to succeed against his enemies when they are largely defenseless, just as his most famous gambit—the wooden horse—allowed the Achaeans to defeat the Trojans while their defenses were down. While Odysseus might very well be both a master mariner and a great tactician, the *Odyssey* is not about celebrating those particular attributes; they are not the principal reasons that he is a Homeric hero. What's more, Odysseus is portrayed as the hero who prizes *nostos* [νόστος; homecoming] above all else, including the classically celebrated *kléos*. But this is another way in which being *polytropos* serves Odysseus well, as he is actually driven to achieve *nostos* at least in part *because* he values *kléos*. In this way, being *polytropos* allows Odysseus to seem like Achilles—a doer of great deeds—even though the *kléos* he ultimately achieves *actually* centers around his ability to endure a great deal more suffering than others in order to accomplish his *nostos* rather than some set of great deeds that he accomplishes.

In chapter 4, "Plato's Philosophic Vision: The Difficult Choices of the Socratic Life," I investigate the third—and very different—classical example of heroism, that of Socrates. While the sequence of dialogues that culminate in Socrates' execution might not seem to be the most obvious place to look for evidence of heroism, I take Plato's portrayal of his mentor there to be the centerpiece of his portrayal of Socrates as not only heroic but also the best of the heroes. Faced with charges of impiety and corruption of the youth, Socrates attempts a defense designed to vindicate the philosophic way of life. In this, he seems to be successful, as Socrates is today highly regarded for his description of the good life and for his unwillingness to live any other sort of life, a position that is most obviously exemplified by his defense in the *Apology*. After his sentencing, Socrates' arguments and actions—in the *Crito* and the *Phaedo*—also lend considerable support to the idea that the philosopher is committed to living a particularly good sort of life, both for himself and for others. Thus, I argue that these dialogues are intended serve to enshrine the character of Socrates as the best of the classical heroes for two reasons: first, the philosopher has an intimate understanding (or even appreciation) of his mortality and actively chooses to die. In this, he mirrors the choices of Achilles and Odysseus. But secondly, in choosing to give up his life, Socrates sacrifices himself for those with whom he identifies, both his friends and even the Athenians at large who seem to be his enemies. In this, he puts a philosophical commitment to others at the heart of the heroic experience in a way that the Homeric heroes—for whom sympathy or fellow feeling is at best tangential to their heroic deeds—do not.

After carefully exploring the characters of Achilles, Odysseus, and Socrates separately, I turn in chapters 5 and 6 to comparisons of Achilles and Odysseus with Socrates. In doing so, I point to their similarities but also highlight the important differences that make Achilles a battlefield hero who chooses to fight and die to gain *kléos*, Odysseus a suffering hero who endures humiliation to achieve *nostos*, and Socrates an other-regarding hero whose actions are undertaken on behalf of others.[5] From the preceding chapters it might be tempting to see them as nothing more than three contrasting exemplars of heroism: Achilles seems to be a brash man of action, Odysseus a scheming survivor, and Socrates a pensive man devoted to the life of the mind. Indeed, in the *Republic*, Achilles is singled out for derision from among all of the Homeric heroes and, in the *Lesser Hippias*, Odysseus' lying ways are defended even though doing so proves "repellent" (Lampert 2002: 231). And yet, in the *Apology*, Socrates famously compares himself quite favorably to Achilles and, in the *Republic*, Socrates seems to argue that Odysseus' soul makes a choice that is nearest to that of the just man. In sorting through this Platonic puzzle, I contend that Socrates is meant to stand alongside Achilles and Odysseus insofar as he possesses many of the same classically heroic qualities. Looking back on these heroic archetypes today, however, the philosopher seems to us to surpass the warrior and the survivor by giving his life on behalf of others rather than in pursuit of his own very personal *kléos* or *nostos*. And ultimately, I argue that Plato presents Socrates as a model of heroic behavior that is not only more worthy of emulation but also far more accessible to us as mortal human beings than is Homer's Achilles or Odysseus.

In the concluding chapter, "The Shifting Sands of Contemporary Heroism," I reflect on the ways in which the Socratic model of heroism has entirely overtaken the Homeric models of heroism today. Indeed, what accounts for Plato's success is more than his ability to twist the examples of Achilles and Odysseus so that they shine less brightly once Socrates gets his rhetorical hooks into them. Looking closely at the way in which the distinctions I have identified throughout between Socrates and the Homeric heroes actually impact our thinking about heroic behavior today, I explore in detail four cases of contemporary heroism that highlight Plato's success. The chapter revolves around the aforementioned stories of John Kerry and John McCain, in order to consider the shadow of Socrates that covers all of our contemporary heroes, followed by two examples—of Janusz Korczak, who was murdered by the Nazis at Treblinka in 1942, and of Father Wenceslas Munyeshyaka, a Catholic priest at the Church of Sainte Famille in Kigali, Rwanda, in 1994—that speak directly to the question of how we might choose to live when confronted by our own mortality.

All four of these cases illustrate the central lesson about heroism that holds true for all three classical heroes: the actions that one takes—and the stories that are told about them—are ultimately all that will remain of this fleeting existence. In coming to grips with the inevitable fact of human mortality, heroes are able to open up a space in which they might act in particularly impressive ways. Those who never fully appreciate the gravity of the human condition can never act heroically; instead, when the moment comes for decisive action, they barter away their chance to act heroically for a few more minutes, hours, days, or even years of life, seemingly unaware that the quantity of our lives cannot be compared with its quality. What moves us beyond that common lesson—and what finally elevates Socrates' heroism above that of Achilles and Odysseus—is also borne out by these contemporary examples—namely, that in a post-Socratic world we have chosen to place a premium on heroes who make other-regarding choices over self-interested ones. What we learn, ultimately, is that the most heroic behavior—that which casts the best reflection back on the life of the hero— puts a premium on providing assistance to others, even when doing so puts the hero's own life directly at risk. When human beings face the fact of their mortality, when they give up all hope for continued existence, then they are able to think most clearly about the sort of life they want to have lived. It is only in doing so that heroic action becomes a possibility.

It is small wonder, then, that we prefer the other-regarding heroism of Socrates today even though in his own day very few—if any—would have considered his actions to be particularly heroic. Plato, of course, crafts his dialogues to reshape the way that foundational texts in the canon of Western literature would henceforth be viewed.[6] But he is able to do so with such overwhelming success because the arguments in favor of other-regarding heroism are, in fact, strong ones. Of the three classical archetypes, it is the most difficult to undertake because it divorces one's own preferences from the actions one feels ought to be undertaken. It is also, seemingly, the type of heroism that could be undertaken by anyone; one need not be born a demi-god or fall victim to something particularly awful in order to be this sort of hero. In that sense, and even though all three archetypes make choices, the other-regarding hero seems to us to be the one who does a difficult thing that he or she need never do. And thus the other-regarding hero seems to us the most impressive of the three—except, of course, that the other forms of heroism have become so occluded by it that other-regarding heroism seems to be the only valid sort of heroism today. This has led to the sort of confusion about our heroes described earlier in the examples of Kerry and McCain—and which I will examine in much greater detail ahead—even as our society has devoted a great deal of time, energy, and resources to encourage more people to act heroically. Disentangling one heroic archetype from another can help us to understand exactly what it is about *other-regarding* heroism that we find so compelling—namely, that each life, no matter how long or short, can have great significance if lived well. This is, at bottom, the lesson we can take away from a careful reading of the Homeric epic poems, especially when read through the lens of the Platonic dialogues.

2 Heroism in Homer's *Iliad*
Violence, Mortality, and Difficult Choices

> Good and bad are for a time the same as noble and low, master and slave. But the *enemy* is not considered evil, he can repay. Trojan and Greek are both good in Homer. Not he that does us harm but he that is contemptible is considered bad. (Nietzsche 1992b: §45)

In Hollywood, most stories have traditionally had happy endings. But not even the best attempts by Hollywood filmmakers would be able to turn the *Iliad* into a feel-good film. Indeed, perhaps the greatest virtue of the recent film called *Troy*—but based largely on Homer's epic poem—is that David Benioff and Wolfgang Petersen, the writer and director, do not try to do so. Instead, the film—like the poem—focuses on the heroic duel between Achilles, the greatest warrior among the invading Achaeans, and Hector, the defender of Troy.[1] And this larger-than-life struggle between two such champions cannot possibly end well for either; as any high school student well knows, both Achilles and Hector will meet their fates in this confrontation with one another. Hector cannot survive his confrontation with the *daimon* [δαιμόν; demigod] Achilles, irrespective of the courage he displays prior to their meeting. Achilles, on the other hand, will emerge victorious from this battle, but he cannot survive the war against Troy if he chooses to fight in it, as he has been forewarned on multiple occasions.

Strangely, however, *Troy* diverges from the *Iliad* in what might be considered one of the most decisive respects. We might quibble about the merits of making Hector so sympathetic a character and seemingly downplaying the heroism of Achilles by extension, as the filmmakers have done. But this is a matter of interpretation, and it is possible to read such sympathy for Hector into Homer's tale. What is unjustifiable, in my opinion, is the complete absence of the Greek gods from *Troy*, for their role in Homer's epic is not a minimal one by any stretch of the imagination. Of course, it is certainly possible to conclude that Homer employs the gods to account for some of the overwhelming excellence of the heroes or to lend additional *pathos* to the unfolding drama by connecting the changing fortunes of the characters to the whims of the denizens of Olympus. But regardless of whether Homer meant for the gods to be taken literally or only figuratively, he certainly meant for them to be prominently featured because their actions bear not only on the plot but also on our perceptions of the human beings at the heart of the *Iliad* (cf. Alvis 1995: 51–53). As Seth L. Schein (1984: 53) points out, "Despite, or because of, their perfection, the gods serve as a foil to clarify by contrast the seriousness, or one might say the tragedy, of the human condition." Most importantly, then, without the presence of the gods, the story of Achilles is entirely lacking the comparative perspective that makes his decision to fight Hector so compelling.

In contrast to the choices made by the Olympians, which have no real costs for them one way or the other, Achilles' decision is a truly difficult one because of the serious consequences that attend it. Although he seems to abstain from the fighting because he has been insulted by Agamemnon, he has another compelling reason to stay by his ships or to sail home from Troy entirely. When Odysseus, Phoenix, and Ajax attempt to convince him to join the war effort instead of sulking by his ships, Achilles explains to his friends that his decision to sail home is not meant solely as a rebuke to Agamemnon:

> My mother, Thetis of the silvery feet, / tells me of two possible destinies / carrying me toward death: two ways: / if on the one hand I remain to fight / around Troy town, I lose all hope of home / but gain unfading glory; on the other, / if I sail back to my own land my glory / fails—but a long life ahead for me. (Homer 1974: IX.499–506)

Thus we learn that Achilles is fated to die at Troy if he chooses to fight, though such a fate is suggested repeatedly prior to this clear statement in book 9 (cf. Homer 1974: I.408–410, 477–482, 578–579). Of course, in dying at Troy, he would also achieve eternal glory—in large measure because the poets would tell his story. Alternatively, if he chooses not to fight, he is destined to live a long life and then to be forgotten.[2]

It is this choice, then, that lies at the heart of this chapter, as I explore the first of Homer's two classical archetypes, that of the battlefield hero, and consider the connection between an appreciation of the necessity of death and the decision to take heroic action. While it might seem counterintuitive that recognizing one's mortality could lead to actions that result more immediately in death, I argue that it is *only* in recognizing the limits of our existence that we can open up a space for heroic behavior. The most striking classical example, of course, is Homer's Achilles, as his understanding of the limits of his existence leads to the question of the kind of life he will choose to live. In the end, Achilles chooses the glory of heroic deeds despite the recognition that doing so will lead to his untimely death. That said, it is important to think carefully about the fact that many of Achilles' heroic deeds—including the most famous, his victory over Hector—would likely be considered infamous today: both his desire for vengeance and the violence that he exhibits in attaining it are overwhelming. But this is not the end of the story, for Achilles experiences a noteworthy rehabilitation later in *The*

Iliad. This shift away from being simply a murderous warrior is most apparent when he meets with Priam to negotiate the return of Hector's body. In particular, I consider here the role played by Achilles' reintegration into the community of human beings like himself, and I argue that his ultimate acceptance of the norms of his day is of fundamental importance to the glory that he achieves through the poets' chronicling of his great deeds. Finally, in comparing Achilles with Coriolanus, one of the most infamous warriors of Rome's republican era, I demonstrate the priority of embracing societal norms to the classical understanding of heroism. Achilles, the battlefield hero *par excellence*, experiences a transformation toward the end of his short life that Coriolanus does not, and this allows for his extremely brutal deeds—which hearken back to an earlier, more violent age—to be seen in a more positive light.

ACHILLES BY THE SHIPS; ACHILLES IN THE WAR

For the majority of the action of the *Iliad*, Achilles seems not to be much of a hero. Despite everything that the other characters say about him, the reader begins to wonder whether the great champion of the Achaeans is really all that he is reputed to be. Quite clearly, Achilles has been heavily involved in the fighting—recently sacking the "ancient town Eëtion called Thebe"—and in his quarrel with Agamemnon, he notes that he has "seen more action / hand to hand in those assaults than you have" (Homer 1974: I.424, 192–193). Further, his virtue as a warrior is extolled throughout the poem by Homer (1974: I.421, 559; XVI.663; II.916–919), who refers to him, for example, as "fast in battle as a lion," "the godlike athlete," and a "breaker of men"; he also notes that "of all the fighting men, most formidable / was Telamonian Ajax—that is / while great Achilles raged apart. Achilles / towered above them all." All of the Achaeans recognize his supremacy: Patroclus says that "he is the greatest captain on the beach"; Ajax tells Hector that soon he'll "realize that we Danaans, / have our champions too—I mean besides / the lionhearted breaker of men, Achilles"; and Agamemnon tries to dissuade his brother from fighting Hector by noting that "even Achilles shivered when for glory he met this man in combat— and he had more driving power than you, by far" (Homer 1974: XVI.320; VII.267–269, 129–132). The Trojans, likewise, proclaim his skill in battle; the clearest expression comes from Hector's wife, Andromache, who details the destruction of her family:

> My father great Achilles killed when he / besieged and plundered Thebe, our high town, / citadel of Kilikians. He killed him, / but, reverent at last in this, did not / despoil him . . . Then seven brothers that I had at home / in one day entered Death's dark place. Achilles, / prince and powerful runner, killed all seven. (Homer 1974: VI.484–494)

Even the gods acknowledge Achilles' pride of place in warfare, as both Apollo and Hera note that the Trojans can defeat the Achaeans only while Achilles is absent from the battle (cf. Homer 1974: IV.620–621; V.899–902). Given this general consensus among both gods and men, it should be no surprise that Achilles knows himself to be "peerless among Achaians"[3] and can confidently prophesize that "a day will come when every Achaian solider / will groan to have Achilles back. That day / you shall no more prevail on me than this / dry wood shall flourish—driven though you are, / and though a thousand men perish before / the killer, Hektor" (Homer 1974: I.475, 284–289).

Despite this impressive reputation, Achilles does very little fighting in the *Iliad*. Indeed, the great hero is most often thought of—today—as sulking in his tent while his friends are slaughtered in the battle that rages nearby. He makes the first of three critical choices—not to fight—as a consequence of his confrontation with Agamemnon over Briseis, a slave girl given to him as a spoil of war and then taken back. Worse still, in the aftermath of this falling-out, he asks that his mother, the goddess Thetis, beg Zeus to bring about his friends' defeat at the hands of the Trojans so that they might better recognize the debt they owe to him:

> Cling to his knees and tell him your good pleasure / if he will take the Trojan side / and roll the Achaians back to the water's edge, / back on the ships with slaughter! All the troops / may savor what their king has won for them, / and he may know his madness, what he lost / when he dishonored me, peerless among Achaians. (Homer 1974: I.469–475)

This seems to be decidedly unheroic behavior, and it might be thought of as particularly problematic for my argument that Achilles is an archetype of heroism at all (cf. Lloyd-Jones 1984: 26; MacCary 1982: 55–56).[4] Of course, Achilles rejects warfare not out of cowardice but out of pride; his desire, were it not for the quarrel with Agamemnon, would be to join his friends in battle. On this point, Homer (1974: I.561–564) says, "He would not enter the assembly / of emulous men, nor ever go to war, / but felt his valor staling in his breast / with idleness, and missed the cries of battle." I want to contend, however, that this sort of behavior is not particularly out of character for protagonists of heroic stories (cf. Campbell 1972: 64–68). Indeed, as both John Evan Seery (1988: 231) and Eric Voegelin (1966: 53) point out, the theme of heroic descent and return can also be found in both Homer's *Odyssey* (in Odysseus' journey to Hades) and Plato's *Republic* (in the Allegory of the Cave and the Myth of Er).

While Achilles does not physically descend and reascend in the *Iliad*, his choice makes him seem less impressive (and less visible) for a time, only to then reappear and seem even more glorious. The same concept is prominently featured in Shakespeare's four histories detailing the rise of King Henry V from his origin as a notoriously riotous prince. As Henry explains in a soliloquy in *1 Henry IV*,

Herein will I imitate the sun, / Who doth permit the base contagious clouds / To smother up his beauty from the world, / That, when he please again to be himself, / Being wanted, he may be more wondered at, / By breaking through the foul and ugly mists / Of vapors that did seem to strangle him. / If all the year were playing holidays, / To sport would be as tedious as to work; / But when they seldom come, they wished-for come, / And nothing pleaseth but rare accidents. / So, when this loose behavior I throw off / And pay the debt I never promisèd, / By how much better than my word I am, / By so much shall I falsify men's hopes; / And, like bright metal on a sullen ground, / My reformation, glitt'ring o'er my fault, / Shall show more goodly and attract more eyes / Than that which hath no foil to set it off. / I'll so offend, to make offense a skill; / Redeeming time when men think least I will. (Shakespeare 1994: 1.2.204–224)

Thus, the prince's descent into England's dark underside, carousing with thieves and prostitutes, is an intentional action that is designed to make an impression when he returns to behavior and company more appropriate to his station (Shakespeare 1994: 5.4.48–50, 64–74). Elsewhere in the Western literary canon, the theme of a protagonist's descent and restoration features prominently, for example, in *Les Misérables* (with Jean Valjean) and *The Count of Monte Cristo* (with Edmond Dantès).

Achilles, then, is not particularly unusual when compared to many of the literary heroes who came after him and, in some cases, were modeled on him. Many scholars have read him as a decidedly tragic figure, with Bernard Knox (1983: 51) arguing that, for example, Sophocles modeled his heroes on the "situation, mood, and action" of Achilles (cf. Motto and Clark 1969: 120n2; Parry 1989: 1–7; Wade-Gery 1952: 44). But, importantly, his heroism seems not to be uncommon for the time in which the *Iliad* itself was written (likely the eighth century BCE). Schein (1984: 17) points out that Achilles has much in common with the main character in the Sumerian *Epic of Gilgamesh*, probably as old as the third millennium BCE, who "is a great warrior-king, of partly divine and partly human parentage but definitely mortal; he experiences profound grief at the death (due in part to his own desire for glory) of his beloved warrior-companion, Enkidu."[5] Thus, the connection between a hero's failings and his return to preeminence might well have been transmitted to Greece (and, thereby, to us) through retellings of Eastern myths. Achilles seems to fit this mold, as do numerous other Greek heroes who are featured in the various epics that describe the conflict between the Achaeans and the Trojans.[6]

Of course, Achilles is famous for far more than his reputation as a warrior and his decision not to participate in the war against Troy in the aftermath of his argument with Agamemnon. He is the greatest warrior, and much of the *Iliad* is spent in attempts to coax him back to the battlefield. It is not long after their quarrel that Agamemnon realizes his folly, in large measure because the Greeks have suffered serious losses and because others are quick to point out to him the costs of Achilles' absence. As Nestor, the most respected elder, points out, "You gave way to your pride, / and you dishonored a great prince, / a hero to whom the gods themselves do honor. / Taking his prize, you kept her and still do" (Homer 1974: IX.129–132). However, the situation might still be remedied because Achilles has not sailed for home as he first suggested he would do. Thus, Nestor counsels that "even so, and even now, we may / contrive some way of making peace with him / by friendly gifts, and by affectionate words" (Homer 1974: IX.133–135). By sending emissaries to Achilles, Agamemnon might be able to coax him back; doing so, everyone agrees, would undoubtedly change their fortunes against the Trojans who are now camped so nearby.

It is in this spirit, then, that Odysseus, Phoenix, and Ajax are sent to inform Achilles of both Agamemnon's apology and the myriad gifts that will be his—including Briseis, who was taken from him—should he give up his anger and rejoin the army.[7] But these emissaries, despite either being held in high esteem by Achilles or else well known for making convincing speeches, have little success in changing his mind. Instead, his responses to their separate pleas, as Schein (1984: 107) points out, highlight "his alienation from the values of his society."[8] In fact, his reply to Odysseus is striking in its departure from everything that he and his comrades-in-arms have taken for granted about the virtues of heroic action:

> Give in to Agamemnon? I think not / neither to him nor to the rest. I had / small thanks for fighting, fighting without truce / against hard enemies here. The portion's equal / whether a man hangs back or fights his best; / the same respect, or lack of it, is given / brave man and coward. One who's active dies / like the do-nothing. What least thing have I / to show for it, for harsh days undergone / and my life gambled, all these years of war? (Homer 1974: IX.385–394)

He continues at great length, rejecting all of the gifts promised by Agamemnon, and then asserts that treasures of this sort lack any serious value for him when compared with the cost of attaining them. He says,

> Now I think / no riches can compare with being alive, / not even those they say this well-built Ilion / stored up in peace before the Achaians came. / Neither could all the Archer's shrine contains / at rocky Pytho, in the crypt of stone. / A man may come by cattle and sheep in raids; / tripods he buys, and tawny-headed horses; / but his life's breath cannot be hunted back / or be recaptured once it pass his lips. (Homer 1974: IX.490–498)

The explanation for these very unusual feelings follows immediately on their heels, for here Achilles explains the two possible destinies, quoted earlier, that have been foretold to him by Thetis. As Schein (1984: 106) astutely points out, "Achilles is led away from a hero's usual preoccupation with what he can do or win to a most atypical, but characteristically Achillean consideration of what he *can't* do: both live to old age and win imperishable glory." Although the other two men also attempt to convince Achilles to rejoin the army and, indeed, to embrace again the traditional heroic value system, both are ultimately unsuccessful. That said, the emissaries are able to achieve some measure of success, in that Achilles decides to postpone his decision to sail home despite his numerous assertions that he would leave immediately.

And, indeed, his decision to remain on the beach, convinced in large measure by Phoenix, is a momentous one. In the end, despite his speeches and although he spends much of the *Iliad* brooding by his ships rather than attaining glory on the battlefield, Achilles is finally brought back into the war after tragedy strikes his closest companion, Patroclus. After Achilles rejects the pleas of Agamemnon's emissaries, the Trojans—assisted further by Zeus—press their advantage and Hector is overwhelmingly successful in battle against the Achaeans. Even this, however, is insufficient to rouse Achilles; indeed, when Patroclus weeps for the misfortune of the Greeks, his friend gently chides him:

> Like a small girlchild / who runs beside her mother and cries and cries / to be taken up, and catches at her gown, / and will not let her go, looking up in tears / until she has her wish: that's how you seem, / Patroklos, winking out your glimmering tears. / . . . is this weeping / over the Argives, seeing how they perish / at the long ships by their own bloody fault! (Homer 1974: XVI.8–22)

Determined that Hector's advances should be turned back, however, Patroclus assumes the position he feels that Achilles should, dons his friend's armor, and leads Achilles' men, the Myrmidons, into battle. While this decisive action is praised by Achilles, and although he prays for Patroclus' success, only one part of his petition is granted and this ultimately proves to be Achilles' undoing: "Zeus who views the wide world / heard him. Part he granted, part denied: / he let Patroklos push the heavy fighting / back from the ships, but would not let him come / unscathed from battle" (Homer 1974: XVI.295–299).

ACHILLES' MORTALITY

A hallmark of Greek tragedy, which might well have its roots in Homeric poetry, is that the hero's most prominent feature—his best attribute—also famously leads to his eventual downfall. In this case, despite his well-known skill as a warrior, Achilles must desist from the fighting in order for others to truly recognize his virtues, and his return to battle spells certain doom for him. In Sophoclean drama, the tragic hero remains unaware of the way that everything will end. In the most famous example, Oedipus is informed that his fate is to kill his father and marry his mother; he sets out with the express purpose of defying that prophesy and, in so doing, fulfills it. In the case of Achilles, however, the hero is fully aware of everything that will happen. While one could argue, then, that Oedipus is not acting independently because he cannot escape his fate regardless of his choices, it is clear that Achilles must make a difficult choice that will determine the sort of life he will lead and for how much longer. And, for much of the *Iliad*, Achilles suggests that he will choose a life where he can "marry someone of congenial mind / and take my ease, enjoying the great estate / my father had acquired" (Homer 1974: IX.487–489).

However, after Hector kills Patroclus and takes Achilles' famed armor from the body, Achilles vows revenge. While there is no doubt, then, that Achilles will kill Hector and avenge Patroclus, neither is there any doubt of the consequences of his doing so. As he mourns Patroclus' death, his mother mourns for him because she knows that this first death—at the hands of Hector—will lead, before long, to Achilles' own: "You'll be / swift to meet your end, child, as you say: / your doom comes close on the heels of Hektor's own" (Homer 1974: XVIII.108–109). And, indeed, Schein points out that the majority of the action after Achilles receives the news of Patroclus' death symbolizes his own death. Homer "makes Achilles die symbolically, when both Patroklos and Hektor are killed in the armor so intimately bound up with his identity" (Schein 1984: 129). Further, Achilles calls to mind his own mortality when he speaks about the armor that Hector took from Patroclus, noting that his "arms, massive and fine, a wonder / in all men's eyes" (Homer 1974: XVIII.93–94) were a gift from the gods to his mortal father, Peleus, when Thetis, a goddess, married him.

Indeed, the imagery that Homer uses to describe the reactions of various characters to Patroclus' death actually suggests their grief for Achilles. For example, Homer (1974: XVIII.30–34) says that "from the hut / the women who had been spoils of war to him / and to Patroklos flocked in haste around him, / crying loud in grief. All beat their breasts, / and trembling came upon their knees." Given this description, the women could well be mourning Achilles in this passage instead of Patroclus. As Schein (1984: 130) notes, "This effect is enhanced by the parallel passage a few lines further on, when Achilles' terrible cry of grief reaches Thetis" and the Nereids all "now beat their breasts" (Homer 1974: XVIII.56). Hearing the lamentation of her son from her home in the sea, Thetis expresses her own grief: "Now my life is pain / for my great son's dark destiny! I bore / a child flawless and strong beyond all men. . . . Now I shall never see him / entering Peleus' hall, his home, again. / But even while he lives, beholding sunlight, / suffering is his lot" (Homer 1974: XVIII.58–67). Finally, the description of Achilles' reaction to the news of Patroclus' death is itself laden with imagery that suggests his own death. As Homer (1974: XVIII.25–30) depicts it, "A black stormcloud of pain shrouded Achilles, / On his bowed head he scattered dust and ash / in handfuls and befouled his beautiful face, / letting black ash sift on his fragrant khiton. / Then in the dust he stretched his giant length / and tore his hair with both hands." Schein argues that this vision of the mourning Achilles is one that is closely tied, linguistically, to those of heroes who have been killed in battle. Though the translation is a bit different, Schein's (1984: 130) main point remains clear: "'Darkness' often 'covers' a man's eyes when he is killed; a 'dark cloud covers' the dying Patroklos. . . . On five occasions a man 'grasps' the earth with his hand as he falls 'in the dust.' The verb 'he lay' . . . is commonly used of warriors 'lying dead,' including Patroklos a few lines earlier . . . as well as of Achilles himself."[9]

For Achilles, however, the constant reminders of his imminent doom are inconsequential when measured against both his grief and his pride. He says, "For me there's no return to my own country. / Not the slightest gleam of hope did I / afford Patroklos or the other men / whom Hektor overpowered. Here I sat, / my weight a useless burden to the earth, / and I am one who has no peer in war / among Achaian captains" (Homer 1974: XVIII.115–121). His desire for vengeance, even though it will be quenched at a terrible personal price, now outstrips his earlier rage at Agamemnon. Though the insult is not overlooked and his anger is not forgotten (Homer 1974: XVIII.122–130), he is finally returned to the more traditional way of thinking for warriors like himself—namely, that "loyalty to a comrade and heroic honor are satisfied by the death of the slayer of the comrade" (Schein 1984: 132).

To this point in the *Iliad*, Achilles has been more concerned with his wounded pride than with attaining glory in battle. Now, however, he returns to his former self, concerned with battle and glory, precisely because Patroclus' death forces him to confront his own mortality.[10] Achilles' recognition of his mortality, made especially poignant by the death of his beloved companion, leads him to think critically about the kind of life he will live before he meets his fate. The choice of a long life with a congenial companion no longer seems particularly compelling to him. He tells Thetis,

> Now I must go look for the destroyer / of my great friend. I shall confront the dark / drear spirit of death at any hour Zeus / and the other gods may wish to make an end. / Not even Heracles escaped that terror / though cherished by the Lord Zeus. Destiny / and Hera's bitter anger mastered him. / Likewise with me, if destiny like his / awaits me, I shall rest when I have fallen! / Now, though, may I win my perfect glory / and make some wife of Troy break down, / or some deep-breasted Dardan woman sob / and wipe tears from her soft cheeks. They'll know then / how long they had been spared the deaths of men, / while I abstained from war! (Homer 1974: XVIII.131–145)

In the end, Achilles rethinks his first choice—to abstain from fighting—and this time chooses to embrace the second of his possible destinies, to live a short life that is filled with glory, and to die at the hands of an enemy in a foreign land. In comparing himself to Hercules while making his second choice, he recalls the greatest of all the well-known Greek heroes. As Schein (1984: 134) argues, Hercules "represents the highest possible heroic achievement, including a previous sack of Troy. . . . This comparison prepares the way for Achilles' fierce battlefield exploits in Books 20–22, which in effect constitute a second sack of Troy; it expresses Achilles' recognition of his own special greatness." In addition, of course, "it also sets a seal on his decision to die, since Heracles in the *Iliad*, for all his supreme heroism, is in the end nonetheless a mortal who died" (Schein 1984: 134).[11]

In making this decision to face his mortality head on, Achilles' differentiation from the gods from whom he is partially descended is brought into sharp focus. Because the gods are immortal, everything they say and do must be considered in this light. Their unceasing interpersonal quarrels, for example, lose some element of seriousness—especially when compared to those of human beings—because they really have nothing at stake in the grand scheme of things. As Schein (1984: 53) correctly points out, "The honor they are obsessed with winning and losing is not truly significant. In this respect, their existence is trivial compared with that of humans, who seek to make their lives meaningful by fighting for this reward until they are finally killed." Sarpedon, one of Zeus' mortal sons, speaks exactly to this point: "Could we but survive this war / to live forever deathless, without age, / I would not ever go again to battle, / nor would I send you there for honor's sake! / But now a thousand shapes of death surround us, / and no man can escape them, or be safe. / Let us attack—whether to give some fellow / glory or to win it from him" (Homer 1974: XII.362–369). Of course, the gods are clearly far superior to human beings in power, knowledge, and even possessions; as Zeus says, "Of all creatures that breathe and move on earth / none is more to be pitied than a man" (Homer 1974: XVII.500–501). Nonetheless, the idea of changing places with the gods remains an unattractive one for heroes. Achilles himself points this out to Odysseus, when they meet in Hades after the war: "Better, I say, to break sod as a farm hand / for some poor country man, on iron rations, / than lord it over all the exhausted dead" (Homer 1990: XI.579–581). This sentiment is not simply bravado, and it is instructive, in large part, because Achilles is already dead; he has chosen a mortal life filled with glorious deeds, but he says he would also choose a far less glorious mortal life rather than the immortality of the gods.[12]

THE WRATH OF ACHILLES

I have already suggested that Achilles' ability to confront his own mortality is vital to his ability to act heroically, but I want to focus now on the substance of his heroism because his deeds are not conventionally heroic, in our day or even for a warrior of his time and place. Rather than doing battle to attain glory and honor, as the other Greek and Trojans heroes do, Achilles fights to quench his terrible rage. Ultimately, I argue here that it is finally Achilles' return to the values of the community from which he withdrew that allows him to become the celebrated hero we know from Homer's retelling of the *Iliad*. Without his rehabilitation, Achilles would more likely have achieved an eternal infamy than the status of preeminent battlefield hero.[13]

Upon learning of Patroclus' death, Achilles knows with relative clarity what will happen next: he will fight gloriously, avenge Patroclus by killing Hector, and then he will be killed before he can return home. Achilles' behavior is characterized, from this point, by an intense rage that is directed not at Agamemnon, who previously bore the brunt of his anger, but at Hector and the Trojans. His personality is markedly altered by his rage, and Homer symbolizes that change through his portrayal of the hero. As Schein (1984: 128) argues,

> Firstly, he emphasizes his alienation from his earlier humane self by symbolically representing him as dead, and therefore less than fully human. Secondly, he depicts him as behaving like an extreme version of a conventional warrior-hero of a kind that was familiar from the poetic tradition but that the *Iliad*, for the most part, is not concerned with. Thirdly, he represents him as increasingly daemonic, not merely human, in his actions and the values these actions imply.

While Achilles might still act in a conventionally heroic manner, his portrayal as both more than and less than fully human jeopardizes the *kléos* [κλέος; glory] he desires because his rage separates him so completely from his community. As I have already considered in some detail Homer's use of language to symbolically portray Achilles as dead and to repeatedly foreshadow his death, the remainder of this section will focus on Homer's attribution of *daimonic* powers and animalistic features to Achilles, as well as his portrayal of him as a distinctly Herculean hero.

More and Less Than Human

Immediately after learning that Patroclus is dead and deciding that he must kill Hector, Achilles is transformed. He is, alternately, godlike and bestial. When Achilles' mother leaves the Myrmidon camp to arrange new armor for him from Hephaestus, the god of metallurgy, to replace the divine set taken by Hector, he learns that the Achaeans are engaged in a losing struggle for Patroclus' body against the Trojans. To prevent this disgrace and to ensure a proper burial for his companion, Achilles is instructed by Hera to show himself in all of his rage in an attempt to both frighten the Trojans and rally the Achaeans. Though he is without any armor and cannot enter the battle itself, he stands at the moat that surrounds the camp and—at that moment—"Around his shoulders / Athena hung her shield, like a thunderhead / with trailing fringe. Goddess of goddesses, / she bound his head with golden cloud, and made / his very body blaze with fiery light" (Homer 1974: XVIII.233–237). In addition to this impressive display, Achilles shouts three times, each one echoed by Athena, and "The great sound shocked the Trojans / into tumult, as a trumpet blown / by a savage foe shocks an encircled town, / so harsh and clarion was Achilles' cry" (Homer 1974: XVIII.251–254).

The supernatural voice and fiery visage are part of the first in a series of transformative moments for Achilles, who is portrayed by Homer, on the one hand, as having died and, on the other hand, as having powers reserved for the gods (cf. King 1987: 17–19). Here, with Athena's assistance, Achilles is able to alter the course of a battle in which he is not a participant; his presence alone is sufficient to allow the Achaeans to rescue Patroclus' body from Hector. Schein (1984: 138) argues that "from this point to the end of the poem, Achilles is sustained by the gods in such a way that he seems more a divine force than a human one." Indeed, when Thetis returns with a divinely created suit of armor, Achilles is anxious to return to the fighting from which he has long abstained. He attempts to rally the Achaeans to go back to war immediately rather than eating a meal first; there will be plenty of time to feast, he says, once "our shame has been avenged!" (Homer 1974: XIX.229). Although Odysseus is ultimately persuasive in arguing for the importance of eating to sustain the soldiers for another day of fighting, Achilles refuses to join the others in their meal, choosing to fast as a sign of mourning for Patroclus. That said, he also seems not to need food to sustain himself, for, as he stands apart from the rest of the Achaeans, Athena is sent by Zeus to sustain him with the food of the gods: "Nectar and ambrosia she instilled / within Achilles, that his knees be not / assailed by hollow famine" (Homer 1974: XIX.387–388). As Schein (1984: 139) suggests, "On the one hand, he no longer is a man who eats, and to this degree is no longer a mortal. On the other hand, he has no place in the community of the army, for whom a meal is a shared social ritual."[14]

Then, in a series of battle scenes, discussed in detail below, Achilles is three times described as behaving "like a wild god" (Homer 1974: XX.572; XXI.21, 266) and he is even compared to "the implacable god of war" (Homer 1974: XXII.158). Further, his battle with Scamander, the river god, seems to confirm his new status.[15] The river god, speaking to Achilles "in likeness of a man" (Homer 1974: XXI.247), temporarily halts his killing of Trojans, many of whom he has dispatched into the river. When Achilles refuses to yield, Scamander attacks him—as the river—and attempts to drown him. After chasing him across the plain, flooding it, the river "surged in turbulence upon Achilles, / tossing his crest, roaring with spume and blood / and corpses rolling, and a dark wave towering / out of the river fed by heaven swept / downward to overwhelm the son of Peleus" (Homer 1974: XXI.380–384). This battle results in additional divine intervention on Achilles' behalf, as Hera sends Hephaestus to confront the river with fire, fanned by winds that she sends herself. Overmatched by two such powerful gods, Scamander gives up the fight and Achilles goes on to confront Hector. While the great warrior is overmatched in his battle with the river god, it is instructive that he is neither defeated nor does he have to alter his behavior in response to Scamander's anger.

But not all of Achilles' behavior is powerful in a godlike sense; indeed, Homer also portrays his hero as animalistic in a variety of scenes. Most obvious is the direct comparison of Achilles in battle to a lion, a dolphin swallowing fish, a "black eagle . . . / strongest and swiftest of all birds," "a racing chariot horse / that holds its form at full stretch on the plain," a hawk, and a hound (Homer 1974: XXII.192–200; XXI.26–28, 296–297; XXII.27–28, 167, 223; cf. King 1987: 13–28). These depictions are largely positive ones that portray Achilles in battle as particularly powerful, fast, and fierce. But, in addition to these comparisons, Achilles also behaves in a way that is bestial and, consequently, unbecoming of a hero. As King (1987: 25) notes, "Homer calls his indiscriminate slaughter *kakà érga* [κακα ἔργα; evil deeds] . . . and terms the groaning that arises from the victims *aeikés* [αεικες; shameful]." Further, when he faces Hector before the walls of Troy, he tells his great foe of his wish that "my passion drove me / to slaughter you and eat you raw, you've caused / such agony to me!" (Homer 1974: XXII.412–414). This suggestion of cannibalism is very uncommon in the *Iliad*, and to have acted on this impulse would have clearly been a violation of a well-understood norm (cf. King 1987: 26).[16] There is, of course, a great deal of talk—especially during the battles—of feeding one's enemies to the dogs, the birds, and even the fish. But this is largely meant as a boast or a way of inspiring fear in one's enemy; such talk is frightening precisely because it is clearly outside the bounds of conventionally heroic behavior that would typically involve ransoming a defeated enemy's corpse. In the end, there are actually very few occasions in the *Iliad* when vanquished opponents are left to be eaten by animals (cf. Homer 1974: XXI.233–238). Thus, the suggestion of cannibalism is particularly outside the bounds of the human community. As Schein (1984: 153) argues, "In wishing he could devour Hektor's meat raw he puts himself outside the ways of distinctively human culture." While the suggestion of cannibalism is disturbing, it is important that Achilles only expresses this desire and does not act on it. Returning from the brink of inhumanity, Achilles can still be rehabilitated despite extended scenes of savagery that surround his victory over Hector. Those deeds, as I argue below, might still be thought of as heroic even though they correspond to a far older and more brutal heroism.

Achilles and Hercules

As briefly discussed earlier, Achilles himself recalls the feats of Hercules when he explains to Thetis his decision to avenge Patroclus. He notes that even this celebrated hero, despite his great deeds and the love of Zeus, could not avoid death. But the comparison between Achilles and Hercules serves a larger purpose than simply highlighting the fate that all men share—even those who are the greatest. Hercules, after all, is a hero from a different age and he is, consequently, very different in his heroism from Achilles. Schein (1984: 135) points out that the "half-savage world" of Hercules' day is far different from Achilles' world, especially in the feats of those bygone heroes, who were "far more powerful and far cruder than those of the *Iliad*'s heroic age." Thus Nestor, who is much older, can legitimately tell Achilles and Agamemnon that "not one man / alive now upon earth could stand against them" (Homer 1974: I.321–322). But this world is also not so far removed from that of the *Iliad*, as Nestor can still recall his interactions with these "champions among men of earth, who fought / with champions, with wild things of the mountains, / great centaurs whom they broke and overpowered" (Homer 1974: I.315–317). Like this reference to the famed battle between men and centaurs, Homer (1974: XX.172–173) also makes mention of the astounding feats of Hercules, like his fight with "the sea-monster / [who] drove him from beach to plain."

Certainly the greatest difference is that Hercules is also one who fought with the gods and achieved some measure of success: "Then think how Hera suffered, too, / when Amphitryon's mighty son let fly / his triple-barbed arrow into her right breast: unappeasable pain came over her. / And Hades, great lord of undergloom, / bore a shot from the same strong son of Zeus / at Pylos, amid the dead. That arrow stroke / delivered him to anguish" (Homer 1974: V.451–458). While warriors in the *Iliad* are largely at the mercy of the gods for their success or failure, Hercules is said to have wounded two of the most imposing of the gods, Hera and Hades.[17] Indeed, when Diomedes attempts to fight with Aeneas—who is protected by the gods—Apollo "raised a bloodcurdling cry: 'Look out! Give way! / Enough of this, this craze to vie with gods! / Our kind, immortals of the open sky, / will never be like yours, earth-faring men" (Homer 1974: V.503–506).

In recalling the heroism of Hercules and attributing the same sort of behavior to Achilles, Homer is not suggesting that his hero can contend with the gods; he is instead highlighting the transformation undergone by Achilles. In particular, the rage that drives his behavior throughout the remainder of the *Iliad* also motivates him to greater acts of brutality than he would normally perform. He is a sacker of cities, to be sure, but to this point he has been portrayed—even by his enemies—as a relatively humane conqueror. As noted earlier, it is Andromache—a victim of Achilles' victory at Thebe—who notes that he killed her father "but, reverent at last in this, did not / despoil him. Body, gear, and weapons forged / so handsomely, he burned, and heaped a barrow / over the ashes" (Homer 1974: VI.487–490). When Achilles returns to battle, however, Homer portrays his extreme brutality; after he kills numerous Trojans in the river, Homer (1974: XXI.30–39) says,

Arm-wearied / by butchery, Achilles from the stream / picked twelve young men alive to pay the price / for dead Patroklos. He led these ashore, / startled as fawns, and bound their hands behind them, / using the well-cut thongs they wore as belts / round braided combat-shirts. He turned them over / to men of his command to be led back / to the decked ships, then launched himself again / on furious killing.

These young men will later be sacrificed on Patroclus' funeral pyre (Homer 1974: XXIII.206–208), an act that Schein (1984: 79) argues serves to show that "Achilles at this stage of the poem [is] beyond a boundary that humans in the *Iliad* normally do not cross."[18]

While this particular act is notable in its cruelty because it is premeditated and takes place outside the boundary of the battlefield, the language of extreme violence that attends Achilles' return to the war is far more obvious when he is actively engaged with the Trojans. In his first fight, Achilles nearly kills Aeneas; only the direct intercession of Poseidon saves the Trojan from the Achaean's spear. Immediately thereafter, Achilles single-handedly kills fourteen Trojan warriors and Homer chronicles their terrible deaths, noting that one's head was "split in two" while another was wounded "on the temple through the helmet / fitted with bronze cheek-pieces, and the metal / could not hold; the driven / spearhead cleft it, broke the temple-bone, / so that his brains were spattered in the helm" (Homer 1974: XX.452–456). Yet another Achilles killed with "a sword cut at his neck / and knocked both head and helmet far away. / The fluid throbbed out of his vertebrae / as he lay stretched upon the earth," while Polydoros, the youngest of Priam's sons, was "hit where the golden buckles of his belt / and both halves of his cuirass linked together. / Passing through the man, out at the navel / the spearhead came, and on his knees he fell / with a loud cry. The blinding cloud of death / enveloped him as he sprawled out, his entrails / held in his hands before him" (Homer 1974: XX.556–558, 475–481).

Despite the savagery of these deaths, they occur on the battlefield, and such violence is not overly surprising when warriors, armed with swords and spears, face one another. That said, Achilles, driven by his rage, also refuses the pleas of a number of supplicants; where he might earlier have ransomed the Trojans who pled with him for their lives, he is now unpitying.[19] In the first instance, Homer (1974: XX.533–543) both describes the action and editorializes a bit on the folly of begging for mercy from Achilles in his present state:

Then Tros, Alastor's son, sank at his knees / and begged the Achaian to take him prisoner, / to spare a man his own age, not to kill / but pity him. How witless, to imagine / Achilles could be swayed! No moderate temper, / no mild heart was in this man, but harsh / and deadly purpose. Tros embraced his knees, / beseeching him, but with his blade he opened / a wound below the liver. Out it slipped / with red blood flowing downward from the wound, / filling his lap.

In the second instance, Achilles comes upon an unarmed man, Priam's son Lycaon, who he had previously sold into slavery on the Isle of Lemnos. Rather than pitying one who "had no helm, no shield, not even a spear,"

Achilles is "taken aback" to see him, thinks for a moment, and then decides to "let him taste our spearhead now" to see if "he'll come / back from the grave" as he came back from Lemnos (Homer 1974: XXI.58–59, 62, 70, 71–72). On his knees, Lycaon begs for mercy, reminding Achilles that—by custom—his plea should be respected as the two men have broken bread together, but the latter is no longer a man who acts as custom dictates that he should. Instead of sparing him, he says, "Come, friend, face your death, you too, / And why are you so piteous about it? / Patroklos died, and he was a finer man / by far than you. You see, don't you, how large / I am, and how well-made? My father is noble, / a goddess bore me. Yet death waits for me, / for me as well" (Homer 1974: XXI.122–128). Achilles has become obsessed with death—Patroclus', Hector's, the Trojans', and his own—and he tells Lycaon that their shared meal is of no consequence; all they have in common now is their mortality.

And yet this commonality is a lot, as there is a sort of solidarity in the way that Achilles speaks to—and ultimately kills—Lycaon. Though Achilles is not ultimately sympathetic to Lycaon's sad state, Schein (1984: 148) argues that "he does not speak sarcastically when he addresses Lycaon as 'friend.' Rather, he invites the Trojan youth to join him in the only solidarity and shared humanity that mean anything to him, the solidarity of their shared mortality, the solidarity of death." When Achilles faces Hector, in the climactic scene of the *Iliad*, there are no such expressions of solidarity or recognition of a common humanity. Indeed, his famous mistreatment of Hector's corpse, after he kills him, is indicative of his final descent into a world where heroic norms were very different and far more brutal. When the two celebrated warriors finally meet, through a ruse by Athena that stops Hector from fleeing, Achilles has no desire to reach any agreements on terms for their single combat: "I'll have no talk of pacts with you, / forever unforgiven as you are. / As between men and lions there are none, / no concord between wolves and sheep, but all / hold one another hateful through and through, / so there can be no courtesy between us" (Homer 1974: XXII.308–313).

The solidarity that Achilles felt for other Trojan warriors—though it did not save them from death—does not extend to Hector, whose actions are responsible both for his return to the war and, ultimately, his own death.[20] Schein's (1984: 150–151) articulation of this moment is particularly helpful: "The utter inhumanity with which he responds to Hektor's suggestion that they agree in advance to return for burial the body of whoever is killed, and the savage hatred that leads him both to spurn the dying Hektor's final plea for burial and to treat his corpse so foully, are a fitting climax to the fury that has marked his words and actions since his reentry into battle." In the end, of course, Achilles defeats Hector—as the former knew he would from the beginning and as the latter comes to realize during their battle. As he lies dying, Hector again appeals to Achilles for the routine courtesy of returning his body to his family for a proper funeral:

I beg you by your soul and by your parents, / do not let the dogs feed on me / in your encampment by the ships. Accept / the bronze and gold my father will provide / as gifts, my father and her ladyship / my mother. Let them have my body back, / so that our men and women may accord me / decency of fire when I am dead. (Homer 1974: XXII.402–409)

He seeks to revive here the solidarity that Achilles, as a great battlefield hero, ought to feel for a fellow warrior. But Achilles is no longer behaving like a conventional hero by this point in the poem, and he angrily replies, "Beg me no beggary by soul or parents, / whining dog! . . . No man exists / who could defend you from the carrion pack— / not if they spread for me ten times your ransom, / twenty times, / and promise more as well" (Homer 1974: XXII.411–417).

What follows is well known: Achilles strips Hector's body of the armor that was only recently taken from Patroclus, and a number of the other Achaeans take turns stabbing the corpse. Then, as Hector's parents watch helplessly from the city walls, Achilles heaps further shame on the corpse:

Behind both feet he pierced / the tendons, heel to ankle. Rawhide cords / he drew through both and lashed them to his chariot, / letting the man's head trail. Stepping aboard, / bearing the great trophy of the arms, / he shook the reins, and whipped the team ahead / into a willing run. A dustcloud rose / above the furrowing body; the dark tresses / flowed behind, and the head so princely once / lay back in dust. (Homer 1974: XXII.468–477)

This defiling of Hector's body continues at the Achaeans' camp, as Achilles refuses to allow a burial service; at the same time, he conducts an elaborate funeral for Patroclus, which includes both the previously mentioned human sacrifice of twelve Trojans and also highly structured feats of speed and strength. Not content with these measures, he continues to drag Hector's body around Patroclus' tomb; he does this three times a day for twelve days, leaving the body facedown in the dust the rest of the time. Although this is indicative of Achilles' wrath and its connection to the more brutal heroism of a bygone age, it also offers a telling insight into his grief at Patroclus' death. Schein (1984: 156–157) notes that Achilles "is fruitlessly still trying to exact revenge from Hektor's corpse for the death of Patroklos, still wanting to be paid back for what he has suffered in a way that is clearly impossible." This barbaric behavior is ultimately futile; Achilles cannot properly be paid back for all that he has lost, and, further, the gods will not allow Hector's corpse to be desecrated. And, because Achilles is a hero of a different age from Hercules, these brutal actions serve to entirely divorce him from the value system of his time. He is, therefore, in dire need of rehabilitation after he has accomplished the goal of avenging Patroclus that will define his life.

CORIOLANUS: A LESSON IN EXCESS

There are few warriors—if any—who can properly be compared to Achilles. But one candidate might be Caius Martius, who is the subject of *Coriolanus*, the first play in Shakespeare's Roman trilogy. Martius first achieved fame as a youth of only sixteen fighting valiantly against Tarquin to preserve Rome's freedom and went on to a number of other singularly impressive military triumphs as a Roman general, including the one—against the Volscian army at Corioles—that earned him the honorary title of Coriolanus (cf. Shakespeare 1967: 2.2.85–120, 1.9.61–65). But Martius, like Achilles, is a celebrated warrior who is deeply at odds with the value system of his time and whose great deeds border quite closely on the infamous rather than the heroic.

The heroic value system of Homer's Greece seems to require turmoil and conflict to give meaning to the lives of men. In some sense, as Schein (1984: 71) argues, this is the great tragedy at the heart of the *Iliad*: "The very activity—killing—that confers honor and glory necessarily involves the death not only of other warriors who live and die by the same values as their conquerors, but eventually, in most cases, also of the conquerors themselves." The same can be said of Shakespeare's Rome, as *Coriolanus* focuses on a city that requires the prospect of war to maintain the virtue of spiritedness—a pride that arises from the assertion of selfhood—it fosters in its citizens. Only through warfare can a patrician be rewarded with great honors; Coriolanus' martial virtue needs great opponents to realize itself. Further, under the pressure of almost constant warfare, men are forced to abandon their private interests and dedicate themselves entirely to the maintenance of the city's public good. Indeed, even the servants of great men recognize the virtue of warfare:

> Let me have war, say I. It exceeds / peace as far as day does night. It's sprightly walking, / audible, and full of vent. Peace is a very apoplexy, / lethargy; mulled, deaf, sleepy, insensible; a getter of / more bastard children than war's a destroyer of men. (Shakespeare 1967: 4.5.228–232)

In the absence of warfare, men are able to indulge their appetites unfettered by the drive to band together against a common foe. As Carl Schmitt (1996: 35) would later formulate the problem,

> A world in which the possibility of war is utterly eliminated, a completely pacified globe, would be a world without the distinction of friend and enemy and hence a world without politics. It is conceivable that such a world might contain many very interesting antitheses and contrasts, competitions and intrigues of every kind, but there would not be a meaningful antithesis whereby men could be required to sacrifice life, authorized to shed blood, and kill other human beings.

The destruction of spiritedness—and the consequent unleashing of *eros*, the self-interested concern with bodily welfare—is inexorably and unfavorably linked with the indefinite preservation of peace.

In the republic of *Coriolanus*, then, the purpose of the Roman government is twofold: spiritedness must be encouraged among the citizens and the vitality of *eros* must be constantly checked. At the same time, however, the former cannot be allowed to exist without some restraint and the latter must not be squelched entirely. Clearly, Rome's position is precarious; if these tasks are not adequately accomplished there are dire consequences for the fledgling republic. To that end, the regime attempts to institute an instructive process for its citizens—an indoctrination of the best way of life for men—and at its heart is Coriolanus. As Cominius notes, "It is held / That valor is the chiefest virtue, and / Most dignifies the haver. If it be, / The man I speak of cannot in the world / Be singly counterpoised" (Shakespeare 1967: 2.2.81–85). The veneration conferred on him throughout by well-respected Romans like Menenius and Cominius works as a means of instruction for the other citizens, especially the city's youth, about the value of martial virtue in Rome.[21] Along with the grand speeches commemorating his deeds, the noble Roman warrior is offered spoils of battle, the "war's garland," his general's horse, and a title by which to remember the victory (Shakespeare 1967: 1.9.59–64). Further, his return from battle is marked by a military parade, additional speeches of praise, and the Senate's hope that he will be made a consul. By rewarding its military heroes with public offices, the republican regime is able to foster the spiritedness they seek, drawing each citizen into Roman military and political life.

At this moment, before any decisions have been made, Coriolanus is at the very pinnacle of his power. He appears in Rome, godlike, after the defeat of the Volsces, and the city is his to do with as he pleases.[22] Patricians and plebeians alike worship him: "The nobles bended / As to Jove's statue, and the commons made / A shower and thunder with their caps and shouts" (Shakespeare 1967: 2.1.257–259). But Coriolanus' bid to become a Roman political figure fails because he cannot be at home in republican Rome with the plebeians. He sees that the potential exists for the multitude to become greedy and misuse any power afforded to it by the Senate. Further, he criticizes the numerous compromises made with the plebeians, which he feels undermine the patricians' ability to devote themselves entirely to the cultivation of a warrior class. For Coriolanus, the word "Roman" has too many applications; the only proper Romans are those warriors who achieve distinction for themselves and their city. The plebeians are no better than animals, therefore bastardizing the term "Roman" and incurring Coriolanus' wrath: "I would they were barbarians, as they are, / Though in Rome littered; not Romans, as they are not, / Though calved i'th' porch o'th' Capitol" (Shakespeare 1967: 3.1.237–239).[23]

On this topic, Paul A. Cantor makes an interesting comparison of Coriolanus' ideas to those of the Spartan rulers, specifically that city's founder,

Lycurgus. For Coriolanus to achieve his perfect Rome, "he would reduce the number of citizens . . . and concentrate on making every citizen fully a Roman in his sense, namely a public-spirited warrior" (Cantor 1976: 82). Overall, his critique of the republican regime is a powerful one, highlighting a potential flaw: "the absence of a legislator, not simply at its founding, but throughout its history" (Cantor 1976: 84). Coriolanus is poised to become the Roman equivalent of Lycurgus, but he must first come to terms with the system of class struggle he criticizes. Only in playing to the masses, whom he despises, can Coriolanus gain the political power necessary to relegate them to the status of slaves and build his pseudo-Spartan regime. Cantor maintains that Coriolanus' failure ultimately stems from his inability to differentiate between leading people in war and peace. He notes that even Aufidius, Rome's Volscian enemy, sees that the problem Coriolanus has in commanding is an inability "to be other than one thing, not moving / From th' casque to th' cushion, but commanding peace / Even with the same austerity and garb / As he controlled the war" (Shakespeare 1967: 4.7.42–45). I would argue, however, that Coriolanus understands the difference well, but refuses to change his martial ways. To become consul, he must flatter the plebeians; if he decides to do so, he would admit that they have some power over him and then could never stop humbling himself to please them. Thus he says, "I will not do't, / Lest I surcease to honor mine own truth, / And by my body's action teach my mind / A most inherent baseness" (Shakespeare 1967: 3.2.120–123). Considering Coriolanus' deeds, as presented during the initial conquest of Corioles, it might be no boast that "on fair ground / I could beat forty of them" (Shakespeare 1967: 3.1.241–242); politics, however, is nowhere heralded as fair ground. In fact, Shakespeare presents illusion as the permanent way of life for the Roman politician, and Coriolanus—who loves honor above all else—must reject it.[24] Like Achilles, who refuses to bow to Agamemnon for the good of the community, Coriolanus is too great a warrior to act the part of a politician; he cannot even attempt it long enough to dissolve the game of politics entirely, because doing so would throw into question the honorable deeds through which he has achieved his glorious name.[25]

Because Coriolanus' honor derives from his heroic deeds in fighting for Rome, he is particularly stricken by the flaw that he sees in his having done so—namely, that he must fight for the worthless plebeians as well as the noble patricians who live there. With this in mind, the hero considers the possibility that there exists another place—away from Rome—where he can properly achieve the uncorrupted honor he desires. In choosing to leave the city, Coriolanus makes clear that he would rather live outside the community than fight for and then humble himself to the plebian masses: "Despising / For you the city, thus I turn my back. / There is a world elsewhere" (Shakespeare 1967: 3.3.133–135). At this moment, as Coriolanus banishes the city, he takes up the image of himself as a god that the Romans had only recently abandoned. Leaving the city behind to suffer without him for its failure to honor him in the manner he deserved, Coriolanus seeks an independence hitherto unknown and unimagined while under Roman rule. Like Achilles—whose brutality placed him outside the community—the story of Coriolanus' banishment calls to mind Aristotle's (1984: I.2.9–14) claim that

> he who is without a city through nature rather than chance is either a mean sort or superior to man; he is 'without clan, without law, without hearth,' like the person reproved by Homer; for the one who is such by nature has by this fact a desire for war, as if he were an isolated piece in a game of chess. . . . One who is incapable of participating or who is in need of nothing through being self-sufficient is no part of a city, and so it either a beast or a god.

It is clear that both Coriolanus and Achilles have an inherent desire for war; by their natures they seem incomplete when they are not fighting. And, of course, both men believe that it is only in battle that they can do great things, even though doing so means that they are isolated from their communities. As Seth Benardete (2005: 75) notes, "Achilles is Coriolanus: both are gods in their wrath."

That said, Coriolanus is not destined to live out his life by himself, just as Achilles could not indefinitely ignore the suffering of his comrades; neither man is a beast or a god, though they act both bestially and divinely at times. Turning his back on one city, here, Coriolanus must find another to serve; much to his displeasure, the only measure of his heroism is the response of the political community to deeds he undertakes on its behalf. However, in choosing to join his former enemies, the Volsces, Coriolanus makes the sort of mistake that Achilles makes in dishonoring Hector's corpse. Leading a successful campaign against Rome, like sacking Troy, is a particularly impressive act for heroes of this age. Indeed, in his return to Rome leading the Volscian army, Coriolanus seems to have at least partially accomplished his goal: "He is their god. He leads them like a thing / Made by some other deity than nature, / That shapes man better" (Shakespeare 1967: 4.6.91–93). But Coriolanus is still mortal and, even at his most godlike, he is brought back to the ground. Like Achilles, whose almost divine conquest of the Trojans is intimately bound up with savagery and lack of fellow feeling, Coriolanus—Rome's one-time favorite son—returns as a potential conqueror.

Of course, the desire to destroy what he has so recently fought to save is not necessarily a bestial act, even though it might be a difficult one for most people to understand. What ties Coriolanus' act in its cruelty to those of Achilles is that his own family members, left behind in Rome, must come to the Volscian camp and beg him not to destroy the city. His mother, Volumnia, explains the terrible predicament he has created for them:

> Alack, or we must lose / The country, our dear nurse, or else thy person, / Our comfort in the country. We must find / An evident calamity, though we had / Our wish which side should win. For either thou / Must as a foreign recreant be led / With manacles through our streets,

or else / Triumphantly tread on thy country's ruin, / And bear the palm
for having bravely shed / Thy wife and children's blood. (Shakespeare
1967: 5.3.109–118)

But even worse, undoubtedly, is that Coriolanus is loathe to listen to their
pleas (Shakespeare 1967: 5.3.78–86). He refuses a private audience with
his wife, mother, and young son, forcing them to plead with him in front
of the entire Volscian army. Confronted in this manner, he says, "I'll never
/ Be such a gosling to obey instinct, but stand / As if a man were author of
himself," attempting to maintain his godlike distance from all such human
entanglements, and urging "All bond and privilege of nature break" (Shakespeare 1967: 5.3.34–36, 25).

In the end, however, his godlike stature proves too weak and crumbles
despite his incredible efforts to the contrary, as it must: he may be temporarily without law or hearth as he joins his former enemy to fight against his
former home, but he cannot help pitying the family he left behind in Rome.
Cantor (1976: 103) is correct in noting that "Coriolanus . . . does not have
the choice of becoming either a beast or a god: his fate is to be a god only
by acting like a beast." If he were to ignore the pleas of his family, Coriolanus would have entirely rejected every bit of his humanity; doing so would
make him most like a god in his detachment, but to contribute to his family's
destruction would strike everyone, at the same time, as startlingly brutal and
bestial. Further, Volumnia tells her son that, in conquering Rome, "the benefit / Which thou shalt thereby reap is such a name / Whose repetition will
be dogged with curses, / Whose chronicle thus writ: 'The man was noble, /
But with his last attempt he wiped it out, / Destroyed his country, and his
name remains / To th'ensuing age abhorred'" (Shakespeare 1967: 5.3.142–
148). With his reputation and the lives of his family hanging in the balance,
then, Coriolanus elects to spare Rome, as he seemed to know he would
when his family first arrived at the camp. In doing so, however, he seals his
own fate, and he seems to know this as well, telling his mother, "You have
won a happy victory to Rome; / But for your son, believe it, O believe it, /
Most dangerously you have with him prevailed, / If not most mortal to him
(Shakespeare 1967: 5.3.187–190). He remains divorced from the Roman
community that created him, unable to count himself as a Roman or find
any common ground with the values of the city. Then, like Achilles, who is
ultimately felled by a lesser enemy far from his home, Coriolanus is murdered by Aufidius and several conspirators when he returns to the Volscian
city of Antium after having made an advantageous peace for them.

ACHILLES' REHABILITATION

Perhaps the greatest similarity—and one of the most important features—of
Achilles and Coriolanus, both of whom do the greatest and most terrible
deeds of their time, must be attributed to the change they undergo toward

the end of their lives. Coriolanus cannot abandon his family and must finally grant a reprieve to all of Rome on their behalf. Though this is a somewhat unexpected decision, it is important to note that Coriolanus' sympathy extends no further than his own family: the Romans are left in peace because his family members happen to live among them, not because Coriolanus pities them or changes his mind about them. Given this, I argue that Achilles' transformation is a far greater one and fundamentally alters the audience's perception of him as the hero of Homer's *Iliad*. Having completed all of his impressive—and incredibly savage—actions, Achilles takes a brief rest from the war whose course he has single-handedly altered. Once a seeming rout by the defending army of Troy, it is quite clear now—with Hector's death—that the Achaeans will eventually destroy the city. The break from fighting will only be brief, of course, because Achilles knows that his death will follow Hector's in swift succession. In the time that remains, he is completely out of sorts: he has avenged and buried Patroclus, but still Homer (1974: XXIV.3–13) says that "Achilles / thought of his friend, and sleep that quiets all things / would not take hold of him. He tossed and turned / remembering with pain Patroklos' courage . . . He lay / on his right side, then on his back, and then / face downward—but at last he rose, to wander / distractedly along the line of surf." It is at this point that Achilles begins his daily desecration of Hector's body, the savagery of which is even noted by the gods; Apollo, arguing that the corpse be taken from Achilles, says that he "shows no decency, implacable, / barbarous in his ways as a wild lion . . . The man has lost all mercy; / he has no shame" (Homer 1974: XXIV.47–52). Settling the argument between Apollo and Hera, Zeus determines that Achilles should accept ransom from Priam in exchange for Hector's body, and he sends Thetis and Iris as messengers to inform both parties of his will.

It is in this context that the great king of Troy departs for the Achaean camp "to do what no man else / has done before—to lift to my lips the hand / of one who killed my son" (Homer 1974: XXIV.606–609). He has been told by Iris that Achilles will accept his ransom and not kill him, though he remains skeptical of both assurances. Nonetheless, Priam is determined to undertake the dangerous journey, largely because he recognizes that he has little left for which to live: "If I must die alongside / the ships of the Achaians in their bronze, / I die gladly. May I but hold my son / and spend my grief; then let Achilles kill me (Homer 1974: XXIV.270–273). The formerly powerful king has the ability to prevail upon Achilles to return Hector's body, not only because the gods have ordered it but also, although neither one yet realizes it, because the two men are already intimately connected. Like Achilles, who is often reminded that he will die soon and symbolically portrayed as already dead, Priam is one who knows his own fate and will meet it soon. Trying to persuade Hector not to fight Achilles, earlier in the poem, Priam prophesies that

upon the threshold of my age, in misery, / the son of Kronos will destroy my life / after the evil days I shall have seen—/ my sons brought down, my daughters dragged away, / bedchambers ravaged, and small children hurled / to earth in the atrocity of war, / as my sons' wives are taken by Achaians' / ruinous hands. And at the end, I too—/ when someone with a sword-cut or a spear / has had my life—I shall be torn apart / on my own doorstep by the hounds / I trained as watchdogs, fed from my own table. (Homer 1974: XXII.71–82)

And, after Hector's death, he seems almost desirous of meeting his end. At the very least, Priam would rather die than await the assault of the invading Achaeans and the destruction of Troy (Homer 1974: XXIV.295–297).

But more than this similarity in their nearness to and acceptance of death, Priam and Achilles also share a common sorrow. Achilles has killed Priam's son and has prevented him from burying the body; but Achilles' father, Peleus, will suffer in the same manner as Priam, whose son—Paris—will kill Achilles on a battlefield far from his homeland. The king seems to understand this, even in his terrible grief at seeing Achilles kill Hector. Before the body is taken back to the Achaean camp, Priam considers the possibility of appealing to Achilles on the basis of this connection: "He may feel shame before his peers, or pity / my old age. His father, too, is old, / Peleus, who brought him up to be a scourge / to Trojans" (Homer 1974: XXII.492–495). And yet, at this moment, Priam is too filled with grief to make the case to Achilles, who is likely too full of rage to have heard him out. Only later, when Priam arrives at Achilles' tent at Zeus' behest, can the connection be made: "Remember your own father, / Achilles, in your godlike youth: his years / like mine are many, and he stands upon / the fearful doorstep of old age. He, too, / is hard pressed, it may be, by those around him, / there being no one able to defend him / from bane of war and ruin" (Homer 1974: XXIV.82–87). It is at this point that the warrior makes his third choice, taking pity on the king through a recognition of all that has been lost by both of their families.[26] Achilles, after all, knows that Priam's comparison is particularly apt; in the end, neither of these great kings will have a son to comfort him in his old age. As Schein (1984: 160) points out, "The two old men are linked in their sorrows through Achilles." The great warrior knows what Priam does not: Peleus will not see him alive again, precisely because of his decision to fight against and kill Priam's son.

As Homer (1974: XXIV.609–611) writes, "Now in Achilles / the evocation of his father stirred / new longing, and an ache of grief. He lifted / the old man's hand and gently put him by." Moved by the circumstances in which they find themselves, both men are overcome by emotion: "the old king huddled at Achilles' feet / wept, and wept for Hektor, killer of men, / while great Achilles wept for his own father / as for Patroklos once again" (Homer 1974: XXIV.613–616). Having shed these tears together with Priam, Achilles seems transformed; he is neither the *daimon* who killed so many Trojan warriors nor the beast that dragged Hector's corpse around Patroclus' tomb. Rather than the lack of sympathy he felt for Lycaon, now he "raised the old king up, in pity / for his grey head and greybeard cheek," and instead of the curses he shouted at Hector, here he "spoke / in a warm rush of words" to the father of those two warriors and attempts to console him (Homer 1974: XXIV.620–622). But the change is an incomplete one as yet; although he is impressed that Priam has come to the Achaean camp and emotional about his father's similar sorrow, the dangerous and savage killer rages just below Achilles' exterior. When Priam refuses to sit down with Achilles, saying that he cannot rest while Hector's corpse lies in the dust, the warrior reminds the king that his pleas have succeeded only because Zeus has commanded it. And, even then, his position is a precarious one: "I have intended, in my own time, / to yield up Hektor to you. She who bore me, / the daughter of the Ancient of the sea, / has come with word to me from Zeus . . . Therefore, *let me be.* / Sting my sore heart again, and even here, / under my own roof, suppliant though you are, / I may not spare you, sir, but trample on / the express command of Zeus!" (Homer 1974: XXIV.671–674, 680–683). It is unlikely that Achilles would actually defy Zeus—especially as he immediately agreed to the god's order when it came to him from Thetis (Homer 1974: XXIV.165–167)—but it is telling that Achilles continues to vacillate here between the *daimon* who challenges the gods and the mortal hero who understands his place in the community of other men.[27]

At the same time, Achilles leaves his tent to make ready Hector's body for Priam's return journey; although he departs "like a lion" (Homer 1974: XXIV.685), he takes great care in preparing the corpse. Homer (1974: XXIV.697–699) says that Achilles "ordered the body bathed and rubbed with oil—/ but lifted, too, and placed apart, where Priam / could not see his son." He does so, notably, out of concern for Zeus' order and also for Priam, "for seeing Hektor / he might in his great pain give way to rage, / and fury then might rise up in Achilles / to slay the old king, flouting Zeus's word" (Homer 1974: XXIV.699–702). Having done as Zeus commanded, Achilles apologizes to Patroclus' spirit for agreeing to the return of Hector's corpse. He then returns to his tent and convinces the king to join him for a meal. It is at this point, his rage spent and his feelings of fellowship with Priam ascendant, that Achilles fully returns to the human community.[28] After Patroclus was killed, he insisted on abstaining from food, and when he fought with Lycaon, he refused to acknowledge the cultural significance of breaking bread together.[29] These two important incidents signaled the difference between Achilles and all other men; now, however, he returns to the traditional fellowship of the shared meal and of the guest/host relationship that is so vitally important to the Greek value system in the Homeric epics. Schein (1984: 161) argues that "the two break bread together in an expression of their shared humanity; this takes precedence of their previous enmity and acknowledges the necessities of a life that goes on even after such deep losses as they have suffered." He is once again fully human and restored to the values of his community, no longer more—*daimon*—or less—bestial or symbolically dead—than other mortals.

Having eaten together, Achilles and Priam are once again overwhelmed; this time, however, it is not their grief but their awe of one another that causes them to share a very intimate moment. Homer (1974: XXIV.753–758) writes that "when thirst and appetite were turned away, / Priam, the heir of Dardanos, gazed long / in wonder at Achilles' form and scale— / so like the gods in aspect. And Achilles / in his turn gazed in wonder upon Priam, / royal in visage as in speech." While a bed is prepared for Priam, who says that he has not slept since his son's death, Achilles asks how long the Trojans will require in order to conduct a proper funeral for Hector. The king asks for eleven days, and Achilles agrees to suspend the fighting for that time, both men knowing that a resumption on the twelfth day will lead to their deaths. With this, the *Iliad* comes to a close; Achilles goes to sleep and Priam, awoken by Hermes, returns to Troy to conduct Hector's funeral. Schein (1984: 159) argues that, in Priam, "Achilles finally finds a 'father' whom he can accept, one with as great or greater a need than his own for consolation and elemental human solidarity." Achilles, then, is brought back from the brink of infamy by Priam, a most unlikely savior. In making plain their intimate connection, Priam not only succeeds in claiming his son's body but also restores Achilles to the human community from which he has been divorced in what he thought was his singular grief. In concluding this way, "Homer makes us understand that transcendent personal sympathy, not martial prowess, represents quintessential human excellence. It is the *kléos* of this sympathy that wins Achilles in the hearts of later generations the valuation *áristos*, 'the best of the Achaians'" (King 1987: 45).

The same cannot be said for Coriolanus, even though he ultimately decides to spare Rome, for, although Coriolanus does not actually carry out the monstrous action of attacking his own city and family, his rehabilitation is incomplete and comes too late. There has been no real reconciliation for Coriolanus, as there is between Achilles and Priam. He is not restored to Rome, but returns to Antium with the hope—but not the expectation—that his inability to sentence his family to death will not be punished too harshly in his new city. Coriolanus, then, remains opposed to the value system of Rome, and, still a traitor, he cannot return home; he waged a war against Rome and secured a peace that worked to the advantage of his own former enemy. It is his family members, instead, who are welcomed back to Rome as heroes, having saved the city from destruction. Further, when Coriolanus is murdered by Aufidius and his conspirators, it is the Volscian leaders who ultimately recognize that he is a great warrior and that he should be afforded the burial of a hero. The Romans do no such thing, nor is there even any mention that they mourn his ignominious death.

CONCLUSION

There are several possibilities for people who come face-to-face with their own mortality; Achilles' destiny highlights the two most obvious: "if on the one hand I remain to fight / around Troy town, I lose all hope of home / but gain unfading glory; on the other, / if I sail back to my own land my glory / fails—but a long life ahead for me" (Homer 1974: IX.502–506). There are other options, of course: one might do great deeds and be forgotten, one might act badly and still be remembered fondly, and one might simply do nothing at all. We might act on behalf of others or for our own ends; we might cause or alleviate great suffering. Yet the *Iliad* would be a radically incomplete study of Achilles if Homer had ended his poem with Hector's death and not with Achilles' redemption. In that case, the archetypical battlefield hero would have much more in common with Brad Pitt's character in *Troy*, an impressive physical specimen whose defeat of Hector is heavily tainted by sympathy for the suffering of the Trojans.

Hector, after all, has a young family and Achilles is a bachelor; the former is protecting his home while the latter is fighting a war that has little—if anything—to do with him. To make matters worse, Achilles sulks at the loss of Briseis while his friends are killed by Hector, who fights valiantly throughout in a losing cause. But why should the greater warrior, the Homeric hero, vie with Hector, his eventual victim, for our sympathy? Indeed, why sympathize at all with the Trojans, whose spoiled prince still holds Helen—the cause of the war—behind the city's high walls at the end of the poem? In the end, *Troy* is far more concerned with eliciting our sympathy than Homer's *Iliad*; a Hollywood film filled with unlikable characters will not do as well at the box office as one that has sympathetic characters with whom the audience can identify. No one can be like Achilles, the movie acknowledges, but we might be a bit like Hector, and so we ought to cheer for him even though we know he cannot win. Homer's audience, however, cannot identify with either of these warriors; they are heroes of a bygone age, just as Hercules was for those who fought in the Trojan War (cf. Alvis 1995: 3–4).

That none of us can be quite like Achilles or Hector and need not sympathize with them, however, does not affect our ability to learn a lesson from them, a point that Homer knew about his audience. And the lesson that the poet offers, through the tragic story of Achilles, is that our lives are terribly brief and thus our choices are powerfully important. Achilles is ultimately neither a beast nor a god—although he comes close to these extremes at times—and this is precisely what makes him relevant to Homer's audience. Achilles is mortal, like us, and his decisions, like our own, have consequences. It matters, then, that Achilles chooses to fight and do the great deeds of which he is capable, but it matters far more that he is ultimately restored to the value system of his society. To do the former without also accomplishing the latter would jeopardize the *kléos* for which he chooses to court death. If a connection to the human community was truly outmoded or unimportant for a great hero, Achilles might well disobey the order of Zeus and kill Priam when the defenseless old man kneels before him. He acknowledges his ability to do so, and he has, very recently, acted in ways that clearly flouted the norms of his age. But he is restrained from doing so and is ultimately returned to the community by his sympathy for Priam, who reminds him of his own father. Achilles' sympathy saves him from the fate of Coriolanus, a warrior so singularly excellent for his time that he seemed unable to muster any connection to his countrymen or their values. In the absence of that connection, recognizing our mortality might very well open up a nihilistic void that leads us to act as brutally as Achilles in his rage. But Achilles is finally a model of heroic behavior because, irrespective of his savagery, he is a doer of impressive, courageous deeds. In the end, he achieves the *kléos* he desires—and surely deserves—because he is both heroic and a mortal human being who is restored to the values of his community. Though his most impressive deeds occur when he is divorced from these norms, Achilles is ultimately able to achieve the status of archetypical battlefield hero, the greatest—and surely the most complex—of the warriors.

3 The Polytropic Hero
Suffering, Endurance, and Homecoming in Homer's *Odyssey*

> The great sweep of life has always shown itself to be on the side of the most unscrupulous *polytropoi*. (Nietzsche 1974: 282)

There are very few similarities between Achilles and Odysseus, the two great Homeric heroes. The former is unmatched in strength and speed, speaks his mind and does what he says, and even challenges gods in battle; his martial skill sets the stage for an Achaean victory at Troy, and his reward is *kléos* [κλέος; glory] in exchange for an untimely death. The latter proceeds along a different path, in large measure because his primary concern has always been regarded as *nostos* [νόστος; homecoming]. While the *Iliad* is clear about the fighting skill of Odysseus, his preference is always for strategy and subtlety over straightforwardness. His artifice of the wooden horse ultimately ends the war at Troy, but the story that Homer devotes to him instead concerns the ten years spent in his attempted return to his home on the island of Ithaca.[1] Odysseus is undoubtedly a hero, but he is made of very different stuff from Achilles; one is sharp while the other is blunt, and, perhaps consequently, one survives while the other perishes. As Margalit Finkelberg (1995: 2) claims, "There is no way in which Odysseus' behaviour throughout the *Odyssey* can be accounted for as heroic on terms of the *Iliad.*" Given the choice, most people likely would not choose Odysseus' life—due to the terrible suffering he must endure and the reputational costs associated with his choices—even though he survives the Trojan War and achieves *nostos* at the end of his journey. Indeed, Odysseus is singled out for his decidedly unheroic behavior: he makes use of unseemly disguises, employs trickery rather than fighting straightforwardly, and is well known as someone who is willing to lie to achieve his objectives.[2]

Certainly, then, the heroism of Odysseus is unusual, and not simply because it is so distinct from the more classically heroic behavior of Achilles. The very first reference to Odysseus in the *Odyssey* highlights precisely how unusual he is, as Homer refers to him with the epithet *polytropos* [πολύτροπος; of many ways].[3] The word itself is clearly intended to convey two things: first, the many twists and turns that Odysseus must take before returning home to Ithaca, and second, his personality trait of being strategic or wily.[4] While there is general agreement about these two meanings for the epithet, I want to argue that it also provides insight into the distinct type of heroism that Odysseus embodies. By introducing Odysseus as a "man of many ways," Homer (1999: I.1) identifies him as one who is well known and lauded for possessing some classically heroic trait even though it is never clear that he embodies that trait. Thus, Odysseus is often referred to as a "master mariner" and a "great tactician," but nothing that he does in the *Odyssey* suggests that he is particularly deserving of these epithets. Indeed, the *Odyssey* is a story about his inability to sail home, and, during the course of his difficult journey, every single member of his crew dies a distinctly unpleasant death: either eaten by monsters, crushed by giants, or drowned by the gods. Further, the best examples of his tactical brilliance—his blinding of Polyphemus and his elaborate vengeance against Penelope's suitors—allow him to succeed against his enemies when they are largely defenseless. While Odysseus might very well be both a master mariner and a great tactician, the *Odyssey* is not about celebrating those particular attributes; they are not the reason that he is a Homeric hero. What's more, Odysseus is portrayed as the hero who prizes *nostos* above all else, including the classically celebrated *kléos*. But this is another way in which being *polytropos* serves Odysseus well, as he is actually driven to achieve *nostos*, at least in part *because* he values *kléos*. In this way, being *polytropos* allows Odysseus to seem like Achilles—a doer of great deeds—even though the *kléos* he ultimately achieves *actually* centers around his ability to endure a great deal more suffering than others in order to accomplish his *nostos* rather than some set of great deeds that he accomplishes.

MASTER MARINER AND GREAT TACTICIAN

Precisely because he is a "man of many ways," there are several possibilities when it comes to finding a way for Odysseus to compete on the same heroic plane with Achilles, Homer's battlefield hero *par excellence*. The two most obvious stem from the two epithets that are most often applied by Homer. While my sense is that neither one properly describes the heroism of Odysseus, it is important to look closely at both before dismissing them as the source of his heroism. Beginning with the easiest to dismiss, let us consider the claim that Odysseus is, in fact, a "master mariner" before moving to the more difficult question of his tactical acumen.

Although several different characters refer to him as a "master mariner" in at least nine places in the *Odyssey* (cf. Homer 1990: X.447, 505, 541; XI.65, 556, 735; XIV.576; XXII.182; XXIV.216), the important question to ask is whether he actually merits the epithet. Working against him, most obviously, is the fact that it takes him so many years to make his way from Troy to Ithaca, a journey that he should be able to make in a relatively short period of time. Indeed, every other living member of the Achaean force that conquered Troy returns home far more expeditiously, and so much time passes before Odysseus' homecoming that most people—even those who know he was alive at the conclusion of the war and sailed from Troy—assume that he is dead. Of course, Odysseus is not actually at sea for much of the time in question; he is famously waylaid on a series of islands, and, when he is actively engaged in sailing for home, he is continually blown off course by the gods in response to various infractions against them that he and his crew have committed. Indeed, most of Odysseus' delays result from decisions to investigate the various islands where he and his crew find themselves buffeted; these include his famously unpleasant brushes with the Cyclops and with Circe, as well as lesser known escapades on the islands of the languid Lotus-Eaters and the cannibalistic Laestrygonians. In all four of these cases, Odysseus loses a great deal of time and—in three of the four—he also loses a great many of the men who accompanied him to and from the war at Troy. In the least discussed of these four episodes—the disastrous visit to the island of the Laestrygonians—the entirety of his squadron, save his own ship, is destroyed by boulder-throwing giants when "hell's own / crashing rose, and crying from the ships, / as planks and men were smashed to bits—poor gobbets / the wildmen speared like fish and bore away" (Homer 1990: X.135–138).

But leaving aside the amount of time that it takes him to return to Ithaca, since much of that time is not actually spent in the endeavor, let us turn to the actual seafaring that Odysseus recounts to the Phaeacians. We might argue that—in order to be considered a "master mariner"—Odysseus must be able to keep his ships on course. Leaving Troy, his squadron first makes landfall at Ismaros; after a successful raid, they prepare to make their way home but are blown off course by storms. Following the aforementioned increasingly disastrous visits to the islands of the Lotus-Eaters and of the Cyclops Polyphemus, they make landfall on the island of Aeolus, the master of the winds, who presents Odysseus with a bag containing winds as a gift to speed them on their homeward journey. His men, however, believe the bag contains gold and silver that ought to be shared; within sight of Ithaca, the crew opens the bag while Odysseus is asleep, unleashing all of the winds at once and blowing them right back to Aeolus' island. While it is tempting to blame these troubles on the mutinous crew, more telling is the way that the "master mariner" responds to the tempest:

> Roused up, despairing in that gloom, I thought: / 'Should I go overside for a quick finish / or clench my teeth and stay among the living?' / Down in the bilge I lay, pulling my sea cloak / over my head, while the rough gale blew the ships / and rueful crews clear back to Aiolia. (Homer 1990: X.56–61)

Rather than undertaking some heroic action like grabbing the rudder, especially so close to home, Odysseus pulls his cloak over his head in the ship's bilge. Indeed, he admits that he considered only two possible courses of action—drown himself or stay put—that make no use of his supposed skill as a mariner. At no point does Odysseus attempt to exhort his men to keep the ships on course or to take some action that might limit both drifting and damage from the storm.

Indeed, Odysseus' interaction with his men seems more limited than one might expect from a "master mariner" on the open ocean. While he is under no obligation to share with them the gift of the winds by using them, though this was Aeolus' intent in giving them, it is interesting that he falls fast asleep at this particular moment because he also decided against sharing any of the work of sailing with them once they left Aeolus' island. As he says, "I had worked the sheet / nine days alone, and given it to no one, / wishing to spill no wind on the homeward run" (Homer 1990: X.36–38). The ability to do this incredibly difficult work for nine days is an impressive feat, or it would be if he had done it to completion; instead, he falls asleep just before reaching home, and his insistence on sailing the ship by himself convinces the crew that he is holding out on them in other ways as well. Nor is this the only time when Odysseus fails to provide sufficient information to his crew or to enlist their assistance in the work of navigation and sailing; it happens next when they face Scylla and Charybdis—a matter that will be discussed in more detail ahead—and the result is the violent deaths of several of his men.

However, when Odysseus does consult with his crew about what awaits them on their journey, they fare no better; indeed, one might argue that their knowledge of their possible fate makes no appreciable difference regarding the decisions they undertake. Approaching the island on which Helios' cattle grazes, Odysseus tells his men,

> I had forewarning from Teiresias / and Circe, too; both told me I must shun / this island of the Sun, the world's delight. / Nothing but fatal trouble shall we find here. / Pull away, then, and put the land astern. (Homer 1990: XII.351–355)

But, of course, Odysseus cannot convince his men about the prophetic warnings he received, and, facing another possible mutiny, he manages to extract a promise from them that they will abstain from slaughtering any of the Helios' sacred cattle. But problems arise when the "master mariner" is unable to get his ships back out to sea because of a month-long barrage of "onshore gales, blowing / day in, day out—south winds, or south by east" (Homer 1990: XII.415–416). Worse still, after his men eat through the stores on their ships, Odysseus absents himself to pray for assistance from the gods and, once again, falls asleep at a crucial moment. As soon as his men slaughter several of Helios' cattle, Odysseus awakens and, six days later, after they have finally finished eating what they have killed, the weather improves dramatically and they set sail from the island. While none of this is particularly remarkable, the decision to kill cattle they have been expressly forbidden to touch yields the first of two shipwrecks that Odysseus suffers on his way home.

This first shipwreck is absolutely catastrophic and leads to the death of every last member of a crew who had survived the Trojan War and the deadly island-hopping journey homeward. As punishment for their actions, "all the men were flung into the sea. / They came up 'round the wreck, bobbing a while / like petrels on the waves. No more seafaring / homeward for these, no sweet day of return; / the god had turned his face from them" (Homer 1990: XII.530–535). Odysseus, however, survives the shipwreck and, now completely alone, drifts for more than a week before coming ashore on Ogygia, where he will remain the captive and lover of the nymph Calypso for seven years. Of course, each time that Odysseus and his crew have difficulty at sea, the cause seems to be the gods. But when Odysseus triumphs over adversity, it is often portrayed as his own handiwork. In this case, the gods—who destroyed his crew—are not responsible for his survival; he manages to ride out the storm sent by Zeus by lashing parts of the wreckage together.[5]

The same is true in the case of the second shipwreck, when Poseidon attempts to prevent Odysseus from making landfall on Scheria after his release from Calypso's island. It is the god whose handiwork breaks Odysseus' mast and sail, casts the hero into the sea, and holds him underwater. But it is Odysseus' own resourcefulness and seafaring ability that saves him again. Despite the furor of winds and waves, Odysseus remains clear-headed enough to act; after surfacing, he "still bethought him, half-drowned as he was, / to flounder for the boat and get a handhold / into the bilge—to crouch there, foiling death" (Homer 1990: V.335–337). Odysseus then receives a visit from a Nereid who is touched by his suffering and who advises him to abandon his boat and swim for the shore; she provides him with her veil to ensure that he cannot drown or suffer harm. Yet Odysseus decides not to do as he is instructed, waiting instead until his boat is completely destroyed before trying to swim in an attempt to reach land. Even then, he is challenged by an inhospitable coast; as Homer (1990: V.418–423) notes, "When he came in earshot / he heard the trampling roar of sea on rock, / where combers, rising shoreward, thudded down / on the sucking ebb—all sheeted with salt foam. / Here were no coves or harborage or shelter, / only steep headlands, rockfallen reefs and crags." He cannot make up his mind as to whether he should swim until he finds a better spot and risk being taken back out to sea, and he is finally forced to look for a calmer area of coastline by the rough seas that threaten to batter him on the rocks.[6]

While none of this necessarily demonstrates that Odysseus is incompetent with regard to the seafaring art, the examples suggest that perhaps his fame as a "master mariner" was earned prior to the events that unfold in the *Odyssey*. Of course, it might be tempting to argue in favor of Odysseus' skill by noting that he and his crew successfully sail from Circe's island to a harbor at the very edge of the world and back. This event is a central one to the *Odyssey*, as it provides Odysseus with very valuable information about the situation he will face upon his return to Ithaca as well as insight into his own future both in life and in the afterlife. And yet, in looking closely at this important moment on Odysseus' journey, it seems that his sea voyage takes no particular skill. As Homer (1990: XI.6–17) describes it,

> But now a breeze came up for us astern— / a canvas-bellying landbreeze, hale shipmate / sent by the singing nymph with sun-bright hair; / so we made fast the braces, took our thwarts, / and let the wind and steersman work the ship / with full sail spread all day above our coursing, / till the sun dipped, and all the ways grew dark / upon the fathomless unresting sea. By night / our ship ran onward toward the Ocean's bourne, / the realm and region of the Men of Winter, / hidden in mist and cloud.

There is no vivid description of the challenges presented by such a voyage, nor are there any important navigational decisions to be made. Indeed, the sense given to the reader from this passage is that this voyage might have been undertaken by anyone, provided one's "steersman" knew the proper direction in which to point the ship. The more difficult part of journey takes place once Odysseus disembarks from his ship and begins the intricate process of summoning the spirits with whom he needs to converse, but this is much more a spiritual journey than it is a physical one. And, even then, the "master mariner" is essentially just following the careful directions that Circe provides for him.[7] Had Homer desired to do so, he might very easily have portrayed Odysseus as the most skilled mariner just as he portrayed Achilles as the most skilled warrior in the *Iliad*; that he chooses not to do so, and thus to complicate the reader's image of Odysseus, is noteworthy and serves to reinforce his polytropic character.

Having considered the question of Odysseus' expertise at sea, let us now turn to the more difficult matter of his tactical expertise. He is introduced as a "great tactician" at least twelve times by Homer (1990: VII.257; VIII.440; XI.413, 438; XV.464; XVII.18, 455; XIX.52, 579; XXII.481; XXIII.147; XXIV.391), but there is little discussion of the specific tactics that are being lauded. It is clear, from the *Iliad*, that Odysseus is a distinctly clever warrior, especially when contrasted with the more straightforward approach to fighting that Achilles embodies,[8] and his most clever gambit is undoubtedly the wooden horse that results in the destruction of Troy. But since the episode of the Trojan Horse is one to which various characters only allude, the tactical triumphs of Odysseus—especially in the *Odyssey*—need further discussion. As noted earlier, the bulk of Odysseus' squadron is destroyed after his men run afoul of the Laestrygonians; his own ship is subsequently destroyed during a storm, and thus his entire crew perishes on their journey home from Troy. While the hero's tactics are not *directly* to blame in either of these instances—his men dock their ships closer to the island of the Laestrygonians than he does and thus cannot escape, and they choose to kill Helios' cattle against his orders while he is asleep—in two other situations where several of his crew meet violent ends, one of which actually sets the stage for all the other difficulties that befall them, the same certainly cannot be said.

The first is an incident that bridges the difficulties that Odysseus faces as both a "master mariner" and a "great tactician," the monstrous gauntlet of Scylla and Charybdis. After returning to Circe's island from his unusual meeting with the spirits of his deceased family members and comrades-in-arms, and hearing the prophecy of Tiresias, Odysseus and his sailors prepare to continue on their homeward journey. Having received instructions from Circe on the various difficulties they will face, they depart from her island and successfully pass the island of the Sirens without incident.[9] What Odysseus knows—and his crew members are not told—is that far worse awaits them in the form of two sea monsters. As Circe tells Odysseus, he has a choice that is, in some sense, not a choice at all. On the one hand is Charybdis, a monster that "lurks below / to swallow down the dark sea tide. Three times / from dawn to dusk she spews it up / and sucks it down again three times, a whirling / maelstrom" (Homer 1990: XII.122–126). On the other is Scylla, whose "legs—/ and there are twelve—are like great tentacles, / unjointed, and upon her serpent necks / are borne six heads like nightmares of ferocity, / with triple serried rows of fangs and deep / gullets of black death" (Homer 1990: XII.106–111). After describing them in this way, Circe advises Odysseus to turn his ships toward Scylla; doing so will allow him to steer wide enough around Charybdis to escape the fate of having all of his ships sucked under. The problem with sailing too close to Scylla, however, is that she will—without fail—pluck six men from his crew to be eaten by each one of her six heads. Odysseus initially tells Circe that he plans to fight rather than surrendering any of his men to such a terrible fate, but when the time comes and he finds himself facing the two monsters, he chooses to turn his ships toward Scylla and sacrifice six of his men to prevent the possible destruction of his entire squadron. Though he thinks, initially, about fighting Scylla—until Circe advises him against the attempt—he does not consider telling his men about the fate that awaits them. Nor is he able to find an alternative route to take that would allow him to avoid one or the other of these sea monsters. While Circe assures him that there is no alternative, it is surprising that the "master mariner" and "great tactician" is unable to formulate any better plan.

While the incident with Scylla is certainly unfortunate for several of his crew and seems to highlight a lack of ingenuity regarding possible tactics from the "great tactician," it pales in comparison with Odysseus' run-in with Polyphemus, the one-eyed son of Poseidon. Taking several men with him to explore, Odysseus refuses to listen to their counsel about stealing what they find and quickly returning to their ship after they wander into the Cyclops' cave. As he later admits, "Ah, / how sound that was! Yet I refused. I wished / to see the caveman, and what he had to offer— / no pretty sight, it turned out, for my friends" (Homer 1990: IX.247–250). This is something of a radical understatement, as the truth of their meeting with Polyphemus is that

> in one stride he clutched at my companions / and caught two in his hands like squirming puppies / to beat their brains out, spattering the floor. / Then he dismembered them and made his meal, / gaping and crunching like a mountain lion— / everything: innards, flesh, and marrow bones. / We cried aloud, lifting our hands to Zeus, / powerless, looking on at this, appalled; / but Cyclops went on filling up his belly / with man-flesh and great gulps of whey. (Homer 1990: IX.313–322)

The same disaster befalls at least four more of Odysseus' men while he looks on, biding his time and planning some way to save himself and the others who remained uneaten.[10] The difficulty, of course, is that Odysseus seems to be without many options; once he and his men are in the cave with Polyphemus, they cannot escape on their own. As the hero recognizes, "If I killed him / we perished there as well, for we could never / move his ponderous doorway slab aside" (Homer 1990: IX.328–330). And so Odysseus must wait until Polyphemus can be tricked into moving aside the giant stone from the mouth of the cave and allowing them to pass unharmed.

Thus, it would be a mistake not to acknowledge the clever plan that Odysseus hatches and puts into action: his lie that his name is Nobody, his famous blinding of Polyphemus, and finally his exiting the cave under the cover of the sheep put out to graze. Each one of these elements requires the other two or else the men would not make good their escape. If Odysseus does not cleverly lie about his name, the other Cyclopes would come to Polyphemus' aid when he cries out for help after he is blinded, and, of course, the ruse of the sheep is a particularly clever way to get around the blinded giant as he carefully examines his flock before letting them out to graze. That said, the problem is that Odysseus makes a terrible tactical blunder after his seeming triumph over Polyphemus. Having successfully extracted themselves from the cave, the men cast off from the island just as Polyphemus learns of their escape and thievery of his flock. Though his crew strongly advises him against goading their enemy, who is attempting to hit their fleeing ship with enormous boulders, Odysseus cannot leave the island without claiming credit for the brilliant plan that allowed his escape. In this moment, Odysseus seems to forget his desire for *nostos* and—for the first time, but not the last—is clearly caught up in achieving *kléos* instead: "I would not heed them in my glorying spirit, / but let my anger flare and yelled: 'Kyklops, / if ever mortal man inquire / how you were put to shame and blinded, tell him / Odysseus, raider of cities, took your eye: / Laertes' son, whose home's on Ithaka!'" (Homer 1990: IX.446–452). Of course, now that Polyphemus knows the name of his assailant, he can curse him. This he does, calling on Poseidon either to prevent Odysseus from returning home or, at the very least, fill his journey with hardship: "Should destiny / intend that he shall see his roof again / among his family in his father land, / far be that day, and dark the years between. / Let him lose all companions, and return / under strange sail to bitter days at home" (Homer 1990: IX.580–585). From this moment, Poseidon takes a direct interest in Odysseus' quest for home and does all that he can do to make Polyphemus' curse a reality. It is at this moment, just after Odysseus achieves what many would consider a brilliant tactical success, that his suffering truly begins and that his entire crew is doomed.

It is also the case that the second major tactical success of the *Odyssey* relies on Odysseus' employment of behavior that is decidedly less than straightforwardly heroic. In preparation for exacting his long-awaited revenge on the suitors who have run roughshod over his home and threatened his family, he hatches a plan that will enable him to achieve that vengeance in a manner that minimizes the chances he will face any serious threat or challenge from them. After recruiting assistance for his endeavor from Eumaeus and Telemachus, infiltrating the house in disguise, and identifying the primary subjects of his vengeance, Odysseus orchestrates the removal of the suitors' weapons from the great hall and constructs a challenge for them that will ultimately conclude with a quiver of arrows and a bow in his hands. When Odysseus then kills Antinous with a single shot, the other suitors note their unfortunate position while also expressing their outrage at the manner in which the first among them was brought down:

> Wildly they turned and scanned / the walls in the long room for arms; but not a shield, / not a good ashen spear was there for a man to take a throw. All they could do was yell in outrage at Odysseus: "Foul! To shoot at a man! That was your last shot!" / "Your own throat will be slit for this!" (Homer 1990: XXII.24–29)

In the ensuing fight Odysseus has ample opportunity to demonstrate his martial prowess, as there are a great many more enemies in the hall than he has friends. Indeed, that fighting skill is tested when the suitors finally gain access to their weapons, though no reader should be particularly surprised that a battle-hardened warrior is able to get the best of a group of spoiled young men. And yet, while Odysseus' plan ultimately proves quite effective—insofar as he succeeds in exacting his vengeance—and while Odysseus is clearly shown to be a great warrior, it is not at all clear that slaughtering men who are entirely unprepared for a fight should be considered a heroic deed, even to the Greeks in Homer's day. This is not to suggest that Odysseus ought to have declared himself upon entering the hall and then engaged his enemies in a battle pitched very much in their favor; it is only to note that there is something unmistakably sneaky in Odysseus' plan, even if such sneakiness is ultimately a necessary precondition of his success. If Odysseus had devised a plan that was both tactically brilliant and that also allowed him to somehow defeat the suitors without concealing his identity and first removing the spears and shields from the great hall (Homer 1990: XIX.20–26), there would be no doubt about his virtues as a warrior, his tactical acumen, or his overall place in the pantheon of heroes. But this is not how polytropic Odysseus operates: the clever stratagems that he devises are always tinged in some way by the questionable tactics he employs in carrying them out.

What I want to suggest, through an exploration of these episodes, is not that Odysseus is a somehow less than a hero or even that he pales in comparison to Achilles, that other tall peak of Homeric heroism. Instead, I argue that Odysseus should be understood as a very different sort of hero, a survivor whose central character trait—being *polytropos*—allows him to *seem* to possess classically heroic traits even though his heroism in fact revolves around his ability to endure particularly terrible circumstances.[11] On first glance, Homer suggests to his reader that Odysseus is a hero who is worthy of emulation because of his seafaring ability or because he can always craft a clever plan to suit his ends. But a deeper reading points to a different conclusion—namely, that Odysseus is a man of many ways who only *seems* to possess all of these heroic abilities. That deeper reading highlights that he is not characterized by any conventional heroic trope; he is not the best warrior, the best sailor, or even the man with the best laid plans. He is, instead, a very different sort of hero from all of the others who fought at Troy, those who did—or attempted to do—great deeds that were measured in blood and treasure. Odysseus is a man whose heroic feat is endurance; he suffers what others cannot.

ODYSSEUS AS SUFFERER

As Odysseus suggests repeatedly, he is a man who suffers more than most do, and, as Homer clearly seems to agree, he is one whose ability to endure such suffering is unparalleled. Indeed, Finkelberg (1995:2) notes that "Odysseus is the only Homeric hero who, in both the *Iliad* and the *Odyssey*, bears the epithet *polutlas*, 'much-enduring.'" But it is important to make clear the sort of suffering that Odysseus endures, for it isn't simply that he endures twenty years away from his home and family or the shipwrecks that claim the lives of his men. What Odysseus endures is that which no other hero conceivably could—namely, the destruction of his name and reputation. Of course, a glorious name is precisely the reason that most Achaean warriors fought at Troy; its importance to the Greek conception of heroism is made clear by the sheer number of times that it is referenced in both the *Odyssey* and the *Iliad*. Indeed, the latter is the story of Achilles making what seems to be the exact opposite choice of Odysseus in the *Odyssey*, actively choosing the *kléos* of a battlefield death over a long life and a return to his homeland.

With regard to the distinct suffering of Odysseus, there are at least four noteworthy examples where he endures the unique disgrace of losing his name and reputation. The first such instance—his adoption of the persona of Nobody to escape from Polyphemus—is noteworthy because of his inability to sustain the ruse to the necessary extent.[12] Jean-Pierre Vernant (1999: 9) argues, "Because of the close ties between your name, your face (*prosôpon*, the visible aspect of the body), and your renown—the honor (*timê*) you are recognized as having and the glory (*kleos*) that accompanies you—it is impossible to act on one element without touching and transforming them all." Thus, Odysseus remains incognito only briefly in this situation and then quickly reclaims his identity by his own choice—even though identifying himself proves to be the undoing of his companions and ultimately results in his having to endure a decade of invisibility before he can return home to Ithaca. And, as Telemachus points out, the fact that Odysseus has vanished so completely has also done great harm to his family: "the whirlwinds got him, and no glory. / He's gone, no sign, no word of him; and I inherit / trouble and tears" (Homer 1990: I.286–288).

In this first episode, then, Odysseus is cleverly flirting with a loss of identity without—to his mind—actually being forced to divest himself of the glory associated with his name. All of that changes, of course, with Polyphemus' curse because—from that moment forward—Poseidon is committed to making Odysseus "the most invisible among men [*aïston*]" (Vernant 1999: 23). Indeed, when Odysseus next appears to other human beings, on Scheria, it is in decidedly unheroic form, as someone who is *aeikelios* [αεικελιος; degraded, shabby, unseemly], washing ashore after being battered and nearly drowned just off the coast. According to Homer (1990: VI.140–149), the hero appeared to Nausicaa, the Phaeacian princess,

> like a mountain lion, / rain-drenched, wind-buffeted, but in his might at ease, / with burning eyes—who prowls among the herds / or flocks, or after game, his hungry belly / taking him near stout homesteads for his prey. / Odysseus had this look, in his rough skin / advancing on the girls with pretty braids; / and he was driven on by hunger, too. / Streaked with brine, and swollen, he terrified them, / so that they fled, this way and that.

When he speaks, however, Nausicaa recognizes that, despite his appearance, he is a man of some quality, and she invites him to the palace to ask for assistance on his journey from her father. Strangely, she does not ask his name, and neither do her parents when he mysteriously appears in their midst and begs for their assistance. They readily agree to help him on his journey, but then proceed to entertain him with banquets and competitions. Thus Odysseus remains in a state of nameless limbo for several days, until—discontented with his namelessness and the absences of *kléos* that attends it—he asks the court minstrel to sing about the heroes of Troy and specifically about his own exploits. When the tale of the wooden horse gambit is told, he weeps at hearing of his own fame; only then does Alcinous suspect and Odysseus finally confirm his identity.

Of course, this is not the first time that Odysseus sheds his heroic persona, nor will it be the last. Indeed, as Helen tells Telemachus, Odysseus first cleverly adopted the outward appearance of a beggar in order to sneak into Troy on a reconnaissance mission for the Achaeans. As she tells the tale, he did not simply adopt a disguise but went so far as to disfigure himself: "He had, first, given himself an outrageous beating / and thrown some rags on— like a household slave— / then slipped into that city of wide lanes / among his enemies. So changed, he looked / as never before upon the Akhaian beachhead, / but like a beggar, merged in the townspeople / and no one there remarked him" (Homer 1990: IV.262–268). While this is a change that Odysseus undergoes on his own, his most impressive disguise—when he returns to Ithaca and must pass unnoticed in his own home—is provided by Athena. She tells him,

> I shall transform you; not a soul will know you, / the clear skin of your arms and legs shriveled, / your chestnut hair all gone, your body dressed / in sacking that a man would gag to see, / and the two eyes, that were so brilliant, dirtied—/ contemptible, you shall seem to your enemies, / as to the wife and son you left behind. (Homer 1990: XIII.500–506)

Thus transformed into someone who is *aeikelios*, Odysseus can slip into his palace and prepare to exact his vengeance against the suitors who have defiled it. As Vernant (1999:7) points out, "For anyone who looks at him, the beggar that Odysseus has become, rendering himself invisible, is truly nobody." Unknown even to those who have awaited his return for decades, he is able to speak with his servants and his family, noting those who continue to pray for his return and those who have become unfaithful to him during his long absence. Of course, the fact of his obscurity is not all that Odysseus must endure when he returns to Ithaca; disguised as someone so shabby, Odysseus is subjected to ridicule and ill-use by the suitors who have taken up residence in his palace: while eating his food and courting his wife, they insult him, throw footstools at him, and even stage a fight between Odysseus and another beggar (cf. Homer 1990: XVII.583–611; XVIII.404–493). Though he is plotting his revenge during this time—and though he will more than pay back the suitors for the way they have treated him, his home, and his family—it can only be regarded as astonishing that the *nostos* for which he has worked and suffered is yet tinged with a great many additional outrages.

Indeed, it is impossible to imagine a hero like Achilles disfiguring himself (with bruises or in any other way) in order to walk unnoticed through Troy or to be perceived as *aeikelios* in his own home; the disguises—and the outrages suffered—are completely unique to Odysseus. W. B. Stanford (1993: 74) rightly notes that "Ajax or Achilles would never have been willing to undergo some of Odysseus' experiences—his three adventures in beggar's disguise, for instance, and his ignominious escape from the Cyclops' cave by hanging under a ram's belly." What is more, the entire notion of Achilles as someone unnoticed is incomprehensible; the only incidents in which Achilles' form is changed is when the gods make him seem even *more* glorious than he is. For Odysseus, however, things are very different. Vernant (1999: 23) makes this point in a particularly compelling way: "Swallowed up in obscurity and silence, he is eclipsed, *akleios*, without glory. For a hero, whose ideal is to leave behind a *kleos aphthiton*, an undying glory, to disappear *akleios*, without glory, is in fact to be nobody." Only Odysseus is capable of enduring such invisibility in order to achieve his *nostos*.

THE PURSUIT OF *NOSTOS*—AND *KLÉOS*

Of course, Odysseus endures the shame of namelessness not for its own sake but for a distinct purpose, and thus any criticism that might follow from Odysseus' behavior stems from the fact that the hero seems to prize the achievement of *nostos* far more than he prizes other more classically heroic goods.[13] Indeed, Odysseus desires his homecoming to such an extent that he effectively chooses *nostos* over the possibility of immortality. And yet it is precisely the way that this choice unfolds that casts Odysseus' preference for *nostos* over *kléos* into some doubt, as—just like in the previous examples—*kléos* here plays a central role in the achievement of his *nostos*. With that in mind, it remains for us to discuss the final example of Odysseus' invisibility, how it fits with his stated commitment to homecoming, and finally how achieving that homecoming relates to his distinct sort of heroism.

Although Odysseus renders himself temporarily invisible in order to escape from Polyphemus, secure assistance from the Phaeacians, and infiltrate the suitors in his palace, his many years of invisibility on Calypso's island are imposed on him and his condition might have become permanent without the intervention of the gods. In addition to the imposition of invisibility and his lack of choice in the matter, it seems clear that there is a distinct difference in the cost to the hero: in the cases where Odysseus gave up his heroic identity, he endured humiliation and even physical violence, but he could regain his identity in the end. On Calypso's island, however, he faces the very real possibility of oblivion. This distinct type of invisibility is highlighted nicely by Vernant (1999: 22), who notes that, as long as he remains with Calypso, Odysseus is hidden from all other human beings and even from his own identity: "He must renounce his trials, his exploits, and his name—everything that makes up Odysseus. They will remain with him forever hidden, buried in silence; not even their echo will reach the world of men, and no one will be able to celebrate them in song."[14] For a classical hero like Achilles, who prizes *kléos* above even life itself, there is no worse fate than oblivion; as we have seen, Odysseus' distinct form of heroism is based on his endurance, and so he must survive even this final, seemingly all-encompassing assault on his reputation. And yet, Homer suggests, Odysseus is able to survive it precisely because he, like Achilles, prizes *kléos*. If he was not ultimately a classical hero in this respect, he would likely remain with Calypso forever, forfeiting his name and his *nostos*.

We are presented with something of a difficulty here: if Odysseus is able to endure being hidden in obscurity, he might remain on Ogygia rather than achieving his homecoming, and thus the world will never know about his most impressive feat of endurance. As Vernant (1999: 23) suggests, "If Odysseus, forgetting and forgotten, remote from human existence, had remained 'hidden' with Calypso in an unchanging youth, there would have been no *Odyssey* in which to recall the memorable adventures that make up his mortal life in poetic song, generation after generation, in perpetuity." But, on the other hand, if he cannot endure his condition, then he will not survive his time on Ogygia and the same problem of his reputation arises. Indeed, as much as he says he prizes *nostos*, Odysseus has seemingly given up on the possibility after seven years with Calypso. What he seems to want now is not to return home—which he has come to regard as impossible—but to put an end to his condition, which he regards as miserable even though the nymph has attempted to bewitch him to think otherwise. In appealing to Zeus to assist Odysseus, Athena says, "She keeps on coaxing him / with her beguiling talk, to turn his mind / from Ithaca. But such desire is in him / merely to see the hearthsmoke leaping upward / from his own island, that he longs to die" (Homer 1990: I.76–80). In the end, then, the gods must involve themselves and solve the dilemma that has arisen when Odysseus, the hero who endures everything for the sake of *nostos*, seemingly cannot both endure this form of suffering and achieve the *nostos* for which he would endure it.

Of course, the interference of the gods does not necessitate that Odysseus will leave Ogygia—only that Calypso will no longer keep him there against his will. It is at this point that Odysseus faces a particularly daunting challenge—namely, choosing to leave Calypso's island and the immortality that she offers him if he remains there. Vernant (1999: 23) highlights the basic issue that confronts the hero once the gods have taken pity on him and insisted that Calypso free him:

> The dilemma that Odysseus faces is unambiguous: either he must settle down to the everyday life of a love match without end, with each day following upon an identical day, without the passing time eroding his strength or vitality, without ever having to descend to the nocturnal abode of Hades, but without ever shining again in the luminous flash of glory; or else he must return to the harsh life of men with its trials, hardships, inexorable old age, and unavoidable death, while securing for himself an undying glory that lives beyond death.

While the standard reading of the *Odyssey* puts *nostos* at the center of Odysseus' heroism, Vernant here recognizes a critically important point: it is, finally, *kléos* that is responsible for Odysseus' achievement of *nostos*.

Having endured seven years of invisibility, Odysseus knows what it feels like not to age and he knows that this form of immortality—one without any glory—is no substitute for the *nostos* he desires. That said, he also knows the precise costs associated with leaving Ogygia and returning to the mortal life that has been on hold all this time.[15]

Although Calypso is now prepared to assist him in leaving her island, she remains certain that Odysseus would make a different choice if he could see the suffering that remains to be endured. As she says, "You would stay here, and guard this house, and be / immortal—though you wanted her forever, / that bride for whom you pine each day" (Homer 1990: V.217–219). Responding to what is, in effect, a direct offer of immortality from Calypso, he says,

> My quiet Penelope—how well I know—/ would seem a shade before your majesty, / death and old age being unknown to you, / while she must die. Yet, it is true, each day / I long for home, long for the sight of home. / If any god has marked me out again / for shipwreck, my tough heart can undergo it. / What hardship have I not long since endured / at sea, in battle! Let the trial come. (Homer 1990: V.225–233)

If the companionship of a nymph and the gift of immortality will not sway Odysseus from his desired return to Ithaca, surely nothing will do so. After all, Odysseus knows exactly what he is giving up, having spent several years on Calypso's island and—perhaps most importantly—having previously conversed with the shades of his dead family members and comrades-in-arms about their experiences in the afterlife. That visit to the edge of the world—however brief—must be particularly disturbing for one who knows he will make the same trip a second time, after his own death. As Patrick J. Deneen (2000: 43) notes, "Odysseus decides to refuse Calypso's offer of immortality, already having descended to the underworld and already having learned there his fate both in the near term, regarding his return to Ithaca, and in the longer term, concerning his mortal fate." Very few human beings, if any, are given such insight into the decidedly sad state of the deceased, and it is noteworthy that Odysseus, who rejects immortality, is given the opportunity to hear all of these laments about their condition. It is Achilles, for whom immortality is never even an option, who seems to reject the *kléos* for which he fought and died when he tells Odysseus, "Better, I say, to break sod as a farm hand / for some poor country man, on iron rations, / than lord it over all the exhausted dead" (Homer 1990: XI.579–581). If only he had known, in other words, what death would actually entail, he would almost certainly have made a different choice. And yet, quite clearly, Achilles could not be a hero if he had not confronted his mortality and made the choice to live a short but glorious life; classical heroism, as I argued in the previous chapter, is intimately bound up with mortality. Having spent time in conversation with the dead, and having heard the prophecy about his own suffering and death, Odysseus knows better than any other hero what death will actually entail. But he also knows that death is intimately bound up with both the *nostos* for which he has endured so much suffering and the *kléos* that all Homeric heroes ultimately prize. Thus, when he seems to choose *nostos* over immortality, making the choice common to all classical heroes to embrace his mortality, he knows exactly what he is choosing and, indeed, he does so much more explicitly than most men will ever do. But in classic polytropic fashion, Odysseus claims that *nostos* is most important to him when, in fact, *kléos* is also very much on his mind and very much responsible for his decision to continue his difficult journey.

HEROIC SUFFERING

Making the choice to live a mortal life, one filled with suffering and ending in death, opens up the possibility for Odysseus to be considered a hero, albeit one whose heroic qualities are very different from the model offered by Homer in the *Iliad*. As with Achilles, who confronts his own mortality after the death of Patroclus, his beloved companion, Odysseus—stranded on Ogygia—thinks critically about the kind of life he will live before he meets his fate. Despite knowing that he will face a great deal of pain and suffering, and despite attaining first-hand knowledge of the sad state of the dead, he opts for a life full of hardship and eventual death rather than Calypso's proffered immortality because only in doing so can Odysseus achieve his *nostos* and, with it, *kléos*.

To argue that heroic behavior is intimately bound up with mortality is, by this point, likely not so controversial a claim, especially considering the centrality to the preceding chapter of the authoritative work done by Seth L. Schein (1984) on the role of Achilles' mortality in the *Iliad*. More challenging, however, is to make the case that Odysseus—despite not appearing to possess classically heroic characteristics—is nonetheless a Homeric hero of the same stature as Achilles. It is a fairly straight line to draw between the great deeds that Achilles accomplishes on the battlefield and the image of him as decidedly heroic. But Odysseus' actions in the *Odyssey* might detract from claims that he is a "master mariner" or "great tactician," even though he clearly endures a great deal more suffering than other men. The operative question, then, is how Odysseus' endurance makes him similarly a hero, and the answer, perhaps unsurprisingly, is that it is a distinct form of endurance that Odysseus embodies through his actions in the *Odyssey*.

In particular, as Finkelberg (1995) demonstrates, Homer's depiction of Odysseus' endurance is meant to emphasize a connection between his form of heroism and that of the hero *par excellence*, Hercules. She argues that "the only other individual hero besides Odysseus to whom the term *aethlos* [ἄεθλος; labor, ordeal] is consistently applied in the epics is Heracles. . . . The encounter of Odysseus and Heracles in the Underworld shows that it is not mere chance that these two are the only individual heroes characterized in the epics through the word *aethlos*" (Finkelberg 1995: 4). Indeed, the meeting in Hades highlights the many similarities between the two: both are most often depicted as employing the bow as their weapon of choice, rather than the more common sword or spear; both experience a great deal of humiliation as part of the challenge of endurance; and, perhaps most importantly, both have the exceedingly rare opportunity to descend into the world of the dead.[16] Thus, the meeting of Odysseus and Hercules is very much the culmination of the journey undertaken by the former, and the latter directly reinforces the connection between the two heroes when they meet by asking, "Son of Laertes and the gods of old, / Odysseus, master mariner and soldier, / under a cloud, you too? Destined to grinding / labors like my own in the sunny world?" (Homer 1990: XI.734–737). While Odysseus and Hercules are thus linguistically connected in a distinct and important way, it is also noteworthy that the two share a good deal more than just the unique word that describes their particular ability to endure great suffering.

Interestingly, while Odysseus and Hercules are the only epic heroes about whose labors the poets use the term *aethlos*, they are not the only heroes who are celebrated principally for their labors. As Finkelberg (1995: 5) rightly points out, "Heracles is only the most prominent representative of an entire category of such heroes of Greek tradition who, like Perseus, Bellerophon, Jason, Theseus, and others, are mostly conspicuous by the labours they performed. . . . None of the heroes of this group died on the battlefield." Like Hercules—and unlike Odysseus—all of these heroes are best known for completing various quests that, more often than not, have as their centerpiece the slaying of a terrible monster. Perseus, the first of the Greek heroes, kills both Medusa and the sea monster; Bellerophon destroys the Chimera; Theseus kills the Minotaur; and Jason fights with and overcomes the Harpies. None are contemporaries—or even near contemporaries—of Odysseus, though two, Jason and Theseus, are contemporaries of Hercules and one myth suggests that both Theseus and Hercules were Argonauts. Regardless of the exact sequence in which these five great heroes were said to have lived, as Nestor remarks in the *Iliad*, their time has long since passed (Homer 1974: I.307–322). Thus Odysseus, with his heroic endurance and the quest that takes him to unknown lands populated by unusual men, calls to mind these bygone heroes and their epic quests. Indeed, the journeys undertaken by his nearest contemporaries, Theseus and Jason, each contain elements in common with Odysseus' own: in Theseus' journey to Athens, he passes six entrances to the Underworld and defeats the spirits who guard them, while Jason faces numerous challenges—including the Sirens—as he sails from island to island on his quest for the Golden Fleece.

Of course, in the *Iliad*, Achilles' actions also call to mind these heroes of a time long since passed, and so we might ask whether Odysseus' connection to these heroes sets him apart from Achilles or simply establishes him as one more in the long line of Greek heroes. To my mind, the former is the correct view, and I want to argue that an important distinction between the two Homeric heroes is ultimately emphasized by the fact that both are compared to the great heroes of an earlier age. Achilles, after all, is portrayed as most similar to Hercules when he is least like himself. As Schein (1984: 79) argues, the great rage that accounts for Achilles' return to battle is also responsible for pushing "Achilles at this stage of the poem beyond a boundary that humans in the *Iliad* normally do not cross." Because Achilles is a hero of a different age from Hercules, his brutal actions serve to entirely divorce him from the value system of his time and require his rehabilitation and reintegration into his community before the *Iliad* can be considered complete. Odysseus, on the other hand, is never unlike himself—even, as demonstrated earlier, when he is disguised as someone else; his polytropic manner is a distinctly important component of his character. While Achilles can recall these bygone heroes only by acting in an unbecoming manner after his impressive defeat of Hector on the battlefield, Odysseus' great endurance directly calls them to mind with every stop on his quest for *nostos*.

The lesson, then, that we would do well to take away from reading the *Odyssey* and thinking about the life of its hero is that "life is full of toil and suffering, but man should be able not only to endure but also to transform this toil and suffering into supreme achievement. 'To make of this suffering a glorious life'—these words of the deified Heracles of Sophocles, addressed to his friend Philoctetes when the latter is sunk in the agony of despair, sum up everything the heroic life is about" (Finkelberg 1995: 10). While Odysseus might not always excel on the high seas or in a straightforward contest between warriors, he is unmatched in his time where endurance is concerned. And though many today might view Achilles' battlefield actions as more straightforwardly heroic, especially in thinking about the humiliations that Odysseus endures, the same likely cannot be said of the classical view of these heroes. Indeed, Finkelberg (1995: 11) suggests that the comments made to Odysseus by Achilles' shade signal his desire to give up the *kléos* he won for his battlefield death in exchange for a life of laboring:

> The verb θητεύω, 'to be a serf or labourer', used by Achilles here, is the same that designates the labours Poseidon and Apollo endured while serving the Trojan king Laomedon. . . . This verb can function as a synonym of ἀθλεύω, 'to labour' proper; note also that the motif of serving one's inferior is closely connected with the idea of labours in general and the labours of Heracles in particular. . . . This seems to indicate that Achilles' choice in the Underworld is not, as is usually supposed, a choice between heroic death and unheroic life but one between two kinds of heroism.[17]

Thus, Odysseus—insofar as he recalls an earlier form of heroism, albeit without all of its barbarism—represents not only a distinct type of hero, on this reading, but also a type more worthy of emulation than the one represented by Achilles. In the same vein, Susan Neiman (2009: 308–309) argues that Achilles' "words are the eulogy for the old order. . . . If Achilles says it wasn't worth it, it is time to rethink what heroes should be."

On this point, a central one, I think that Finkelberg and Neiman go a bit too far.[18] One would be hard-pressed to make a case for Odysseus as a superior sort of hero to Achilles solely on the basis of a few words in the *Odyssey*. Indeed, by the measures of heroism put forward by the *Iliad*, it is clear that Odysseus cannot compare to Achilles. But we ought not to rate either one of these heroes by measures found in the epic devoted principally to the exploits of the other, just as both Achilles and Odysseus would seem a great deal less impressive than they are when we measure them against Hercules or Perseus. After all, Achilles seems *like* Hercules only when he is thoroughly in the grips of a rage he cannot control. Achilles is the best of the Achaeans in battle, without a doubt, but not even he could compete with the older, more ferocious heroes; as Nestor notes, "Not one man / alive now upon earth could stand against them" (Homer 1974: I.321–322). As for Odysseus, he only *recalls* the heroic endurance of Hercules and the other heroes of old; more than anything else he is a polytropic hero who is best at suffering while also appearing to be a clever and skilled warrior and mariner. Odysseus is not a hero defined by his *aethlos*; he is, instead, a polytropic hero who sees *aethlos* as one more of the many ways that—like navigating, fighting, and even lying—will be needed in order for him to accomplish his ultimate end: *nostos*. Thus, what I want to suggest is not a rank ordering of classical heroism that would prefer Odysseus' endurance of suffering to the great and warlike deeds of Achilles or Odysseus' goal to *nostos* to Achilles' goal of *kléos*. Such a ranking would be problematic for several reasons—for example, that Odysseus' *aethlos* and Achilles' *bie* [βία; might, force] are similar but not comparable to that of Hercules, who possessed both qualities in greater measure.[19]

Instead of setting Odysseus against Achilles—or either one against Hercules—I want to argue for a recognition that the two Homeric characters represent distinct visions of how one might act heroically. This is by no means a novel argument; it is at least as old as Aristotle's discussion of the seemingly distinct heroic virtues of Achilles and Odysseus: *andreia* [ανδρεία; courage, manliness] and *sôphrosunê* [σωφροσύνη; moderation]. As Louis A. Ruprecht Jr. (1998: 48) notes, "Achilles is the epic exemplar of *andreia*, just as Odysseus is of *sôphrosunê*. Asking which man is more heroic is senseless. They embody different, but by no means mutually exclusive, modes of heroic virtue—and our moral task, Aristotle suggests, is to celebrate them both."[20] That said, it remains something of a challenge to put both of the Homeric heroes on pedestals of exactly equal height. While the vast majority of scholars seem to prefer Odysseus, no doubt because he employs reason rather than force to succeed, Achilles remains the truly larger-than-life figure; his heroism is never in question because his actions are bold and straightforward (even as—or perhaps because—they lead inexorably to his death). Odysseus, on the other hand, often seems willing to act in ways we might consider less than heroic in order to survive.[21]

And yet it is Odysseus' will to survive—to suffer and to endure all of the challenges that beset him—that sets him apart as a distinct sort of hero. Indeed, his ability to survive against all odds, and the distinct behavior that allows him to achieve *nostos*, might provide a good role model for young Greek men to emulate. In particular, Finkelberg (1995: 10) argues that "distinct from the Iliadic hero, who sets an example of how one ought to die, all Odysseus' life-experience demonstrates how one ought to live." This position, which provides a reason for preferring the heroism of Odysseus to the heroism of Achilles, stands in contrast to Ruprecht's argument about the position that Aristotle tries to sketch: "that it can be heroic to die, perhaps, but that it can be equally heroic to survive" (1998: 51). As I suggested earlier, even though I am sympathetic to the general preference among scholars for Odysseus over Achilles, I find myself fitting more squarely in Ruprecht's camp on this question, especially insofar as the lesson in how to live that we are taught by polytropic Odysseus involves lying and dissembling. In no small part, I am inclined to agree with Ruprecht because I do not find either of these Homeric characters to be the most compelling of the classical Greek heroes.

As this chapter and the last have demonstrated, both Odysseus and Achilles represent distinct heroic archetypes. Achilles is the most excellent of the Greek warriors who sail to Troy, and his actions win for him eternal glory while also demonstrating the limits and the consequences of human action. To win glory on the battlefield might very well be seen as a worthy goal, though—to be sure—Homer does not present the life of Achilles in an uncomplicated light, especially as the *kléos* he earns cannot be separated from his mortality. Odysseus, on the other hand, survives the Trojan War and ultimately achieves both the *nostos* that he prizes and also the *kléos* that is bound up with it. But few who have a choice in the matter would likely choose his life, characterized as it is by great suffering and humiliation, just as few would voluntarily face Achilles' choice between earning a glorious name or living a long life. What we know is that most people will not decide the exact path that will be set out before them. But what we learn from the heroes of Homer's epic poems is that we *have* choices when it comes to dealing with the difficulties that beset us and that these choices, ultimately, will determine how we are remembered.

4 Plato's Philosophic Vision
The Difficult Choices of the Socratic Life

Socrates *wanted* to die: not Athens, but he himself chose the hemlock; he forced Athens to sentence him. (Nietzsche 1968: 479)

There are few books or articles, if any, that praise the Athenians for having convicted and executed Socrates. Such an argument is particularly difficult to find in the West today, where freedom of thought and expression reigns supreme. Indeed, to suggest that Socrates truly was guilty of corrupting the youth of Athens and of not believing in the gods of the city is a great deal less controversial than agreeing with the Athenians that death is an appropriate punishment for those actions. While he might well have been guilty of the crimes for which he stood accused, few today believe these things ought to be crimes in the first place. Thus, when I teach Plato's *Apology,* my students are generally outraged by the fact that impiety was a capital crime, and that the first political philosopher went to his death largely for encouraging the Athenians to question authority and received opinion. And yet it is a rather large leap from that position to one that extols Socrates' virtues or to the belief that Socrates is someone to be emulated. In general, the classic portrait of Socrates is not a particularly inspiring one; in the dialogues that deal with his trial and execution, he treats his accusers with scorn, he speaks ironically to his interlocutors (even his friends, students, and jurors), and his arguments often seem designed to confuse rather than to persuade. For all of that, however, I want to argue that the Platonic Socrates—especially of the *Apology, Crito,* and *Phaedo*—is a character meant to do much more than simply move readers to feelings of great sympathy; rather, he is carefully crafted to serve as a new model of heroism whose behavior ought to be emulated by others. Indeed, his speeches and deeds—including the often confusing and unpersuasive arguments—call attention to the self-sacrifice of Socrates on behalf of his friends, the Athenians who condemn him, and, more broadly, the life of the mind.[1]

Given the unflattering picture that emerges in several dialogues, a good deal must be said in order to defend the claim that Socrates is a character who is designed to engender feelings of admiration. Allan Bloom (1987: 269) notes that, in the *Clouds,* Aristophanes presents the philosopher as one who "spends his life investigating nature, worrying about gnats and stars, denying the existence of the gods because they are not to be found in nature. . . . His companions are pale-faced young men totally devoid of common sense. In this academy, which has established itself in the free atmosphere of Athens, these eccentrics carry on their activities without appearing to be other than harmless cranks." For Bloom, this portrayal is not overly problematic; one can celebrate and seek to emulate the life of Socrates while also laughing along with Aristophanes. And, indeed, there is undeniably something amusing about the *Clouds;* in part, it is that "Aristophanes recaptures for us the absurdity of a grown man who spends his time thinking about gnats' anuses" (Bloom 1987: 270). But it might also be that Bloom (1987: 269) is correct in noting that Socrates would have found the portrayal amusing, as "he and Aristophanes share a certain levity." That said, many readers are seriously troubled by the connection between the charges leveled against Socrates in the *Clouds* and those that ultimately resulted in his execution.[2] And, of course, Aristophanes' portrayal is not the only one that paints Socrates in a less than flattering light.

In several of Plato's dialogues, Socrates is described by his interlocutors as weak, cowardly, and disingenuous. Perhaps the most famous negative description is put forward by Callicles in the *Gorgias* (Plato 1996a: 480a–487e). There, the life of the philosopher is subjected to serious scorn and ridicule. Angela Hobbs (2000: 139) aptly describes Callicles' devastating critique:

> The adult philosopher is utterly ignorant of the ways of the world, and entirely inexperienced in the pleasures, desires and characters of men. If he ever has to engage in any public business, he is thus bound to make a fool of himself; he is equally bound to lack manliness, since he spends his days huddled in a corner with a few callow youths, avoiding the social centres where, as Homer notes, men win glory. Unable to protect himself or his own if wrongfully accused, he is both a boy amongst men and a slave amongst the free.

While a great deal more will be said ahead about the Platonic response to these disparaging comments, it is immediately noteworthy that Callicles directly mentions the inability of the philosopher to defend himself against potential accusers or to act heroically. Plato will need to answer both of these challenges in order to present Socrates' philosophic way of life as one worthy of emulation, especially insofar as Callicles' critique alludes to the glory of the Homeric heroes. In addition to this denunciation, the *Republic* also presents a critique of Socrates' character. There, Thrasymachus chastises Socrates for speaking about nonsense, debating in an inane manner, and being ironic (Plato 1991: 336c–d). Further, when Socrates begins to question his definition of justice as the advantage of the stronger, Thrasymachus retorts, "You are disgusting, Socrates. . . . You take hold of the argument in the way you can work it the most harm" (Plato 1991: 338d).3 While we might dismiss as sour grapes the obvious contempt for Socrates that Thrasymachus displays, it is also noteworthy that book 1 of the *Republic* ends with the former unable to convincingly refute the argument about justice made by the latter.[4]

In so many ways, then, Socrates seems to be the central figure in a cautionary tale that fathers might present to their sons. Given these critiques, what about him might be seen as heroic or worthy of emulation? In this chapter, I put forward an answer to this question through an exploration of the three Platonic dialogues that deal with Socrates' trial, imprisonment, and execution. Faced with charges of impiety and corruption of the youth, Socrates attempts a defense designed to vindicate the philosophic way of life. In this, he seems to be successful, as Socrates is today highly regarded for his description of the good life and for his unwillingness to live any other sort of life, a position that is most obviously exemplified by his defense in the *Apology*. After his sentencing, Socrates' arguments and actions—in the *Crito* and the *Phaedo*—also lend considerable support to the idea that the philosopher is committed to living a particularly good sort of life. While the sequence of dialogues that culminate in Socrates' execution might seem to be the most obviously critical of the life of the philosopher, I argue that these dialogues actually serve to enshrine the character of Socrates as the quintessential other-regarding hero, the third of the classical heroic archetypes that inform Western thought. After all, the critical position taken by Aristophanes, Callicles, and Thrasymachus is distinctly in the minority today, and even the Athenians who condemned Socrates erected statues in his honor almost immediately after his execution (cf. Kofman 1998: 47).

In turning the ignoble death of his mentor into a virtuous triumph and defining other-regarding heroism in the process, Plato makes an important contribution to the debate about heroic behavior and motivation that stands at the center of this project. He is successful in this, I argue, for two reasons: first, he suggests that Socrates has an intimate understanding—and perhaps even an appreciation—of his mortality and actively chooses to die. Secondly, he demonstrates that—in choosing to give up his life—Socrates sacrifices himself for the good of others, both his friends and even the Athenians at large who seem to be his enemies. He explains his decision to several of his students in ways that set an example of proper decision making and also encourage them to continue to see the life of the philosopher as choiceworthy. In his depiction of Socrates' trial and execution, Plato establishes him as a hero whose actions are distinctly other-regarding while, at the same time, like Homer's heroes, Socrates effectively demonstrates that the kind of life one lives—rather than its duration—is of primary importance. But unlike them, he chooses to give up his life not to attain some personal good—like *kléos* [κλέος; glory] or *nostos* [νόστος; homecoming]—but in order to do some good for others. In thus rehabilitating the life of the philosopher— one devoted both to the pursuit of wisdom and to assisting others—Plato provides a new model of heroism that can stand alongside Homer's Achilles and Odysseus, and even compete with them for the attention of young people who seek role models to emulate.

THE TRIAL OF SOCRATES

The arguments found in Plato's *Apology* are well known and much discussed, as is the idea that Socrates' character is crafted to be seen as a martyred hero.[5] There is little debate about whether Socrates defended himself successfully against the charges that he faced, even if Socrates himself wants to debate why his accusers have brought him to trial in the first place. Similarly, few people seriously question whether Socrates believes that his jury will accept his proposed punishment after convicting him; instead, most assume that he is either speaking ironically or actively seeking the death penalty proposed by his accusers.[6] Somewhat less well-worn, however, is a discussion of Socrates' initial defense, and so it is to that discussion that I turn in this section, as I want to suggest that Socrates' defense cannot possibly succeed in refuting the charge of impiety (or of corrupting the youth, which stemmed from it) and is not intended to do so.

Socrates' contemporaries believed that philosophy was a useless and dangerous activity; indeed, the danger of the philosopher stemmed, at least in part, from his uselessness. The philosopher, they argued, was thoroughly self-interested and was, therefore, not a contributing member of the political community.[7] In the *Clouds,* Socrates is characterized by his selfish concerns for others' money and his own reputation. He and his students spend their time engaged in outrageous arguments and the examination of the things in the heavens and below the earth, rather than with those things—like working, governing, or fighting—that would fall within the traditional purview of other Athenians (Aristophanes 1984: 187–206). In contemplating the eternal things, Socrates does little—if anything—that would serve to benefit his community and challenges the very idea that human beings should concern themselves only with their own small world. Worse still, in discussing ephemeral topics with the youth of Athens in the *agora,* Socrates might come to be seen as a role model for these young Athenians to emulate. His endeavor—amusing and provocative as it is—actually seems designed to ensure this possibility, as he questions the best-known and most respected men of Athens, and systematically displays how little they truly know about the very topics in which they claim expertise. In doing so, he bolsters his own reputation for wisdom while denigrating all others. Thus, the philosopher is not simply a lazy or arrogant annoyance, one who challenges received opinion while contributing precious little of substance: he is also a potential subversive. If he successfully presents his way of life as worthwhile, the consequences for Athens could be disastrous. A good number of young men might choose to follow the example of Socrates and thereby neglect their duties as citizens. While Socrates would not regard this behavior as a corruption of the youth, it seems clear that his jurors should. And yet Socrates agrees that the youth follow him, but he says that they do so of their own free will. He takes pains to demonstrate that he does not charge them for the lessons they learn and proceeds to argue that his influence does not corrupt them. Indeed, neither the parents nor the children who are directly concerned have ever come forward to argue against him and even now, at his trial, his accusers cannot bring forward any witnesses against him (Plato 1984a: 33e–34a). Therefore, he argues, the parents must not actually believe their children to be corrupt and the children with whom he spoke in their youth must not have grown into corrupt adults.

Regardless of whether the jurors could conceivably be convinced by this argument, it seems clear that anyone who spends a significant amount of time with Socrates likely runs the risk of corruption. After all, his stated goal in the *Republic* is to demonstrate the virtue of living a life devoted to philosophy, and he clearly reiterates that position during his trial. Anyone who might be convinced—either by his arguments or by his lifestyle—would be following an example that is distinctly troubling for Athens, for in living a life devoted to questioning and thinking about what happens in those places that are above and below the earth, Socrates wants to subject Olympus and Hades to the same sort of examination for which he is known in Athens. But this amounts to claiming that the world of the gods can be made intelligible to human beings in the same way as the natural world, which likely ought to be read as a direct challenge to the gods. After all, the natural world around us is clearly observable and measurable, while the world of the gods is considered to be mysterious and so presumably unknowable. In asking questions about the realm of the gods, Socrates is likely blaspheming; in claiming that he might make sense of it he is unquestionably displaying that classic tragic vice, hubris. While we might well question whether Aristophanes' portrayal of Socrates is a fair or accurate one, it is noteworthy that Plato's Socrates is undoubtedly acting either blasphemously or hubristically in the *Apology* as well.[8]

In his own defense against the charge of impiety, Socrates tells an unusual story about how he came to be on trial (cf. Plato 1984a: 21b–23e). He argues that Chaerephon, a deceased friend of his who appeared in the *Clouds* and was also well known to the jurors, once visited the Oracle at Delphi and was told there that Socrates was the wisest man. Upon hearing what he perceives as an outrageous claim about his own intelligence, Socrates sets out on a quest to find wiser men than himself. He is either puzzled by or else he simply does not believe the words of the Oracle; either way, he decides that he must now spend his time publicly interviewing the most respected men of Athens in order to demonstrate the inaccuracy of the Oracle's claim. He begins with the politicians, moves next to the poets, and finally concludes with the artisans. Unfortunately—though perhaps unsurprisingly—Socrates discovers that "those with the best reputations seemed to me nearly the most deficient" (Plato 1984a: 22a). Of course, in asking questions of those people who are considered wise by everyone and then demonstrating their shortcomings, Socrates recognizes that he is not winning any friends among the men of Athens. Despite both the personal and financial costs to him, he cannot give up his examination of those men who are purported to be wise, as he argues that his activity is done in the service of Apollo.

Brickhouse and Smith (1989: 96) view Socrates' mission as a pious one, as "Socrates' attempt to refute the apparent meaning of the oracle only reinforces the view that he sees piety as requiring that he always make 'the god's business' take first priority." The trouble with this argument—and with the entire story that Socrates tells about Chaerephon—is that human beings simply do not have the option of disputing the Delphic Oracle. As is well known from the majority of Greek tragedy—most notably the tale of Oedipus—horrible misfortune always ensues when mortals attempt to question what the gods have decreed. As Michael Zuckert (1984: 284) notes, "Like Oedipus, he sets off on his 'wanderings' in order to show that the oracle is false. Socrates' 'service to the god' consists in an Oedipean rebellion against the god." And just as Oedipus cannot outrun his fate, it seems like a tragic mistake for Socrates to question the accuracy of the Oracle. In defending himself with this story about what he sees as his overwhelming devotion to Apollo, Socrates seems to be embracing the charge of impiety by displaying his hubristic attitude (even if we might argue that he does so fairly subtly). His goal, in all that he has done, has always been to find a man wiser than himself. This quest both infuriates the individuals with whom he speaks and also serves as a challenge to the validity of the Delphic Oracle. In other words, Socrates either acts with hubris by seeing the words of the god as a puzzle he can piece together or is guilty of impiety, as charged, because he just does not believe in the god's omniscience. Regardless of whether the former or the latter is correct—and it seems impossible to decide which is the actual position that Socrates takes—both are incredibly dangerous and have obviously negative implications for the outcome of his trial.

In thinking through the charge of impiety and Socrates' defense against it, one would be hard-pressed to argue that the philosopher is successful in demonstrating his innocence. And yet it is also important to note that Socrates seems less interested in proving that he is pious than a normal defendant likely ought to be. Instead, a good portion of his defense—after the story described earlier—is given over to a demonstration of the ignorance of his accusers, as well as their envy and personal animosity toward him. Thomas West (1979: 147) argues that, instead of attempting to defend himself against the charges, Socrates jokes with Meletus, who "cannot help being ridiculous because he woodenly persists in trying to be serious." While he then pronounces his answer to Meletus "sufficient," he immediately claims that "this is what will convict me, if it does convict me: not Meletus or Anytus, but the slander and envy of the many. This has convicted many other good men too, and I suppose it will also convict me" (Plato 1984a:

28a–b). Thus, although he might be successful in highlighting the true motivation behind his trial—namely, that Meletus, Anytus, and even his jurors desire that he be publicly punished—it is also possible to argue that neither Socrates' behavior nor that of his accusers prior to the trial ultimately accounts for his conviction.[9] Indeed, it seems just as likely that the jurors find him guilty by virtue of his behavior during the trial.[10] After all, much of his defense is spent reminding his jurors that he is allegedly the wisest man in the world and certainly wiser than they are. The remainder focuses the attention of the jury on the consequences of the trial's outcome, for Socrates effectively raises the stakes for himself and for the city before the jurors have even considered whether he should be judged guilty or innocent.

While any reader of the *Apology* would already know that the historical Socrates was convicted and ultimately executed, it is unusual that Plato's Socrates seems to force the hand of the jury in the matter even as he should be defending himself. Rather than focusing solely on the question of his guilt or innocence, Socrates argues that the jury must either find his actions blameless or kill him. Central to this point is Socrates' argument that he has not intentionally harmed anyone and that, if has done any unintentional harm, he did so only with the hope of teaching others how to live virtuously. Given his view of both his innocence and the rectitude of his actions, Socrates believes that he cannot do anything other than what he has done. Even more than arguing for the perceived rightness of his actions, however, Socrates suggests that he will not flatter his jurors or seek to arouse their sympathy in ways that might have been expected. To do so would be inappropriate for someone with the reputation for virtue that he believes he possesses. V. J. Gray (1989: 139) writes, "Socrates does not conform to the accepted psychology of a man on trial for his life. He preferred to die by *megalēgoria* [μεγαληγορια; lit. 'big talk,' high-mindedness, boastfulness] than live by appeasement."[11] Though Socrates does make reference to his military service on behalf of the city and also to his poverty as proof that he does not charge the youth who learn from him, N. A. Greenberg (1965: 70) argues that his "major defense, whether the result of Machiavellian planning . . . or the result of an absolute confidence in the rightness of his past life . . . is a tremendous stipulation in the form of a counterchallenge flung at the jurors: Either kill me or acquit me." The increased risk that he faces from this gamble is calculated to make clear to the jury that Socrates means what he says. He does this by neglecting an actual defense, as described earlier, and by arguing that he will not back down by altering his behavior. As he says,

So that not even if you let me go now and if you disobey Anytus—who said that either I should not have been brought in here at the beginning, or, since I was brought in, that it is not possible not to kill me (he said before you that if I am acquitted, soon your sons, pursuing what Socrates teaches, will all be completely corrupted)—if you would say to me with regard to this, "Socrates, for now we will not obey Anytus; we will let you go, but on this condition: that you no longer spend time in this investigation or phi-losophize; and if you are caught still doing this, you will die"—if you would let me go, then, as I said, on these conditions, I would say to you, "I, men of Athens, salute you and love you, but I will obey the god rather than you; and as long as I breathe and am able to, I will certainly not stop philosophizing." (Plato 1984a: 29c–d)

In other words, the only way for the city to ensure that Socrates will desist from philosophizing is by executing him; more traditional punishments—like exile or a steep fine—would be unacceptable both to him and to them.

And, indeed, Socrates spends a great deal of time and energy demonstrat-ing that he does not fear the death that might well result from the gamble he takes. The tack that he takes with regard to dying is straightforward and fits nicely with his position about the virtues of the philosophical life. Socrates notes that no one knows what happens to people after they die and, for that reason, most people—fearing the unknown—fear death. The philosopher, however, is principally concerned with examining the unknown, and so, rather than fearing death, he might well anticipate the unlocking of its mys-teries. As he says, "To fear death, men, is in fact nothing other than to seem to be wise, but not to be so. For it is to seem to know what one does not know: no one knows whether death does not even happen to be the greatest of all goods for the human being; but people fear it as though they knew well that it is the greatest of evils" (Plato 1984a: 29a). While Socrates will speak to this point in further detail in both the *Crito* and the *Phaedo*, he notes here that death is the eventual fate of every living thing and, as a consequence, one might consider how best to die. Rather than hoping to squeeze a few more years of life from his jurors by pleading with them or bringing his family forward on his behalf, Socrates argues that "as to reputation, mine and yours and the whole city's, to me it does not seem to be noble for me to do any of these things. . . . I have often seen some who are just like this when they are judged: although they are reputed to be something, they do wondrous deeds, since they suppose that they will suffer something terrible if they die—as though they would be immortal if you did not kill them" (Plato 1984a: 34e–35a). This line of thought, characterized by Greenberg (1965: 56) as choosing to live "not life, but a good life," is an important component of my argument that Socrates' behavior should be regarded as distinctly heroic. Because he could likely avoid death and instead chooses to embrace it, Socrates is able to make a statement with his death. As Costica Bradatan (2007: 589) points out, "Socrates' death was the most effective means of persuasion he ever used, and over the centuries he has come to be venerated not so much for what he did when he was alive, but for the way in which he died."[12]

That said, Bradatan (2007: 591) puts forward a reading of Socrates' aggressive stance toward his jurors that is quite at odds with the one I have been advocating: "By the age of seventy, one has grown deep enough into the world and the world has grown deep into one; any separation cannot but be painful, so Socrates had good reason for being afraid of dying." Thus, Socrates is exceptionally heroic in electing to die now rather than later. For Bradatan (2007: 591), "a Socrates who had to make efforts to overcome his fear of death, who had to find his courage in the depths of his fear, is even more glorious." While it is quite likely that many (and perhaps most) septuagenarians fear death, it is noteworthy that the Platonic Socrates repeatedly tells us that he does not. For Bradatan (2007: 591) this amounts to excessive protestation that must be a signpost of his concern: "Socrates is simply *too* insistent on his not being afraid of death not to draw our attention to it." The more straightforward reading, however, is one that takes Socrates at his word: he tells his jurors that he does not fear death not to convince himself but because he wants to impress upon them that he truly does not.[13] Of course, on either reading, there is something distinctly impressive about Socrates. As I argue, Plato provides his readers with a role model who emulates the Homeric heroes in facing the afterlife without trepidation.[14] Just as Achilles announces his unwillingness to leave Troy for a life of safety once Hector has killed Patroclus and just as Odysseus abjures Calypso's offer of immortality, so too does Socrates embrace death without fear, putting on a defense that is very likely to lead to his execution. Further, his arguments about death and his actions surrounding his impending execution—in the *Crito* and the *Phaedo,* the jailhouse dialogues—seem to lend considerable support to this claim. It is to those dialogues that I now turn.

THE POSSIBILITY OF ESCAPING FATE

The *Crito* is perhaps best known for Socrates' argument that one must obey the laws. He makes this case in a jailhouse discussion with his friend Crito, who actively seeks a way to mitigate the punishment that Socrates faces in the aftermath of his unsuccessful defense. While Crito is frustrated that Socrates has gotten himself—and, by extension, all of his friends—into this situation in the first place, he is not above resorting to extrajudicial means to keep the philosopher alive. The possibilities of bribery, escape, and exile are all raised in the course of the dialogue, but Socrates cannot be turned from the path he has chosen. For Greenberg (1965: 51), this amounts to a distinction between the way practical and impractical men choose to approach a problem:

> Crito takes a practical view of the situation. In his opinion, the trial should have been avoided or at least conducted differently, but all that is past. At the moment, as he sees it, Socrates has a choice between certain death and the attempt to escape, and he argues strongly for the latter. . . . For Socrates, the impractical man, it becomes important not only to defend his decision to remain and die, but also to defend his past decisions and actions, for the present and the past are closely and indissolubly connected for him.

Regardless of whether we view the Socratic position as impractical, it is clear that the philosopher is very much driven, in the *Crito*, by arguments he made previously. His claims, here, echo those made in both the *Apology* and the *Republic*, creating a coherent picture of a Socrates who is heroic in his steadfast commitment to living justly.

The impending execution is an obvious evil to Crito and to most readers of Plato's dialogues, but for Socrates there are clearly several outcomes that would be worse still. Indeed, as he repeatedly argues in the *Apology*, "The unexamined life is not worth living for a human being" (Plato 1984a: 38a). This argument is reiterated in the *Crito*, as Socrates says that "not living, but living well, is to be regarded as most important" (Plato 1984b: 48b). That said, there is considerably less time spent in the *Crito* on making a case for living a particular sort of life, especially in comparison with the *Apology* or the *Republic*. Instead, the focus of Socrates' argument here is on whether it would be acceptable for him to escape the fate that has been decreed for him by the members of his jury.

The numerous points put forward by Crito seem to be at least moderately compelling, both on their own merits and because readers would prefer that Socrates be saved from execution. The various claims are nicely articulated elsewhere (cf. Greenberg 1965: 48–49) and need not be rehearsed here in great detail. Suffice it to say that Crito approaches the problem from several angles and that Socrates eventually either ignores or deflects each one. At the center of the dialogue, however, is the seemingly straightforward case for obeying the laws, which Socrates employs to serve both his argument against escape and, more importantly, his larger point about justice. It is important to ask, then, whether Plato makes a compelling case on behalf of the laws—which are personified here in discussion with Socrates—or whether Socrates' decision not to resist his punishment rests on some other argument. To my mind, the idea that the laws must always be obeyed simply does not hold up to scrutiny; thus, I argue that Socrates has already decided to remain in prison prior to Crito's visit. Despite his good intentions, Crito's case is never seriously considered and Socrates' argument is meant to mollify his friend and instruct other like-minded Athenians.

In thinking through Socrates' discussion with Crito about the possibility of escape, it is important to note that he claims a willingness to *try* to escape if he can be persuaded that such an attempt would be right. At issue, then, is not the success or failure of the escape, but whether the proposed action itself (even if the attempted escape failed) can be shown to be the correct one. Thus, Socrates is not concerned with avoiding his punishment; he is, instead, interested in whether one can legitimately set out to subvert the law under which he has been convicted and sentenced. In the end, he argues that attempting to escape is impermissible because of the harm that would be caused by that attempt. The argument, then, revolves around the idea of harm and the claim that a just man ought not to harm anyone (an echo of the *Republic*). In the first place, it is clear that Crito is confused by Socrates' assertion that no one would be harmed if he decided to remain in prison and face execution. Leaving aside the question of whether Socrates himself ought to be considered (as Crito would likely assume that he would be harmed by his own death, even though Socrates might not think so), there seem to be several people who would suffer from Socrates' death. Most obviously, Crito points out that the family and friends of the philosopher would be greatly injured by his execution. While his family would clearly suffer from the loss of husband and father, Crito also argues that the reputations of his friends—and of his family too—would be harmed. By way of a response, Socrates says that "these are considerations of those who easily kill and, if they could, would bring back to life again, acting mindlessly: namely the many" (Plato 1984b: 48c). As Greenberg (1965: 60) argues, this passage both conveys a deep contempt for those things—like reputation—that are prized by the masses and seems to fail to consider Crito's argument in any serious way. Is it not, in fact, the case that Socrates' friends and family will be harmed by his death, even if he is unwilling to agree that he is being personally harmed? And would the harm to these people not be substantially mitigated by his escape from the death penalty? While Socrates might be opposed to putting much weight on the loss of these things that are prized by the many, his friends and family will almost certainly feel differently in the aftermath of his execution. Crito is thoroughly perplexed by this discussion, as Socrates seems to ignore the harm done to himself, his friends, and his family, while focusing on the possible harm done to those who seek to execute him. In doing so, of course, Socrates clearly refutes the notion that he acts selfishly, for this would certainly be the time to think principally of oneself and one's loved ones if ever there was one. As Ernest J. Weinrib (1982: 97) points out, "Now Socrates is suggesting, without so far explaining himself, that by escaping he will be harming precisely those who he least ought to. Those whom Socrates has in mind have an even stronger claim to immunity from harm than his friends and family, but who could those be?"

As far as Socrates is concerned, the only serious consideration seems to be the harm that he would cause by attempting to escape from his judicial punishment. In the attempt, after all, Socrates would be expressing his opposition to the laws of Athens, and this would presumably cause a great deal of harm (both to the laws and, by extension, to the city). Thus, the philosopher devotes a considerable amount of time in the *Crito* to thinking through the various ways in which his actions would do harm to the laws. To do so, he imagines a discussion where the laws, personified, ask him,

> By this deed that are you attempting, what do you think you're doing, if not destroying us laws and the whole city, as far as it lies in you? Or does it seem possible to you for a city to continue to exist, and not to be overturned, in which the judgments that are reached have no strength, but are rendered ineffective and are corrupted by private men? (Plato 1984b: 50a–b)

While these questions are certainly interesting and challenging ones, there are a number of problems that arise from them. Indeed, A.D. Woozley (1979: vii) argues that "the arguments given in *Crito* why it is wrong to break the law are interestingly bad rather than uninterestingly good." Thus, we might ask whether it is necessarily the case that any violation of the law spells disaster for the city as a whole, whether an attempted escape would thoroughly invalidate the power of the laws in general, and also whether it is therefore imperative to follow even unjust laws.

In responding to Crito, Socrates seems to be arguing something very similar to the idea that one cannot choose to obey the law when it stands in one's favor and then ignore it when it stands opposed. If the Athenians voted, in accordance with the laws, in favor of his execution, he must go along with that decision; after all, in all other decisions, Socrates has respected the will of the voting majority without complaint. Thus, the argument seems to be that if proper procedures are followed, one cannot now dispute the outcome. As the laws themselves ask, "Are you not transgressing . . . your contracts and agreements with us, although you did not agree to them under necessity and were not deceived? Nor were you compelled to take counsel in a short time, but during seventy years in which you could have gone away if we were not satisfactory or if the agreements did not appear to be just to you" (Plato 1984b: 52d–e). Further, Socrates—as a citizen of Athens—has benefited a great deal from the order, security, and prosperity that can be traced back to the laws of the city. It might be human nature to complain when the laws now condone a judgment against him, but one must consider the fact that he never complained about any other judgment concerning others. Justice, then, would seem to demand that Socrates follow the dictates of the law in his own case, just as he has done in every other case.

But this is likely not the central claim he wants to make, for one might well argue that Socrates can safely disobey the laws in this case because the Athenians have arrived at an unjust outcome, even if they have followed the laws in doing so.[15] Indeed, the essence of his discussion with Crito seems to be Socrates' opposition to exchanging injustice for injustice, which is further developed in book 1 of the *Republic* in his rebuttal of Polemarchus' claim that a just person "gives benefits and harms to friends and enemies" (Plato 1991: 332d). The argument about owing obedience to the laws of Athens, then, accords with the principle that one should not commit a wrong in response to a wrong. Of course, as Weinrib (1982: 97) notes, this also implies "the rejection of the converse popular notion that the doing of good is owed only to one's friends." While Socrates demonstrates for Polemarchus in the *Republic* that one cannot make a person more just by acting unjustly toward him, he also concludes in the *Crito* that he must do good to those who condemn him—his seeming enemies—and thereby provide them with further instruction. He speaks of honoring Athens and her laws, and in so doing, he is acting justly toward Athens as the city should be just to him, while refusing to do anything unjust (cf. Zuckert 2009:

237–238). He believes that Athens has wronged him, but—as he loves Athens—he will not harm the city in return. There are two problems with this position, however. The first is that the principle under which Socrates has long been proceeding applies to *people* and not to *laws*. As Weinrib (1982: 98) astutely argues,

> the Laws are not persons but personifications, abstractions conjured up by Socrates and endowed with the power of speech, suffering, and action. The shift is unobtrusive but not insignificant, since the . . . principle is derived from, and thus tied to, the supposition that there is something supremely human which is injured and destroyed by injustice in the same way that the body is destroyed by disease.[16]

Indeed, the laws themselves accuse Socrates of working for their "destruction," if he attempts to escape, rather than causing them "harm" (cf. Plato 1984b: 50b). And so Socrates has altered the argument in a way that would seemingly allow him to attempt an escape in his demonstration that such an attempt is impermissible.

The second problem, of course, is that the entire argument holds only if it is the case that disobedience to the laws constitutes a harm to the city. The question of whether Socrates would do harm to Athens by disobeying the laws in an attempt to save his life is not as easily assessed as it might initially appear. As noted earlier, Socrates argues that he loves Athens and will not exchange harm for harm with her citizens. An escape attempt would be a clear harm to Athens by undermining the power of her laws. This is the position put forward by the laws themselves, and Socrates seems to agree insofar as he refuses Crito's pleas. And yet Socrates does not appear to be nearly as caring in the *Apology,* where he argues that he loves Athens and also that his execution will damage the city by depriving her of someone who cares most deeply for her well-being (cf. Plato 1984a: 30c). Further, Athens will incur a negative reputation by executing him and her citizens will remain in ignorance. It is fair, then, to ask why he would refuse Crito's assistance in attempting to escape, if he truly loves Athens and believes that his death will have an adverse effect on her. The answer seems to rely on the argument that the laws have a special, parental relationship to the citizenry and that, in fact, one must treat the city and her laws with even more respect than one's parents (cf. Plato 1984b: 50e–51b). Faced with these two competing claims, Socrates must choose between continuing to challenge the people of Athens by denouncing their unjust punishment and circumventing their laws, on the one hand, and respecting the traditional values of the city, on the other. As everyone knows, he will select the latter and accept his punishment.

That said, even this choice is more complicated than it appears, for Socrates only moments earlier told Crito that he did not respect the traditional judgments and values of the multitude. Why should he now respect the laws as the voice of the authority figures he has been challenging throughout his life? This seems especially surprising as the laws themselves echo an unfair criticism of Socrates, about sons unnaturally beating their fathers, found in the *Clouds*.[17] While the laws seem to suggest that Socrates is liable to act unnaturally, they also seek to impress upon him that citizens ought not to do so. But, as Weinrib (1982: 99) argues, "The violation is . . . of the tenet of popular morality that one should help one's friends and harm one's enemies. And it is precisely this tenet which Socrates was rejecting." Of course, in choosing to circumvent the laws of Athens, he would violate his own principle of not harming anyone, provided that one accepts that breaking the law will harm the Athenians. Even though, as Weinrib (1982: 106) points out, "Socrates' disobedience is expected because it is possible, regardless of his innocence," his escape would constitute a harm by validating the Athenians' oversimplified understanding of justice as doing good to friends and harm to enemies. In doing so, Socrates would accept the position that the Athenians are able to condemn him to death, on the one hand, and also—as Crito fears—to criticize his friends for failing to rescue him from that fate. Thus, in either case, Socrates seems to run headlong into one of the two principles he sought to impress upon Crito as being of grave importance. If he flees, he violates both principles by harming the Athenians insofar as their laws are circumvented and also by accepting the outlook of the many: "just as they used the opportunity to convict him, so Socrates should use the opportunity to escape" (Weinrib 1982: 106). If he stays, he violates both principles by harming the Athenians insofar as they are deprived of him and also by accepting the outlook of the many: the laws "are his friends and it would be ingratitude on his part to destroy, so far as in him lies, those who had rendered him such signal services in the past. He would be requiting benefit with harm" (Weinrib 1982: 99).

In an attempt to sort out what Socrates ought to do and why he chooses to remain, it is important to recall that he changes the terms of his second principle in the course of his discussion with Crito. Rather than avoiding all harm to all people, Socrates asks, "If we go away from here without persuading the city, do we do evil to some—indeed, to those whom it should least be done to—or not?" (Plato 1984b: 49e–50a). It seems, then, that Socrates is willing to compromise the principle a bit, acknowledging that some people will inevitably be harmed to some degree, though the harm might not be as serious as those people might imagine. On the one hand, it seems to be principally important to persuade the Athenians of the veracity of all that he has said prior to his conviction. The most obvious way to accomplish this task, of course, is to sacrifice himself, for he already averred—in the *Apology*—that he would not change his ways "even if I were going to die many times" (Plato 1984a: 30c). In order to demonstrate his stated commitment to living a good life, Socrates chooses to "express himself by the most radical means, namely, his own body, *letting it die* in a most spectacular manner, so that nobody could ignore or not 'listen to' it" (Bradatan 2007: 592). Zuckert (1984: 293) makes a very similar point:

"Socrates' dying for his philosophy, while upholding at once his own justice and the justice of the city, can prove to the Athenians that philosophy is not the sort of thing they suspect it to be." And yet, on the other hand, Socrates also seeks to provide for his friends even as he leaves them in a way that might harm them. Indeed, the arguments he makes in the final hours of his final day—chronicled in the *Phaedo*—speak to this goal.

THE LONGING FOR IMMORTALITY

The *Phaedo* is a story within a story, as Phaedo—who was present at the execution—recounts to Echecrates—who was not—all that took place on the day of Socrates' death. There are several interesting points that might be discussed, including the philosopher's apparent lack of concern for his wife and children, and the fact that he has begun writing poetry despite vehemently arguing—especially in the *Republic*—against the influence of the poets. But the majority of the dialogue is devoted to a discussion of whether it makes sense to live a life devoted to philosophy, especially in the face of Socrates' execution that day. In order to make his case to two skeptical friends, Simmias and Cebes, Socrates puts forward a series of arguments to suggest both that the soul is immortal, and that the philosopher will be rewarded after his death for his devotion to wisdom and justice.

In the first place, Socrates claims that death is actually the principal goal of the philosopher because only by dying can he attain true wisdom. As Eric Voegelin (1952: 65–66) asserts, "Under the aspect of death the life of the philosophical man becomes for Plato the practice of dying . . . and, when the philosopher speaks as the representative of truth, he does so with the authority of death over the shortsightedness of life." For this position to be tenable, Socrates must go on to demonstrate that the soul will continue to exist, separately, after the death of the body. He begins by pointing out that, in all the time that a philosopher is alive, he is restricted from achieving his goal of truly knowing anything; Socrates' reason is that the senses are deceptive and the many bodily needs distract the philosopher unmercifully throughout life. He says,

> So long as we have the body with us in our enquiry, and our soul is mixed up with so great an evil, we shall never attain sufficiently what we desire, and that, we say, is the truth. . . . Chief of all is that if we do have some leisure, and turn away from the body to speculate on something, in our searches it is everywhere interfering, it causes confusion and disturbance, and dazzles us so that it will not let us see the truth; so in fact we see that if we are ever to know anything purely we must get rid of it, and examine the real things by the soul alone; and then, it seems, after we are dead, as the reasoning shows, not while we live, we shall possess that which we desire, lovers of which we say we are, namely wisdom. (Plato 1999b: 66b)

Given all of the problems life presents for the philosopher, we might conclude that Socrates is looking forward to his impending execution as a great benefit. He goes so far as to argue, in fact, that the philosopher alone deserves the reward that will come to him after his soul is finally free of its impure body. One reason is the philosopher's extreme devotion to wisdom, even at the expense of bodily desires. And, indeed, his way of life seems to lend support to this conclusion, as Socrates famously lived ascetically so that, presumably, he could ignore as many of the body's demands as possible. But does Socrates truly believe his own rhetoric here or is he simply attempting to shore up his distraught friends at a particularly difficult time? On my reading, Socrates does welcome his own death, seeing it as a necessity, but he seems to be doing much more in the *Phaedo* than simply encouraging Simmias and Cebes to look forward to their own deaths.

The difficulty in making this case, as with the previous discussion of the *Crito*, lies in the fact that my interpretation runs counter to the claims made by Socrates in the dialogue. In other words, when Socrates attempts to demonstrate that the soul is immortal, I point to the weakness of his arguments in order to suggest that he does not, in fact, believe that the soul is immortal. Nevertheless, in the *Phaedo*, Socrates has several reasons to hope that others will believe his arguments about the immortality of the soul. These include a desire to calm his friends and to demonstrate the virtues of the philosophic life; after all, he has been arguing that his death is not an evil because the philosopher deserves a reward after death, which hinges on an afterlife in which the philosopher can actually be rewarded. Thus, he puts forward several possible arguments and submits each to questioning. First, he suggests to Cebes that "the living are born again from the dead" (Plato 1999b: 70a–b).[18] Asking only a few questions—do all beings who have opposites come into being out of their opposites and is death the opposite of life?—Socrates gains assent from Cebes. The trouble, however, is that the points to which he readily agrees do not actually demonstrate the immortality of our souls; instead, they demonstrate that death comes into being out of life. To take the argument further, Socrates provides examples of the connection or similarity between living and dead things, and also gets Cebes to agree that death is akin to sleep. Peter J. Ahrensdorf (1995: 67) does a particularly nice job of setting out the problem: "insofar as we are living beings, that is, warm, fully grown beings whose soul and body are combined, and insofar as death transforms us into cold and decayed beings whose soul and body are separate, we no longer exist once our lives have come to an end. And . . . insofar as we are thinking beings and insofar as death is a form of sleep for the soul, we no longer truly exist once we have died." In the end, not even Cebes is particularly convinced of the argument, saying only, "It seems to me . . . from our admissions that must of necessity be true" (Plato 1999b: 72a). He has given his agreement to each of the points made by Socrates, but even if he is now convinced about the immortality of the soul, he is disappointed in the sort of immortality that Socrates has put forward.

The reason that Cebes remains unhappy—and the reason that the dialogue continues with a new argument for the immortality of the soul—is that he desires a particular sort of immortality. Rather than simply being content with the idea that the soul never perishes, Cebes' "deepest hope is not merely for an everlasting existence but also, and above all, for a perfect and everlasting happiness" (Ahrensdorf 1995: 68). Thus, Cebes suggests that Socrates might put forward another argument in favor of the immortality of the soul, one that he has made in the past. This is the argument that learning is a form of recollection, previously outlined in the *Meno* (cf. Plato 1999a: 81c). And, indeed, as Ahrensdorf (1995: 73) rightly highlights, "The argument that learning is recollection is not only an argument for the immortality of the soul; it is also an argument which seeks to defend the goodness of the life devoted to learning and to the pursuit of wisdom." At this point in the dialogue, Cebes becomes an ally of Socrates while Simmias takes on the role of an extreme skeptic, arguing not only against the notion that learning is recollection but also—in fact—against the idea that learning the truth about these important things is even possible for human beings. While Cebes seems genuinely hopeful that Socrates can persuade him, Simmias seems not to be overly concerned. Of course, in some sense, Simmias' skeptical position is an echo of Socrates' own assertion about death and the afterlife in the *Apology,* quoted earlier (cf. Plato 1984a: 29a–b). And yet, as Ahrensdorf (1995: 77–78) points out, there is a key difference between the two: while Socrates tells the jurors that he welcomes death out of a genuine curiosity about the afterlife, "Simmias . . . does not regard his ignorance about such matters as the immortality of the soul as an evil and hence . . . he believes that he knows all that he needs to know about such matters." Clearly, this is a notion about which Socrates must disabuse him.

He does so by encouraging Simmias in his belief that he is sufficiently wise, even comparable to Socrates. In each step of the discussion, he equates himself with the young man and argues that they must have acquired all of their knowledge about equality, beauty, and goodness before they both were born because they have never seen, in their lives, things that are perfectly equal, beautiful, or good. Moving away from the discussion at hand, about recollection, Socrates suggests that they have had this knowledge all of their lives. Having gained acceptance of this point, Socrates goes on to suggest the possibility that all of this knowledge was forgotten when they were born and has since been recollected. Once Simmias agrees with this assessment, Socrates proceeds to challenge his conception of himself as possessing sufficient wisdom by asking him a question he did not anticipate—namely, "Were we born knowing, or do we remember afterwards what we had got knowledge of before?" (Plato 1999b: 75e). Simmias admits that he is unable to answer because he does not possess sufficient knowledge of what we were like before birth, when our souls dwelled among the eternal things, precisely the matter that is up for discussion in the *Phaedo*. While this might be viewed as a cruel trick, it serves its purpose well. "For, by expressing the wish that all men were wise, Simmias seems to express the wish that he were wise. And by expressing the fear that all men, other than Socrates, are unable to become wise, Simmias seems to express the fear that he may never be able to escape from his ignorance and thereby seems to acknowledge that his ignorance is an evil" (Ahrensdorf 1995: 84). In suggesting that Socrates is wise, however, Simmias presents an objection to any claim that wisdom forever eludes human beings. But he remains reluctant to follow in the philosopher's footsteps, as the conversation is taking place in the very deep shadow of Socrates' impending execution and it is therefore impossible not to be mindful of the consequences of leading a philosophic life. That said, Simmias does not want to think of himself as cowardly, any more than he wanted to think of himself as ignorant; yet if he abandons the philosophic way of life, he will clearly be doing so because of the fear that he will end his days in the same manner as Socrates. As Ahrensdorf (1995: 86) argues, "He must see how important it is for him to know whether or not there is an afterlife in which the philosopher is rewarded for his virtue, that is, for the sacrifices he has made in this life." Simmias now turns to a serious consideration of the immortality of the soul in order to mitigate the dangers of philosophy.

The argument that learning is recollection, then, serves less as a way to persuade his interlocutors of the immortality of the soul than to encourage Simmias that he ought to care about the question of whether the soul is immortal. As proof of Socrates' success in this task, Simmias now rejoins the conversation in earnest, putting forward the cogent objection that the existence of souls before birth does not provide evidence that they survive after death (cf. Plato 1999b: 77b). While Socrates argues that Simmias and Cebes will not accept anything he says because, at bottom, they simply fear death and this colors all of their discussion, he proceeds to make a third argument for the soul's permanence—namely, that the soul resembles all those things that are immortal and is therefore likely immortal itself. In brief, "Socrates' third argument for immortality consists of three parts. First, he explains the nature of mortal and immortal beings (78c1–79a11). Then he argues that the soul is similar to what is divine and immortal (79b1–80b7). Finally, he concludes that the soul 'is altogether indissoluble or nearly so' (80b7–10)" (Ahrensdorf 1995: 91). While this argument might provide some comfort to his friends at a most difficult time, it is clear that Socrates has not adequately demonstrated that the soul is immortal. Instead, as Ahrensdorf (1995: 99) correctly argues, "While the soul may be very similar to what is immortal and hence may be 'nearly' immortal, it is not, in the end, immortal." Much like in his discussion with Crito, Socrates again seems to be making arguments that are either suspiciously incomplete or about things he does not actually believe.

Despite their interest in his arguments, their personal devotion to him, and their desire to be persuaded, then, Simmias and Cebes are reluctant to accept what Socrates says, both about the immortality of the soul and about the likelihood that the philosopher will be rewarded after his death. Of course, this might be due in part to the fact that Socrates openly acknowledges that his interlocutors have good reason to doubt what he says (Plato 1999b: 84d). Why does Socrates so readily admit that his argument is a weak one? Perhaps he notices that Simmias and Cebes are not persuaded, as they are whispering among themselves after he concludes his argument. Perhaps he is fearful—despite everything he has said to the contrary—and desires his friends to assist in making a persuasive case about the possibility that his soul will survive his impending death. More likely, though, is that Socrates' style of discussion in the *Phaedo* is specifically suited to Simmias and Cebes. As Ahrensdorf (1995: 110) notes, "By awakening in them the desire to know that the soul is immortal and by letting them see for themselves the reasons for doubting that the soul is immortal . . . Socrates encourages Cebes and Simmias most effectively to examine the question of the immortality of the soul for themselves and on their own." Given that he will soon be absent from their lives, and given their uncertainty about the virtue of living a life devoted to the search for wisdom, Socrates addresses his primary concern that they will reject the philosophic way of life as a consequence of his execution.

SOCRATES' LAST INTERLOCUTORS

Rather than writing a philosophic text and ascribing it to his mentor, Plato chooses to present the character of Socrates in dialogue with people for whom he has specific messages. As David Bolotin (1987: 39) notes, "Socrates' primary intention, it seems, on many or even most occasions was to impart opinions that would be salutary for his particular interlocutors, rather than to teach them what he regarded as the truth." In the *Apology,* for example, Plato takes pains to answer the two sets of charges put forward against Socrates, even mimicking the structure used by Aristophanes in the *Clouds.* Though his principal interlocutor is Meletus, one of his three accusers, Socrates also speaks directly to his jurors about Anytus, his second accuser, and then about an imagined interlocutor.[19] Zuckert (1984: 280) argues that there are two instances in the *Apology* where Socrates responds to these hypothetical arguments: "In the first exchange, 'one of you' personifies the Just Speech and Socrates, surprisingly perhaps, the Unjust Speech. The second exchange, reversing the order of the Aristophanic model which the first exchange had followed, finds 'someone' taking the part of the Unjust Speech while Socrates apparently has the last word in his Just Speech." In doing so, Plato attempts to use the occasion of Socrates' trial to demonstrate the innocence of philosophy in the face of the charges arrayed against it. As Zuckert (1984: 293–294) argues,

> If philosophy leads Socrates to die, willingly, then philosophy does not, as Aristophanes' and the *Apology*'s Unjust Speech did, decree self-preservation the highest good. To complete his Just Speech before the city, to acquit philosophy from the charges leveled against it first by Aristophanes and later by his other accusers, Socrates must actually die; nothing else will do, for philosophy's identification with the thesis of the Unjust Speech can be decisively broken only if there remains no doubt about Socrates' stance toward that thesis.[20]

If readers were unfamiliar with the *Clouds*, Plato's construction of Socrates' defense would have missed its mark, but given that virtually all would have been well acquainted with it, the mimicry is particularly useful. The aim of the dialogue is not to prove Socrates' innocence in the face of the various charges, but instead to demonstrate the innocence of philosophy as a way of life. Thus, as Zuckert (1984: 296–297) notes, "The *Apology* suggests that Socrates could have 'gotten off' by being less provocative, but had he done so he would not have mitigated the strong prejudice against philosophy that existed in Athens and elsewhere." Knowing his audience, Plato crafts the *Apology* in such a way that Socrates' death is revealed as the noble choice of an other-regarding hero.

This choice is emphasized again in both the *Crito* and the *Phaedo*, where Socrates meets with his friends and justifies his decision to accept the fate that awaits him. And again, in both cases, his speeches are crafted for the benefit of his interlocutors. Thus, in the *Crito*, Socrates presents the argument of the laws as justification for his decision to remain in prison, despite the fact that these arguments seem hollow and unconvincing. Why, then, does Socrates present them at all and, importantly, why does he portray them as decisive in his decision not to escape? According to Weinrib (1982: 103–104), the arguments of the laws are designed for Crito, who is not himself a philosopher: "Crito and the Laws share the same view of the world, a view based on respect for the views of the many, helping friends and harming enemies, and the avoidance of ridicule and shame. . . . Although the speeches of Crito and of the Laws are separated by the conversation establishing the two principles, these principles are reflected in neither set of speeches." Just as Plato uses both the speeches and the actions of the *Apology* to demonstrate Socrates' commitment to philosophy over self-interest and self-preservation, he makes a similar case by putting forward and then refuting the argument of the many as presented by Crito. Weinrib (1982: 107) argues that "Crito pleads as a friend, but his arguments show that the disordered randomness of popular morality was not only destructive of law but that it also rendered irrelevent [sic] considerations of real justice." Crito believes that Socrates *ought* to escape from prison because it *could* be arranged for him to do so.

This dangerous argument, if followed, suggests that actions are prohibited only if they cannot be successfully accomplished, leading—ultimately—to the self-interested extreme of the tyrant who does whatever he can (cf. Plato 1991: 343d–344c). Of course, "it is only because of Crito's unphilosophic nature that Socrates can both sketch a position which is at odds with the opinion of the many and then justify obedience to the law in terms which correspond to the opinion of the many" (Weinrib 1984: 104).

Rather than reject Crito along with his position, Socrates attempts to use the same argument to refute him. Thus, the laws—who speak for the many—enjoin Crito not to violate principles with which he already agrees and with which Socrates now suggests his agreement (cf. Allen 1980: 112–113).[21] Socrates is not persuaded by the argument of the laws, but Crito will be because, in large part, the laws make the same case for obedience that he attempts to make for disobedience. While the philosopher rejects the argument of the many, he does not dispute the conclusion put forward by the laws, for he is committed to obeying the laws for his own reasons and has already chosen to accept his punishment. In this way, Socrates is able to maintain his friendship with Crito by seeming to accept the argument that his principles explicitly reject. Underlying that acceptance, however, is a refutation of the opinion of the many, as Weinrib (1982: 108) notes that "only the self-abnegation involved in deciding to remain in prison and drink the hemlock could bring home the significance of the enterprise on which Socrates was engaged." Just as in the *Apology*, Socrates' actions are necessary to validate the arguments about justice and virtue that he has made throughout his life and to invalidate the charges leveled against the philosophic way of life.

The arguments put forward in the *Phaedo* are substantially different from those of the *Apology* and the *Crito*, and they seem not to fit neatly into the position I am sketching here. Indeed, it might be claimed that Socrates suggests he is approaching death in a self-interested manner, emphasizing a position to which he briefly alluded in the *Apology*. As noted earlier, Socrates argues there that he does not fear death because he does not know much about it; in addition, he claims that "no one knows whether death does not even happen to be the greatest of all goods for the human being" (Plato 1984a: 29a). Now, on the day of his death, Socrates directly states that philosophers should not only not fear death but also welcome it (cf. Plato 1999b: 63b–c). As Ahrensdorf (1995: 37) says, "Socrates here reveals to his friends that the philosopher is not only ready or even eager to die but that he devotes his whole life to learning how to die and that he longs throughout his life for nothing but death." In this discussion with Simmias and Cebes, where Socrates takes as his final subject the immortality of the soul, one might well argue that his position is distinctly self-interested insofar as he argues that he need not fear death because it will be good for him to die. And yet I believe that this would be too narrow a reading of the *Phaedo*, one that does not delve deeply enough into the arguments that Socrates makes.

Instead, I argue that Socrates continues his defense of the philosophic way of life to two friends who are on the verge of rejecting it in the face of the extreme persecution facing philosophers.[22]

More than simply encouraging Simmias and Cebes to think critically during this final conversation, Socrates exhorts everyone present to continue living philosophic lives (cf. Plato 1999b: 88a–c). He then proceeds, in his response to the final objections of his interlocutors, to argue that the philosophic life is the best way of life for human beings, regardless of whether there is an afterlife. "While Socrates responds to Simmias' distrust of the particular argument for immortality by encouraging him in his distrust, he responds to [Cebes'] doubt that it is possible for us, in this life, to attain clear knowledge or wisdom about such questions as the fate of the soul by affirming that such knowledge and such wisdom are indeed available to us in this life" (Ahrensdorf 1995: 186). He does so through an elaborate examination of the existence of the divine ideas, ultimately arguing that they are not able to exist independently of their earthly incarnations. While this argument does not seem to have any bearing on the question of the immortality of the soul, it does speak directly to the question of the goodness of the philosophic way of life, for if the ideas are not separate and divine beings, existing apart from the world occupied by mortals, it would be possible for the philosopher to attain wisdom concerning those ideas while alive. In other words, Simmias and Cebes might well be correct about the mortality of the soul, and, if so, it might also be correct that there is nothing immortal; in that case, "wisdom would consist of the greatest possible knowledge of the world as it is revealed to us by our senses" (Ahrensdorf 1995: 187; cf. Bolotin 1987: 53). Of course, through all of this, Socrates states that he is firmly committed to the belief that the soul is immortal, and he concludes the discussion with mythical accounts of the soul's existence after death.

I contend that, in making these statements, Socrates once again leaves aside self-interested considerations and focuses instead on achieving some good for others. At a time when he would surely be comforted by simply believing that some great reward awaits him after his death, Socrates instead undermines that position in favor of one that will instill in his surviving friends a desire to continue living philosophically. Yet, in concluding with myths and underscoring his commitment to a belief in the afterlife with his final words,[23] he seems to undermine precisely the position he has been advocating throughout his life. Rather than continuing to urge them to question received opinion about the most important things, he now simply tells them to believe in the immortality of the soul, provides a myth rather than an argument for them to consider, and reminds Crito to perform a sacrifice for him.[24] According to Ahrensdorf (1995: 203), "Both the speeches and deeds of Socrates in the *Phaedo* appear to demonstrate his piety. The dialogue in which the Athenians execute Socrates for impiety is the dialogue in which Socrates appears to be most pious." While there continued to be some harassment of individual philosophers in the years after Socrates' death, it is noteworthy that the vocation or lifestyle of philosophy began to be viewed in a far more positive light (cf. Bolotin 1987: 54; Ahrensdorf 1995: 202; Kofman 1998: 47). In addition to the fame of Plato and Aristotle, achieved in their own lifetimes, Ahrensdorf (1995: 202) points out,

> when Aristotle's student Theophrastus was accused of impiety and a law was passed restricting the activities of philosophers in Athens, the Athenians shortly thereafter fined his accuser and repealed the antiphilosophic law so that Theophrastus, who had fled, would return to Athens and live there as before. The Cynic Diogenes and the Stoic Zeno were honored and cherished by the Athenians. And Pyrrho, whose students founded the Sceptics, was appointed the chief priest of Elis. Eventually, the philosophers won renown in the most powerful city in the ancient world, Rome. . . . The reputation of philosophy grew so great there that such students of philosophy as Scipio Aemilianus Africanus, Cato the Younger, and Marcus Aurelius became its leaders. Philosophy, then, which had been an activity engaged in by a small band of persecuted and despised men at the time of Socrates' death, gradually became a subject of study for preeminent statesmen of the ancient world.

In large part, philosophy owes this remarkable reversal of fortune to Plato and his portrayal of Socrates in the dialogues concerning his trial and execution.

In addition, the very end of his life serves as a model for others to emulate; not only does he approach his death with nobility and courage, but he also encourages his friends to continue to devote themselves to philosophical inquiry. Earlier in the dialogue, Socrates warns everyone present not to lose faith in reason at the moment they seem most discouraged about reasoned argumentation (Plato 1999b: 88a–c). When Simmias and Cebes provide strong arguments against Socrates' claims about the immortality of the soul, all those present despair of ever learning the truth through argumentation, rather than acknowledging that Socrates' arguments might have simply been poor ones or that his interlocutors' speeches might be correct. As Bolotin (1987: 55) notes, "So powerful, in other words, is their attachment to the belief in immortality that they would sooner believe that there is no truth in speeches or arguments than that there is no argument for the immortality of the soul." In order to bolster these young men at such a precarious time, Socrates encourages them in their belief about immortality. At the same time, however, he leaves them with a series of arguments that highlight the trouble with simply believing in the truth about such an important matter instead of using reason to arrive at it. Indeed, rather than using his final breath to utter some sort of profundity that would undoubtedly be followed blindly as Socrates' true and final teaching, Socrates instead directs his interlocutors back to the unresolved argument they have been having about the soul's immortality. In doing so, he encourages them to continue on the path on which he has set them.[25] More broadly, in suggesting that Socrates loved Athens, chose to follow its laws, and believed in its gods, Plato removes the tainted image of impiety and self-interest from philosophy. As David Leibowitz (2010: 143) argues, "Not only is Socrates' activity . . . decent, it shows that he cares for the city and for all of the Athenians, older and especially younger—indeed, that he is devoted to their welfare. . . . He thus implies that they are all worthy of his care, that they have the potential to become good, and that, properly understood, their own standard, virtue, is the correct one." In this way, then, by demonstrating that his mentor was dedicated to the pursuit of justice and wisdom above even his own life—dying in order to benefit others and thereby demonstrating that the kind of life one lives is of far greater importance than its duration—Plato creates an altogether new heroic archetype, that of the other-regarding hero, to stand alongside Homer's conventional heroes, Achilles and Odysseus.

5 Philosophy against Poetry
The Distinct Heroics of Achilles and Socrates

> Plato versus Homer: that is the complete, the genuine antagonism—there the sincerest advocate of the "beyond," the greatest slanderer of life; here the instinctive deifier, the *golden* nature. (Nietzsche 1992c: 590)

At the outset of the *Phaedo*, Plato presents the reader with a surprising sight: Socrates, in his jail cell, composing poetry. Now, the philosopher is not currently engaged in this unusual activity; rather, he has just been released from his bonds in preparation for his execution later that day. In commenting somewhat poetically on the pleasure of release that follows the pain of the irons—and referring directly to Aesop in doing so—Socrates reminds one of his interlocutors, Cebes, of a question he meant to ask on the subject of poetry. Apparently, a great many people—including those present on Socrates' last day—were aware that he had recently written poetic versions of Aesop's fables, as well as a hymn to Apollo. As Paul Stern (1993: 20) points out, "We pay special attention to the last words and deeds of the dying with the thought that at the end of life something about human life as a whole might be revealed. But what Cebes sees when considering Socrates' last days is Socrates' divergence from his lifelong pursuit of philosophy." Thus, in asking his question, Cebes notes precisely how odd it seems that Socrates has been writing poetry: "Many people have asked me . . . what on earth put it in your mind to make those poems after you came into prison, although you never made any before" (Plato 1999b: 60d). The question is an important one for his friends because Socrates is so well known for his contempt when it comes to poetry and those who compose it. As recently as his trial, he condemned the poets because they "say many noble things, but they know nothing of what they speak" and because they believed, "on account of their poetry, that they were the wisest of human beings also in the other things, in which they were not" (Plato 1984a: 22c). But this was not the most famous—and certainly not the first—of the Socratic statements of opposition to the poets.

The designation of most famous—and most vitriolic—arguments against poetry undoubtedly goes to those found in Plato's *Republic*. As Dean Hammer (2002: 3) notes, "In positing a split between epic and philosophic knowledge, Plato contended that the problem with the Homeric epic was that it was an imitation (*mimesis*) of phenomenal appearance since it depicted the shadowy world of human action and emotion." As Socrates sets out to construct the ideal city in speech, then, it becomes imperative to design a special system of education for the warrior class who will protect the city from its enemies. While a traditional Athenian education would have at its core poetry about the gods and heroes, Socrates asserts that the poets offer lessons unsuitable to the guardians of his city. In what has come to be seen as the opening salvo in the enduring battle between philosophy and poetry, he begins to censor the poets—notably Homer and Hesiod—by excising passages that he deems particularly subversive. Socrates' treatment of the poets' presentation of exceptional human beings will be discussed in greater detail below; for the moment, it will suffice to outline his censorship of those treatments of the gods that make them seem less worthy of honor. He argues that "it mustn't be said that gods make war on gods, and plot against them and have battles with them—for it isn't even true—provided that those who are going to guard the city for us must consider it most shameful to be easily angry with one another" (Plato 1991: 378b–c).[1] He proceeds to point out that the gods should be thought of as perfectly good, and thus he takes from the gods the responsibility for evil in the world, removing those passages from Homer that suggest otherwise. Finally, Socrates makes the case that the gods should not be portrayed as tricking human beings by adopting disguises or by lying. The reason for all of these changes to the standard curriculum is that the guardians must be "god-revering and divine insofar as a human being can possibly be" (Plato 1991: 383c). The poets, however, present the gods as capricious, belligerent, and often unjust; anyone educated to revere these gods might well turn out to act like them. In order to ensure that the guardians will behave as the city requires, the gods must be presented quite differently from the way the poets traditionally have done. After their transformation, Seth Benardete (1989: 64) argues that the gods "are so much the models of self-sufficiency that they cease to be models of care. Indeed, since Socrates assigns them hypothetically a will only to deny them the possibility of exercising it, it is not clear whether they are meant to be alive. Perhaps they are beautiful but invisible statues." In so dramatically altering the standard, poetic presentation of the gods, it seems that Socrates attempts to change what his interlocutors think not only about the poets but about the gods as well.

Given these complaints against poetry, why does Socrates spend time, in his final days, writing poems? His answer to Cebes is that he decided to compose poetry in response to a recurring dream in which he is told, "Socrates, get to work and compose music" (Plato 1999b: 60e). This dream is not a new one that has plagued him since his conviction; instead, he has heard this voice for much of his life and has always interpreted it to mean that he should philosophize. He says, "I thought the dream was urging and encouraging me, as people do in cheering on their own men when they are running a race, to compose—which, taking philosophy to be the highest form of composition, I was doing already" (Plato 1999b: 60e–61a). Only now, as his death approaches, does Socrates consider that the dream voice might mean for him to compose poetry rather than to philosophize. He tells Cebes that he is now considering a second interpretation of his dream in order to correct any unintentional impiety he might have committed as a result of his lifelong interpretation.[2] While the philosopher suggests that he is hedging his bets, in some sense, it seems clear that his friends are disturbed by his change of behavior: "Socrates is their hero. Yet at this solemn time of his life, Socrates seems cavalier about his devotion to philosophy, apparently abandoning—or at least ignoring—it in favor of poetry" (Stern 1993: 20). His behavior seems to call directly into question the virtue of philosophy at the very moment when his friends most require an adamant defense of the life he has led. As a result, Socrates spends the remainder of his final day discussing the virtues of the philosophic way of life and nothing else is said about either his attempts at poetry or the dream that initiated them.

In this chapter and the next, then, I explore the connection between Socrates and the poets in detail. Rather than falling back on the traditional interpretation that the philosopher and the poet are natural enemies, sketched briefly earlier, I argue that Socrates has a far more complicated relationship with the poets and that, in some sense, Homer and Plato are engaged in a very similar endeavor. Their main characters—Achilles and Odysseus, on the one hand, and Socrates, on the other—are presented as models of heroic behavior to be emulated by all those who learn about their great words and deeds. In this chapter, I focus on Socrates' complicated relationship with Achilles; in the next, I will turn to Odysseus. From the preceding chapters that focus on Achilles and Socrates, it might be tempting to see them as two contrasting exemplars of heroism: the former seems a brash man of action and the latter a pensive man devoted to the life of the mind. Indeed, in the *Republic*, Achilles is singled out for derision from among all of the Homeric heroes. And yet, in the *Apology*, Socrates famously compares himself quite favorably to Achilles. In this chapter, then, I look closely at the points of agreement and of contention between Achilles and Socrates in order to determine whether the characters are more similar or different. In doing so, I argue that Plato's Socrates is meant to stand alongside Achilles insofar as he possesses many of the same heroic qualities. Ultimately, I demonstrate that these important character traits, shared by Achilles and Socrates, make them both classically heroic, but that Plato presents Socrates as a model of heroic behavior that is far more accessible to human beings than Homer's Achilles and, as an other-regarding hero, far more worthy of emulation in our eyes today.

CRITIQUING ACHILLES IN THE *REPUBLIC*

After excising passages from Homer and Hesiod that might give the guardians a negative impression of the gods, Socrates turns his attention to the treatment of heroes in the epic poems. In doing so, he reserves his sharpest words for the Homeric portrayal of Achilles in both the *Iliad* and the *Odyssey*. Perhaps least devastating is the Socratic critique of the language of immoderation that can be found in both texts, especially about the excesses that heroes enjoy. He argues that the poets put words into the mouths of their greatest heroes that would be harmful to the guardians. The first such negative example is the disobedience that heroes like Achilles show to their commanders (cf. Plato 1991: 390a). If there is any hope of instilling martial virtue, clearly Achilles' tirade against Agamemnon of book 1 must not be taught to the guardians (cf. Homer 1974: I.175–359). Additionally, Socrates focuses on Odysseus' claim that when people can sit "in a great hall, by rows of tables heaped / with bread and roast meat, while a steward goes / to dip up wine and brim your cups again. / Here is the flower of life, it seems to me!" (Homer 1990: IX.8–11; cf. Plato 1991: 390a–b). The trouble with this statement—and others cited by Socrates—is that it suggests that heroes not only regularly give in to their appetites but also celebrate those occasions that allow them to do so. As Socrates asks, "Aren't these the most important elements of moderation for the multitude: being obedient to the rulers, and being themselves rulers of the pleasures of drink, sex, and eating?" (Plato 1991: 389d–e). While these might well be considered virtues by the citizens of the unhealthy city that Glaucon and Adeimantus have been envisioning, Socrates asserts that they would be properly considered vices in any other city. And, regardless of the city in question, the guardian class must be taught moderation in these things so that the ordinary citizens might be preserved from their enemies—and from the guardians themselves.

Next, Socrates turns his attention more specifically to Achilles and argues forcefully that he "was so full of confusion as to contain within himself two diseases that are opposite to one another—illiberality accompanying love of money, on the one hand, and arrogant disdain for gods and human beings, on the other" (Plato 1991: 391c). With regard to the first allegation, Socrates points to a series of quotations from the *Iliad* that he takes to demonstrate the hero's unseemly acquisitiveness. Achilles should not be desirous of trophies as rewards for his bravery, nor should the emissaries sent from Agamemnon encourage him to accept some gifts in exchange for setting aside his quarrel (cf. Plato 1991: 390d–e; Homer 1974: I.184–199; IX.625–640). Following on these allegations, of course, is the charge that Achilles finally decides to ransom Hector's body back to Priam when it is clear he will be well paid for it (Homer 1974: XXIV.165–167). Of course, as any careful reader of the *Iliad* knows, the latter charge against Achilles is not nearly as accurate as the former. While it is certainly true that Priam brings gifts to Achilles in exchange for Hector's body, Socrates fails to mention that Achilles is compelled by the gods to ransom Hector's body, even before Priam arrives. To say that Achilles will only "give up a corpse when getting paid for it" (Plato 1991: 390e–391a) seems a bit disingenuous, especially in describing the hero after his decision to rejoin the war. It would not, however, be out of character for Achilles at the outset of the *Iliad*, as he is concerned at that time with prizes, rewards, and gifts to the seeming exclusion of anything else. Indeed, one of the least flattering portrayals of Achilles—and one that raises some of the most difficult questions about his heroism, as discussed previously—stems from the opening of the *Iliad*, where he withdraws from the fighting in protest of losing Briseis and calls on the gods to punish all of his friends as a result.[3] That said, whether this amounts to acquisitiveness, as Socrates claims, remains very unclear and, I believe, unlikely. Achilles' anger is aroused only when a particular gift is taken away from him; he does not demand a great deal in exchange for his heroism nor has he complained when Agamemnon has taken more than his share of the spoils of previous battles (cf. Homer 1974: I.190–199). Indeed, he goes so far as to reject the gifts that Agamemnon subsequently sends to him and, along with them, the entire heroic lifestyle built upon winning honors and rewards; if he truly loved money, as Socrates charges, he would quickly accept the bounty brought by Odysseus, Phoenix, and Ajax, and return to the war (Homer 1974: IX.489–517).

With regard to the claim that Achilles acts arrogantly toward gods and men, the situation is again far more complicated than Socrates allows. There is no doubt that the behavior cited by Socrates is unacceptable, by the standards of both Socrates' time and also Achilles' own. In dishonoring Hector's corpse and sacrificing twelve young men on Patroclus' funeral pyre, Achilles recalls much earlier forms of warfare and heroism, divorcing himself entirely from the prevailing value system.[4] And while it is certainly true that Achilles holds himself above other men, the trouble lies in figuring out how he *ought* to view himself given that he is the son of a goddess. Though he often refers to his own strength and skill as being the greatest, one would need to doubt the validity of his origins in order to challenge these claims. But with regard to his interaction with the gods, Achilles seems to have been generally hard done by Socrates. He is certainly portrayed in a relatively complex manner by Homer, far more than Socrates suggests by the three examples he employs in his critique. Though he undeniably vies with Scamander, the river god, and expresses his desire to avenge himself on Apollo (Homer 1974: XXI.259–265; XXII.18–25), it is clear that Achilles also recognizes his limitations: he is not a god himself and cannot succeed against them when push comes to shove. Just as important, Achilles is portrayed as doing the bidding of the gods on several meaningful occasions. At the outset, rather than raise his sword against Agamemnon, he checks his anger as instructed by Athena (Homer 1974: I.242–260). And, near the conclusion, he agrees to obey the command of Zeus to release Hector's body when Priam arrives at his camp to claim it (Homer 1974: XXIV.159–167). In both cases, Achilles is enraged and seems resolved to act in opposition to the demands of the gods, yet he quickly chooses to moderate his behavior and accept their judgment rather than attempting to defy them.

But the most serious critique is the one that Socrates levels at Achilles after his glorious life has come to an end. To do so, he turns away from the

Iliad, where Achilles' heroic deeds are chronicled, and focuses instead on the very brief passage in which he appears in the *Odyssey*. There, as is well known, Achilles bemoans his fate and rejects the earthly glory that he chose when he battled Hector instead of sailing home from Troy to live a longer life: "Better, I say, to break sod as a farm hand / for some poor country man, on iron rations, / than lord it over all the exhausted dead" (Homer 1990: XI.579–581). This passage, according to Socrates, is the first that must be censored because it calls into question the virtue of Achilles' choice and might well foster the fear of death in the guardians, who must "be fearless in the face of death and choose death in battles above defeat and slavery" (Plato 1991: 386b). Socrates proceeds to list six additional passages, four of which are taken from the *Iliad*, in order to demonstrate that Homer portrays Hades in an overwhelmingly negative light.[5] But, in quoting Achilles from the *Odyssey*, Socrates also highlights his disagreement with the positive treatment the hero receives in the *Iliad*. Patrick J. Deneen (2000: 90) notes that

> this single pronouncement by Achilles marks an interpretive break between the *Iliad* and the *Odyssey*. . . . In Hades, amid the sifting souls of the dead, Achilles eternally bewails his rash action, preferring slavery to death. . . . By highlighting the offensiveness of Achilles' preference for enslavement, Socrates in fact calls attention less to the need for excising those exact words than to questioning the reverence of the hero who pronounced them.

And yet, while Socrates wants to put this quotation forward as evidence that the guardian class (and perhaps others as well) ought not to emulate Achilles, it seems characteristically unfair to do so. After all, though it is unquestionably true that Achilles makes clear his hatred of death, his statement does not imply that he feared it when he was alive.

The living Achilles of the *Iliad* likely would not have spoken in this manner, and it is difficult—if not impossible—to imagine a scenario where he might have lived differently, choosing a withering life over his glorious death at Troy. And, indeed, the result would have been the same for Achilles; regardless of his choice in the aftermath of Patroclus' death, he would still find his way to Hades like all mortals, even the farmhand he now seems to wish he could have been.[6] And yet for all of the unseemliness of these few lines, everything is actually far more muddled in the final analysis. While the dead Achilles seems to repudiate the glorious name he achieved in life, it is noteworthy that he immediately asks for news about the honor accorded to his son and his father. In particular, Achilles wants to know "if rank and honor still belong to Peleus" and also whether Neoptolemus, his son, was able to "come after me to make a name in battle" (Homer 1990: XI.583–585). Further, Robert Schmiel (1987: 37) correctly notes the importance of the fact that Achilles is not the lord of the dead, as Odysseus suggests he is in an attempt at mitigating the pain of death: "If Achilles could have anticipated, not some Achaean Valhalla, but any kind of special status in the Underworld, the price of glory would have become at least that much more reasonable. Odysseus' well-intended but inept attempt to console has the effect of reducing the fearful cost, and therefore the terrible splendor, of Achilles' decision. And that Achilles—Homer—will not allow." Finally, and most importantly on my reading, is the fact that Achilles leaves Odysseus substantially cheered after hearing about the glory won by Neoptolemus after his death (Homer 1990: XI.639–642). All claims to the contrary, the hero remains interested in winning honor—first and foremost—and seems far less pained by his own death when he hears that his son has maintained his legacy as a great warrior.

Perhaps most interesting, of course, is that the passage Socrates expunges here resurfaces later in the *Republic*, when Socrates sets out his famous Allegory of the Cave. In that allegory, the philosopher is portrayed as one who is released from imprisonment and ascends from the cave to the bright world above. Once there, he is able to make out the things as they truly exist, whereas he and his fellow captives had previously known only shadows of the things. Unsurprisingly, Socrates says, the philosopher is reluctant to reenter the cave and release those who are held prisoner for two reasons. First, his preference would be to remain among the things as they truly are rather than returning to the world of shadows, and second, because leaving the cave is a painful process, he has reason to fear that the other prisoners will attempt to harm him in order to remain in the blissful ignorance of bondage. And yet Socrates says to Glaucon,

> "Then our job as founders . . . is to compel the best natures to go to the study which we were saying before is the greatest, to see the good and to go up that ascent; and, when they have gone up and seen sufficiently, not to permit them what is now permitted."
> "What's that?"
> "To remain there . . . and not be willing to go down again among those prisoners or share their labors and honors, whether they be slighter or more serious." (Plato 1991: 519c)

Though Socrates recognizes that the philosopher will have little desire to go down among the people again, and could even be endangered by it, he must be compelled to do so in the best interest of the city and its citizens.

At the heart of the *Republic*, then, is the decision of the philosopher to descend into the world of shadows. Allan Bloom (1977: 317) makes a compelling point about the allegory of the cave:

> The potential philosophers must be compelled to leave the cave as well as return to it. But once out, they recognize how good it is to be out. They never see a reason to go back, and compelling them to go back is said to be for the good of the city, not the philosophers. If they thought it good to go back, they would not be good rulers. It is only by going

out that they became aware that the kallipolis is a cave, nay Hades, and to be in it is as to be a shade.

In setting up the problem in this way, Socrates demonstrates both the need for a philosopher-king and also the difficulty in assuring his rule.[7] But he also raises anew the issue of Achilles and his choice, in the *Odyssey*, of the longer life of a slave over his own brief, glorious life. He does so by asking Glaucon whether the philosopher might be envious of those prisoners in the cave who are accorded some honor by their fellows for excelling at the guessing games that the captives play with the shadows that pass before their eyes. Or, he asks, "Would he be affected as Homer says and want very much 'to be on the soil, a serf to another, to a portionless man,' and to undergo anything whatsoever rather than to opine those things and live that way?" (Plato 1991: 516d). In short, he returns to Achilles—and specifically to the passage that he previously excised from the *Odyssey*—by asking Glaucon whether the philosopher would ever desire to return to the world of the cave. Deneen (2000: 114) points out that "like the serf above the ground, life in the sunlight, no matter what its condition, is preferable to the darkness below." The man who would not return to the cave is compared here to the ghost of Achilles in Hades, and, although his feeling might be perfectly understandable, it is still incorrect.

Given all that Socrates says about ascending and descending here, his own case is both an interesting and instructive one. Glaucon makes clear that he finds it unfair to compel the philosopher to return to the cave after he learns of the pleasures that exist outside. He would behave like the ghost of Achilles, choosing to remain above the earth and living a self-interested life. Thus it is Socrates who imposes the requirement—even to the point of compulsion—that philosophers live a life that is both less pleasurable and also potentially dangerous for them by descending again in order to attempt to free others. The imagery of ascending and descending in book 7, of course, is meant to parallel the original descent in the *Republic*, when Socrates and Glaucon go down to the Piraeus in book 1. In that instance, Socrates goes down voluntarily but very quickly longs to leave again; indeed, he is said to be "hurrying to get away to town" (Plato 1991: 327c). Ultimately, he is either forced or persuaded to remain there by Polemarchus and his group of friends, leading to the central dialogue about justice and the ideal city. But being threatened with force is not the same as being forced to descend in the first place, and, unlike the reluctant philosopher of book 7, Socrates seems to have done that much voluntarily. Thus it is not entirely clear whether Socrates behaves like the shade of Achilles or eschews the hero's argument about life among the shadows.

It might be the case, however, that Socrates is not comparing himself to Achilles at all. And this would make a good deal of sense, especially given his censorship of a great deal of Achilles' character earlier in the *Republic*. As Deneen (2000: 115) points out, "Recalling the initial descent of Socrates to the Piraeus, we find by comparison that his journey is quite voluntary: he seeks to instruct the young gentleman Glaucon. His motion, unlike that of the philosopher of the Cave, is one of descent to ascent; his movement is precisely the opposite of that philosopher who otherwise refuses to descend." It might be the case, then, that Socrates is not the philosopher who escapes from the cave and must be compelled to descend again; instead, it might be Glaucon or any of the other young men to whom Socrates is addressing the Allegory of the Cave and who might aspire to the life of the philosopher. Deneen (2000: 115) expands upon this idea substantially: "Whereas in the first book it appears that Socrates is being 'shackled,' or arrested, by Polemarchus, in the end it is Socrates who literally frees them from opinion. . . . The descent of Socrates to the Piraeus, seeking in this case to instruct a young man and eventually a group of young men, proves itself to be the opposite of that reluctance demonstrated by the philosopher." In that case, Socrates might well be the character about whom he only hints in the allegory, the mysterious person who is responsible for freeing the philosopher from the cave in the first place (cf. Plato 1991: 515e).

All of this leads Deneen to make a very favorable comparison between Socrates and Odysseus, on his reading a more Platonic hero—and thus one more worthy of emulation—than Achilles. And while I find the argument quite interesting and even compelling to an extent, as will be discussed in much greater detail in the next chapter, I think his rejection of the connection with Achilles comes much too quickly and easily. Socrates might well be similar to Odysseus in many ways, as even Aristotle seems to intimate.[8] But for all of his prominence, especially in the *Odyssey*, Odysseus is decidedly not the best role model. As Angela Hobbs (2000: 196–197) argues, "This accords with the common perception of Achilles' act of self-sacrifice as the paradigm example of the *kalon ergon* [καλόν ἔργον; fine and noble deed]: his type of heroism simply appears to have been regarded as more noble than Odysseus' heroics of endurance." Odysseus is not particularly renowned for his physical prowess among the Greek warriors at Troy; while Achilles is regarded by everyone as the best, Odysseus is not even second best: "Of all the fighting men, most formidable / was Telamonian Ajax—that is / while great Achilles raged apart. Achilles / towered above them all" (Homer 1974: II.916–919). Instead, he is best known as a dissembler, a man of disguises, and it is on the basis of this reputation that he is criticized to his face by Achilles: "I hate / as I hate Hell's own gate that man who hides / one thought within him while he speaks another" (Homer 1974: IX.381–383). Further, even Odysseus' portrayal in the *Odyssey* is occasionally less than heroic. As Goldhill (1991: 101–102) notes, "Odysseus not only returns in disguise but also his disguise is the lowest rank in the social hierarchy. This disguise leads to a series of humiliating experiences. Indeed, while heroic evaluation is based on the performance of great deeds, it is being long-suffering that is a hallmark of Odysseus' struggles in the *Odyssey*." Thus the connection of Socrates to Odysseus does not accomplish nearly what a connection to Achilles might—namely, the ability for Plato to subvert the traditional understanding of the greatest hero as a man of action on the battlefield.

EMBRACING ACHILLES IN THE *APOLOGY* AND THE *CRITO*

Though my argument against a possible identification of Socrates with Odysseus is a very brief one here, especially in comparison to Deneen's positive argument, I will expand it considerably in the next chapter. For the moment, I believe that Plato's identification of Socrates with Achilles provides one of the strongest challenges to Deneen's thesis. Although Socrates is clearly critical of the Homeric portrayal of Achilles in the *Republic*, the relationship of the philosopher and the warrior is wholly different in the *Apology* and the *Crito*. In both of those texts—which I have argued, in the previous chapter, are designed to portray the philosopher as a role model worthy of emulation—Socrates directly and indirectly compares himself with the great hero. Gregory Vlastos (1991: 233) sets out some of the clearest dissimilarities between the two: "Socrates is a plebian, Achilles noblest of the heroes, darling of the aristocracy. Socrates is the voice of reason, Achilles a man of passion rampant over reason. Socrates abjures retaliation, while Achilles, gutting his anger on Hector's corpse, gives the most terrible example of vengeance in the *Iliad*." In these important respects, and others too, Achilles and Socrates seem antithetical to one another, and I do not want to suggest that the two should be understood as being of a piece. That said, I think Vlastos (1991: 233–234) is incorrect in asserting that they have only one thing in common—namely, "absolute subordination of everything each values to one superlatively precious thing: honor for Achilles, virtue for Socrates." Indeed, it is precisely their other similarities that allow Plato to successfully compare the two in a way that redounds favorably to Socrates.

A great many scholars have commented on the importance of the comparison that Socrates draws between himself and Achilles in the *Apology* (cf. Clay 1972; Greenberg 1965; Hobbs 2000; Holway 1994; Leibowitz 2010; Metcalf 2009; Santilli and Santilli 2004; West 1979, 1984). Indeed, the glaring exception seems to be in the work of Thomas C. Brickhouse and Nicholas D. Smith (1989: 129), where the passage is mentioned only in passing to highlight Socrates' piety and regard for the word of the Delphic Oracle. They argue that Socrates is demonstrating his deep commitment to doing what he believes is right—in this case, examining the most respected men of Athens to determine whether he knows more than they do—just as Achilles was committed to avenging Patroclus and just as Socrates was committed to following orders when he was a soldier himself. While Socrates certainly does suggest these things in the *Apology*, I argued in the previous chapter that his obedience to Apollo is suspect; further, it is noteworthy that his greatest attribute as a soldier was known to be his endurance rather than his obedience (cf. Plato 1999c: 219e–220d). The more common reading of Socrates' comparison with Achilles is not quite as straightforward, and its proponents argue that Plato is elevating Socrates at the expense of Achilles. As Thomas G. West (1984: 20) writes, "Socrates implicitly proposes himself as a *successor* of the Homeric hero. The 'real man' must give way to the genuine human being. Socrates' quiet conversations and exhortations to care for prudence, truth, and the good of the soul replace Achilles' bloody deeds of war." West's point is well-taken, though in the end I think the victory that he and several others see for Socrates over Achilles is not quite as simple as they make it out to be.

Before looking into that question, however, a careful consideration of the comparison between the two characters is necessary. It is worth quoting Socrates at some length here, as he is nowhere else so straightforward in connecting himself to Achilles:

> Perhaps, then, someone might say, "Then are you not ashamed, Socrates, of having followed the sort of pursuit from which you now run the risk of dying?"
>
> I would respond to him with a just speech: "What you say is ignoble, fellow, if you suppose that a man who is of even a little benefit should take into account the danger of living or dying, but not rather consider this alone whenever he acts: whether his actions are just or unjust, and the deeds of a good man or a bad. For according to your speech, those of the demigods who met their end at Troy would be paltry, especially the son of Thetis. Rather than endure anything shameful, he despised danger so much that when his mother (a goddess) spoke to him as he was eager to kill Hector—something like this, as I suppose: 'Son, if you avenge the murder of your comrade Patroclus and kill Hector, you yourself will die; for straightaway,' she says, 'after Hector, your fate is ready at hand'—he, upon hearing this, belittled death and danger, fearing much more to live as a bad man and not to avenge his friends. 'Straightaway,' he says, 'may I die, after I inflict a penalty on the doer of injustice, so that I do not stay here ridiculous beside the curved ships, a burden on the land.' Surely you do not suppose that he gave any thought to death and danger?" (Plato 1984a: 28b–d)

In looking at what Socrates says here, it is immediately obvious that he plays a bit fast and loose with both his quotations from Homer and his analysis of Achilles' motivation. He can certainly be excused for errors in quotation—he was, after all, on trial for his life and quoting the *Iliad* from memory—especially as they do not alter Homer's text in any substantial way.[9] The same cannot be said, however, about Socrates' exegesis of the text. As Paul C. Santilli and Kristine S. Santilli (2004: 194–195) rightly point out, "Socrates suggests that Achilles is like the worthy man, who does not weigh the dangers of an action in his own mind, but thinks only of whether he is acting 'rightly or wrongly, like a good man or a bad one.' But these are Socrates' emendations, which 'ethicize' and rationalize Achilles who speaks in the *Iliad*." While it is certainly true that considerations of justice do not seem to play an overly large role in Achilles' decision to avenge Patroclus' death, I want to argue that Achilles does not proceed irrationally or thoughtlessly here.

In truth, Achilles reacts emotionally throughout the *Iliad*, and seems to *fully* consider his options on only one other occasion, when he explains his decision to abstain from fighting to Odysseus, Phoenix, and Ajax. Now he is reminded of that earlier decision to leave for home and changes his mind because the pain of Patroclus' death far exceeds the insult he suffered at the hands of Agamemnon and because he is aware of his own role in Patroclus' death through his decision to avoid fighting. Thus, West (1979: 155–156) argues that "Socrates' version of the story makes Achilles more just, but less noble and godlike. . . . In Socrates' revision Achilles has been domesticated: he is more civilized, less passionate, less splendid, more prosaic—on the whole, more Socratic."[10] It is certainly true that Socrates takes some significant liberties with Achilles' character, downplaying the effect of his grief and including considerations of shame that Homer does not, but West goes a bit too far in claiming that Socrates elevates Achilles with regard to justice and degrades his divinity or nobility. As Angela Hobbs (2000: 183) points out, Achilles "clearly possesses a keen sense of justice: he is certainly bitter that Agamemnon has not given him the honour that he feels he deserves. And as for his specific decision to kill Hector, he is in general . . . a firm believer in the rightness of revenge." On the question of justice, it is Socrates—not Achilles—who has opposed the idea that a just person "gives benefits and harms to friends and enemies" (Plato 1991: 332d). He demonstrates for Polemarchus in the *Republic* that one cannot make a person more just by acting unjustly toward him and forcefully reiterates this position in the *Crito*. And, as outlined earlier, a great many of Achilles' actions—motivated by vengeance—result in behavior so odious that Socrates censors it out of the poetry that can be taught to the guardian class.

And although his mother is a nymph and his exploits in battle eclipse those of other heroes, it is clear that Achilles is intended by Homer to be viewed in the full glare of his humanity—and mortality.[11] Nowhere in the *Iliad* is it suggested that Achilles might somehow gain immortality, and his appearance in Hades in the *Odyssey* confirms his fate; without this emphasis on his mortality, the choice he makes would be as meaningless as the petty squabbles of the gods. Nor is Achilles overwhelmingly noble by Homer's account. He refuses to obey the orders of his commanders, he hurls insults at his friends, and he raises the specter of cannibalism at the extremity of his bestial behavior. More importantly, it is his decision to call down the gods' wrath on his friends and to sulk rather than fight that eventually leads to Patroclus' death. But the key to the comparison between the Homeric hero and the Platonic one is that Achilles is fully aware of the high price he will pay to avenge his friend. In this, an emphasis of both Achilles' humanity and nobility, the comparison that Socrates wants to draw does not miss its mark. In the final analysis, it is not that Achilles is changed by Socrates' description but that Socrates seems to change the image of himself in order to align himself more closely with Achilles in the minds of his jurors.

Yet, for all of this discussion of the unusual connection that Socrates draws between himself and Achilles, it is only the most obvious such comparison. Indeed, Socrates goes a great deal further in drawing attention to Achilles than Brickhouse and Smith acknowledge when they gloss over this reference to the battlefield hero. Indeed, he draws his jurors' attention to Achilles even earlier in the *Apology* by repeatedly stressing that he will speak to them plainly and without pretense. This character trait is celebrated by Achilles, who loathes dissembling and dishonesty, but it marks a significant departure for Socrates, whose penchant for irony is well known. Whether Socrates actually speaks plainly in his defense is debatable, but he certainly makes clear his refusal to flatter his jurors or arouse their pity by referring to his family and friends (Plato 1984a: 34d–35a). Socrates also calls attention to the piety that underlies the trouble in which he now finds himself, arguing that the charges against him are the result of personal animosity arising from the service he is performing to Apollo. Similarly, all of the trouble between Achilles and Agamemnon begins when the former attempts to defend Apollo in the face of the latter's hubris. Given Agamemnon's subsequent punishment of Achilles, Richard Holway (1994: 564) speculates that "perhaps Agamemnon's hostility can be explained in the same way as Socrates' accusers': he is angry at having his shortcomings publicly exposed, or he envies the incomparable son of the goddess Thetis."

More explicitly than in these two references, Socrates also explains—in his interview of Meletus—the belief that "daimons are certain bastard children of gods, whether from nymphs or from certain others of whom it is also said they are born" (Plato 1984a: 27d). Given this veiled reference to Thetis, who was a nymph, Achilles must be the *daimon* that Socrates has in mind. He proceeds to make the claim that one who believes in these *daimonia* [δαιμόνια] must also believe in the gods from whom they descend; to believe otherwise "would be as strange as if someone believed in children of horses or asses—mules—but did not believe that there are horses and asses" (Plato 1984a: 27e). Thus, Socrates attempts to dispute the charge of impiety that Meletus levels against him by connecting the *daimon* who speaks to him with Achilles, the demigod. If we believe that Achilles is a demigod, then we must also believe in Socrates' *daimon*, and we cannot claim—as Meletus does—that believing in his *daimon* is impious. But this analogy of mules and heroes also connects Socrates directly to Achilles. As Clay (1972: 58) argues, "Both Achilles and Socrates are in fact stubborn in face of death, but they are mulish or mule-like only in terms of their mixed parentage: they are ἡμίθεοι [*hemitheoi*; demigods]." The comparison of their parentage requires a bit of work—a reference to the description, in the *Symposium*, of the erotic Socrates as the son of Poros and Penia—but much less is needed to demonstrate that "he is like Achilles in his recklessness in face of death, his sense of justice, and his bravery" (Clay 1972: 58, 59).

Nor does Plato's identification of Socrates with Achilles come to an end with the *Apology*. Perhaps one of the most interesting references to the *Iliad* occurs at the very outset of the *Crito*, when Socrates explains that his execution is not as imminent as Crito believes it to be. The additional day of life about which Socrates is confident is based on his most recent dream. As he tells Crito, "I thought a woman came to me, handsome and well grown, and dressed in white; she called to me and said, 'Socrates, on the third day you'll reach fertile Phthia'" (Plato 1984b: 44b). Crito remarks that the dream is an unusual one, but, rather than explaining it, Socrates tells his friend that the message is quite clear, and then Crito quickly agrees. The reason for Crito's agreement is unclear, as there are a number of possible interpretations of this passage. Each one, of course, begins with the recognition that the woman in white is quoting the *Iliad*. In responding to the emissaries sent by Agamemnon to persuade him to return to the fighting, Achilles says, "Tomorrow at dawn when I have made offering / to Zeus and all the gods, and hauled my ships / for loading in the shallows, if you like / and if it interests you, look out and see / my ships on Helle's waters in the offing / oarsmen in line making the sea-foam scud! / And if the great Earthshaker gives a breeze, / the third day out I'll make it home to Phthia" (Homer 1974: IX.437–444). At this moment, his mind is made up and he will leave Troy in the morning; if all goes well, he can be home in three days.

One interpretation is that both Socrates and Crito understand the dream to mean that Socrates will, in fact, be executed in three days. As G. M. A. Grube (Plato 2000: 44n) asserts, "Socrates takes the dream to mean that he will die, and his soul will find its home, on the third day." This might well account for Crito's immediate attempt to persuade Socrates to escape from prison. Of course, it remains a bit unclear why Socrates and Crito would both understand Phthia, Achilles' home, to be the home of Socrates' soul. Additionally, it is dubious that Socrates might think it obvious that Phthia, where Achilles would live a long but inglorious life, would be equated with his own impending execution. Indeed, in encouraging escape, Crito raises the possibility of another interpretation, as he begs Socrates "to go to Thessaly," where his friends "will make much of you and keep you safe, so that no one in Thessaly shall hurt you" (Plato 1984b: 45c). In this interpretation, Crito understands Socrates' dream to mean that he might escape, and he proceeds to suggest Thessaly because he believes Socrates has just expressed an interest in that location. Thus, Scott Kramer (1988: 196) notes that "the reference to Thessaly is significant if one remembers that Phthia formed one of the geographic tetrads of Thessaly proper. It is therefore quite possible that Crito is merely reiterating the words of the woman in Socrates' dream. If he chooses to escape, Socrates could arrive in Phthia (Thessaly) within 'three days.'"

Of course, there are several possible translations that impact how confident Socrates should be about traveling to Phthia in three days. The word in question is ἵκοιο [*hikoio*], and, as Kramer (1988: 196) points out, "Its range of meaning extends all the way from merely suggesting that something *might* happen to asserting that something certainly *will* happen." Unlike in the *Iliad*, where Homer includes conditional language about a favorable breeze, "Plato has suppressed the protasis of the conditional, and this suggests . . . that it is even more probable for Socrates to be in Phthia in three days than it originally was for Achilles" (Kramer 1988: 197). Thus, while Achilles suggests that he could hypothetically return home in three days, if all goes well on his voyage, Socrates' dream asserts that he *will* be in Phthia in three days. And yet, though the wording is not conditional, the dream is nonetheless presenting Socrates with a choice, just as Crito will do. Like Achilles, Socrates can choose to remain where he is or to depart for Phthia. But because there are multiple interpretations of the dream, it seems that either staying or escaping will lead him to Phthia (either his soul will go to its figurative home or he will literally go to live in Thessaly). And by rejecting Crito's offer, Socrates fully embraces the connection he has been drawing with Achilles: while he could certainly be in Phthia in three days, thereby extending his life, escape would be markedly less heroic and therefore unworthy of him.

A COMPARISON OF HEROIC BEHAVIOR

Having reviewed the treatment of Achilles in three different Platonic dialogues, an obvious question arises. Why does Socrates critique Achilles in the *Republic* and then compare himself so directly with the great warrior in the *Apology* and the *Crito*? This is especially difficult to work through if, as I have been arguing, Plato wants to portray Socrates as being heroic *like* Achilles. After all, there *is* undeniably something compelling about the argument presented by West (1979: 154):

> That Socrates should compare himself with Achilles is, of course, ludicrous. Before the judges stands an ugly old man of seventy who is about to be condemned by them to death. Achilles was the beautiful, strong youth whose courage and skill in battle had no equal. He was held in high repute by both men and gods, while the obscure Socrates is about to die a wretched death by drinking a cup of poison in jail.

That said, like Santilli and Santilli (2004: 189), I do not accept the fairly standard reading of Socrates' praise of Achilles as ironic, "where, in the guise of praising Achilles, he buries the Homeric warrior to create a new form of heroism." If he sought to completely replace the warrior with the philosopher, it seems unnecessary and potentially quite problematic to suggest, in the *Apology*, that the philosopher is like the warrior in some favorable way, especially after his scathing critique of Achilles in the *Republic*. Leaving aside the possible argument that Socrates, in the *Republic*, is merely critical of Homer's portrayal of Achilles rather than of Achilles himself, I want to argue that a more nuanced presentation of their relationship is needed. More specifically, I believe that Plato's portrayal of Socrates is meant to demonstrate that the philosopher is heroic *like* Achilles rather than to replace the warrior outright. That said, I believe that Santilli and Santilli (2004: 190) likely go too far in asserting that "the old hero may also have been a kind of philosopher." On my reading, Achilles is no more a philosopher than Socrates is a warrior, even though the former "demonstrates growth in both wisdom and goodness" (Santilli and Santilli 2004: 200) and the latter remained at his military post "where they stationed me and ran the risk of dying like anyone else" (Plato 1984a: 28e).

Instead of alleging that Achilles and Socrates are either of the same mold or should be thought of purely as rivals, I posit an approach that allows for their existing similarities and differences. Put succinctly, Achilles and Socrates are quite different in several obvious ways, but Plato clearly draws important comparisons between the motivating factors underlying Socrates' heroism and that of Homer's hero. In the first place, both have an uncommon depth of understanding with regard to the limits of their existence; this leads to their thinking critically about the importance of their choices and about the kind of lives they will live before they die. Secondly, a sympathetic connection to others plays a critical role in the stories of both Achilles and Socrates; it is in this second similarity where Socrates ultimately proves to be a more impressive character to us, insofar as his heroic actions are thoroughly other-regarding while Achilles manages only a restoration to the value system of his community in the aftermath of his battlefield heroics.

The first similar characteristic is relatively straightforward; as I have demonstrated earlier, both Achilles and Socrates are viewed as heroes in large part because they chose to sacrifice themselves for an ideal. As J. Peter Euben (1990: 219) notes, "Socrates wants his fellow citizens to see that he, like Achilles, is more concerned with how one ought to live than with calculations of advantage and mere survival, and that for him to abandon these commitments would be cowardly." Of course, the views of the good life held by these two characters are wildly divergent, with Achilles focused almost entirely on *kléos* and Socrates on virtue and wisdom. Nevertheless, in both cases, there is a clear choice to be made and it directly concerns human finitude: either live a shorter, principled life or a longer life that ultimately rejects those principles. And, in both cases, Achilles and Socrates reject a longer life in order to embrace the principles that are of central importance to them. For Greenberg (1965: 73), this amounts to the notion that "heroes have formed a view of the good life which is so strict and so precious that they will accept infinite odds in the risk to preserve it." It is undoubtedly true that the story of the *Iliad* is far more complicated than Euben, Greenberg, and even Plato suggest in their interpretations, as Achilles first chooses not to fight, entirely rejecting the idea of glory, and then later makes a second choice that embraces the connection between classical heroism and a glorious life. And yet there is no doubt that Achilles is seen as straightforwardly heroic in finally choosing to fight at Troy, even though it means certain death for him to do so, just as he would be viewed quite differently had he stuck by his initial choice and sailed home to Phthia. It is to this understanding of the connection between heroism and mortality that Socrates draws his jurors' attention in the *Apology*.

Despite Socrates' favorable comparison, the two characters are, on first blush, quite distinct, and there are certainly differences like those pointed out earlier by West. However, the two are clearly not so different as Greenberg (1965: 74–75) suggests, when he argues that "the philosopher's vocation does not ordinarily demand the choice of certain death. Like other men, he may be placed in situations where he will risk death, but that is not the same thing. . . . Philosophers *qua* philosophers simply do not get the chance to play the rôle of Achilles, because they do not seek to live the life of Achilles." Although Socrates is neither a young man who might otherwise continue to live for a long time nor a warrior who deals in violence and death, he repeatedly claims that his vocation demands a critical knowledge of death and dying. As he tells his interlocutors in the *Phaedo*, "Those who tackle philosophy are simply and solely practising dying, practising death, all the time" (Plato 1999b: 64a). If Achilles and Socrates are more similar in this respect, they seem quite distinct with regard to their interactions with their community. Rather than being highly regarded by those who know him, the vast majority of the Athenians view Socrates as useless and dangerous. Of course, he also adopts a distinctly oppositional position to his fellow citizens because his value system differs so seriously from that of his community, just like Achilles for much of the *Iliad*, even though at no time does Socrates suggest that he might make different, safer life choices, as Achilles does.[12] And yet, whereas Achilles rejects—and even hurls a curse at—his fellow Achaeans, Socrates continues to act in the manner he believes to be consistent with the good of that community.

Indeed, Socrates' behavior highlights the second heroic characteristic, namely the other-regarding behavior that arises from strong personal identification with others. Most people, of course, feel a strong connection with friends, family members, and those who are similar to themselves in some way that, as Richard Rorty (1998) argues, is more immediate—and thus felt more powerfully—than simply being members of the human race. It is no surprise that Jews are more likely to identify with their co-religionists than with Muslims or that black South Africans will more closely identify with members of their own race than with their white neighbors. In cases where someone like us is suffering, we are expected to act on their behalf. But, in some sense, the obvious need (and even desire) to assist those who are tied most closely to us makes it difficult to call an action heroic when it is undertaken on behalf of someone close to us. Indeed, it is precisely for this reason that the biblical Good Samaritan resonates with us as an exemplary actor. Avishai Margalit (2002: 43) highlights the point nicely:

"Living in proximity, being kith and kin, being similar and familiar are correlated features that enhance the chances of mutual sympathy if not full-fledged care. The beauty of the Good Samaritan story is to show that those features may hold but the one who is the true neighbor and who responds to suffering is not the one who bears those features." The case of the Good Samaritan, then, nicely highlights the distinction for us today in the heroic behavior of Achilles and Socrates, as the former's identification with individuals both inside and outside the boundaries of his own immediate group does not amount to very much for the majority of the *Iliad*, whereas the latter consistently acts on behalf of those who would normally fall outside his traditionally understood circle of care.[13]

In the case of Achilles, the most obvious action he undertakes as a result of his sympathy for another would be his decision to avenge the death of Patroclus by killing Hector. In doing so, Achilles both demonstrates compassion for his lost friend and assists all of the Achaeans, who have suffered a great deal as a result of his decision to abstain from the fighting. He certainly identifies closely with Patroclus, both because they are kinsmen and because Patroclus is wearing Achilles' armor when he is killed. But this, like his identification with the Achaeans who are his friends, does not seem obviously heroic to us because it is expected. And even though, by choosing to fight, Achilles embraces his mortality and accepts a short, glorious life, his deeds on the battlefield often border on the bestial or infamous rather than the heroic. What differentiates Achilles from his fellow warriors is that he is both the greatest fighter and able to express a kind of solidarity or fellowship with the enemy. Of course, Achilles' personal identification with Priam is surprising but not a mystery: as discussed in detail earlier, Priam's situation so closely resembles that of Achilles' own father that the great warrior must recognize his connection to the aging, careworn king of Troy. Homer (1974: XXIV.608–611) writes, "Now in Achilles / the evocation of his father stirred / new longing, and an ache of grief. He lifted / the old man's hand and gently put him by." Seeing his enemy in a very different light, he now decides to act toward Priam as he would toward his own father. In doing so, Achilles is finally restored to the community from which he had been divorced throughout the *Iliad*.

While Achilles' ultimate reintegration reflects positively back onto his battlefield heroics, Socrates' heroic deeds are directly informed by his care for the other. In this, his heroism is distinct from Achilles and, to us, seems decidedly impressive. In all that he does, Socrates seems to include a multitude of diverse people in his circle of care. Most obviously, the philosopher spends the majority of his time with a group of men who are unrelated to him, even as his execution approaches. Included in this group, of course, are prospective philosophers—like Phaedo—but also older men—like Crito—who will never be philosophers. It is especially noteworthy that the principal interlocutors in this final dialogue, Simmias and Cebes, are both Thebans rather than Athenians. In making the choice to surround himself with friends, he explicitly rejects his family's claims on both his time and concern. Indeed, his only expressed concern for his family, put forward at the conclusion of the *Apology*, is that his sons be treated in the same manner that he treated the Athenians:

> When my sons grow up, punish them, men, and pain them in the very same way I pained you, if they seem to you to care for money or anything else before virtue. And if they are reputed to be something when they are nothing, reproach them just as I did you: tell them that they do not care for the things they should, and that they suppose they are something when they are worth nothing. (Plato 1984a: 41e)

In prison, when Crito chastises Socrates for choosing death, thereby abandoning his sons and failing to educate them, the philosopher simply replies that—like spending money and caring about reputation—"these are considerations of those who easily kill and, if they could, would bring back to life again, acting mindlessly: namely, the many" (Plato 1984b: 48c). Further, at the very outset of the *Phaedo*, he orders that his wife and young son be taken home "to keep them from making a scene" with their weeping (Plato 1999b: 117d). Thus, none of his family members are present in the hours before his death, and they reappear only briefly to talk to and receive instructions from him; then, they are sent away again and do not witness his execution (Plato 1999b: 116b). Instead of worrying about his loved ones and attending to their needs at this trying time, as might be expected, Socrates chooses to focus on his friends. He is particularly concerned that they will see his execution as confirmation that the life of the philosopher is both excessively risky and not worth that risk. Socrates, of course, views a life devoted to philosophy as the best possible life and wants his friends to make what he believes is the wisest choice; in addition, he recognizes that these young men are particularly devoted to him and have, in some sense, thrown in their lot with him. To abandon them at this time would be akin to abandoning the philosophic life to which he has dedicated himself because his students might well decide that some other way of life is more obviously choice-worthy.

Despite the fact that Socrates spends his final hours discussing the philosophic life with the foreigners Simmias and Cebes, there is also no doubt that he cares a great deal about the average Athenian citizen. Apart from his Athenian friends and disciples, like Crito and Plato, Socrates also speaks about the concern he feels for the average citizen. Although he spends the majority of his time speaking to them ironically and questioning their intelligence—and although he is persecuted by them—Socrates undoubtedly includes even his enemies in his expansive circle of care. He repeatedly tells them, in the *Apology*, that he is neither angry nor indignant that they convicted him and sentenced him to death (cf. Plato 1984a: 35e–36a, 41d–e). That said, he does offer a seemingly harsh prophesy to those who voted for his death: "you have now done this deed supposing that you will be released from giving an account of your life, but it will turn out much the opposite for you, as *I* affirm. There will be more who will refute you, whom I have now been holding back; you did not perceive them. And they will be harsher, inasmuch as they are younger, and you will be more indignant" (Plato 1984a: 39c–d). While this prophecy must be quite unwelcome to his jurors, Socrates believes that the refutation he foresees, while unpleasant, will do a great deal of good for the Athenians. After all, his allegation is that he undertook the very activity for which he now stands trial for the benefit of his fellow citizens and thus he cannot do otherwise. As he says about an Athenian who believes himself to be living virtuously, "I will speak to him and examine and test him. And if he does not seem to me to possess virtue, but only says he does, I will reproach him, saying that he regards the things worth the most as the least important, and the paltrier things as more important" (Plato 1984a: 29e–30a). Just as he argues that his primary concern has been with teaching them to live virtuously, Socrates now likens himself to a gadfly who disturbs "a great and well-born horse": "the god seems to me to have set me upon the city as someone of this sort: I awaken and persuade and reproach each one of you, and I do not stop settling down everywhere upon you the whole day" (Plato 1984a: 30e–31a).[14]

CONCLUSION

While a great many people would view Socrates' attentions as annoying rather than caring—and certainly most of the Athenians did—it is clear that he sees a direct connection between annoyance and care. In questioning his fellow citizens about their beliefs and commitments, Socrates believes himself to be doing a great good by showing them a more virtuous path than the one they are, perhaps unknowingly, walking. As he points out throughout the *Apology*, he could lead a far more comfortable life if he desisted from these activities; however, in abandoning his questioning, he would be abandoning the Athenians to lives that are devoid of wisdom and virtue. That Socrates will not abstain from philosophizing—even when continuing to do it clearly means a death sentence—is a powerful statement about how important he believes philosophy to be, both for himself and also for the Athenians more generally. His inclusion of even his enemies into the circle of those on whose behalf he must act sets Socrates apart from the average citizen and also from Achilles. While the latter is dependent on his extension of sympathy to Priam in order to achieve the *kléos* to which he feels entitled as a result of his accomplishments on the battlefield, Socrates' heroic accomplishments are themselves other-regarding in nature. It is this ability to personally identify with others, and to extend to even the enemy the sort of care that would normally be reserved for family or close friends, that makes Socrates' risk-taking or death-courting behavior heroic. And it is here that Socrates is finally distinguished from Achilles in the most decisive respect.

While both characters are classically heroic, their heroism is clearly distinct. This is not as simple as pointing out that one is a great warrior and the other a great thinker; instead, it involves the motivation behind their heroism. Achilles, of course, is the best of the Achaeans; he is outstanding in every way, including in the fact that his mother is a goddess. His greatness allows him to distance himself from both friends and enemies on the battlefield—none are his equal—but it also distances him from Homer's audience. Though we might be impressed by his abilities and undoubtedly think of him as heroic, we also cannot imagine ourselves in his place. And this is as it should be, for Achilles. When he fights, it is for the purpose of distinguishing himself from all others. And when he chooses to do so, knowing that he will die as a result, his reasoning is that a short, glorious life far exceeds that of a longer, humdrum one. Like Socrates, Achilles is motivated to act heroically because he recognizes that he, like all mortals, must die and so the type of life he chooses to lead gains a new salience; however, unlike Socrates, he chooses to give up his life not for the good of others but for his own *kléos*.

Of course, there is nothing problematic in itself with excelling and thus being worthy of the glory associated with *kléos*. Nor would the Greeks of either Homer's or Plato's day have thought so. But one would be hard-pressed to argue that Achilles' behavior stirs us today in the same way as Socrates', even if his actions might be viewed as more straightforwardly courageous insofar as they are bound up with battle. In the first place, the behavior for which Achilles is celebrated is driven by anger and grief, and is distinguished by its extreme violence. Secondly, when he recognizes a personal connection with Priam, it returns him to the community of human beings and allows him to be celebrated as a Greek hero after a departure from traditional Greek values that includes human sacrifice and desecrating the dead. In contradistinction, and as I have been arguing, Socrates shares important character traits with Achilles but unlike Achilles, Socrates' heroic actions are inseparably bound up with his fellow feeling or care for others; he chooses to die in the name of his commitment to wisdom and virtue, but also with the express purpose of assisting others, both future philosophers and also his Athenian jurors.

Finally, while both heroes are meant to be worthy role models, only Socrates is presented as a person whose actions might be emulated by all others. In part this is a function of Achilles' inhumanity, both in the fact that his heroic actions are beyond the realm of normal human action and, of course, in his lineage. But Socrates is also sketched as someone who desires emulation far more than adoration. He surrounds himself with young men, those who are most likely to imitate his activities, and his goal is to convince those students that the best possible life is one dedicated to philosophy. Achilles, on the other hand, is portrayed by Homer as someone who both believes himself to be inimitable and is correct in his belief. Though he is mortal, like the rest of the Achaeans, he has no equal from among them. He expects their adulation, and he is angered in the extreme by Agamemnon's refusal to properly honor him for his heroic deeds. And, even more importantly for this project, Achilles would clearly be horrified by the suggestion that others might emulate him; not only would it be impossible for anyone to do so, but even the attempt would be something akin to hubris. The suggestion that anyone might be like Achilles denigrates him and directly threatens the *kléos* for which he chooses to give up his life. In this sense, Socrates can be thought of as a democratic figure and Achilles an aristocratic one. Certainly, a careful reading of the *Republic* makes clear that not everyone can be a philosopher. Yet the position Socrates stakes out in the *Apology*—that "the unexamined life is not worth living for a human being" (Plato 1984a: 38a)—suggests that anyone might (and perhaps ought to) be dedicated to the critical experimentation that the philosopher illustrates in both his life and his death. Few people, if any, are capable of the heroism of Achilles, but anyone might make the Socratic choice of putting the greater good above one's own. In sacrificing himself and serving as an example for the Athenians and for future generations, Socrates achieves a sort of *kléos* that Achilles, in his singular excellence, cannot: a great many people pattern their lives after his, dedicating themselves to the search for wisdom and longing to be thought of as one of his intellectual heirs.

6 Philosophy against Poetry
The Complicated Relationship of Odysseus and Socrates

The journey to Hades.—I, too, have been in the underworld, like Odysseus, and shall be there often yet; and not only rams have I sacrificed to be able to speak with a few of the dead, but I have not spared my own blood. (Nietzsche 1992d: 159)

At the beginning of my class on ancient political thought, before students have begun to read Homer's *Iliad* and *Odyssey*, I suggest that one of the great Homeric heroes will be certain to appeal to them and the other will not. I say this from experience, but they cannot imagine that they will really have much interest in the exploits of *any* of the characters in these ancient poems. And yet, semester after semester, my comments turn out to be prescient, and, semester after semester, it is the *Odyssey* they most enjoy and Odysseus who strikes them as the more compelling character. Despite all the problems with Odysseus as a straightforwardly heroic character—he lies, he cheats, he fails, he cries—people seem to like him and to root for his success. It is no secret, of course, that Achilles' complaints—when he appears as a shade in Hades in the middle of the *Odyssey*—do not endear readers to him. Nor is it too far-fetched to argue, with Max Horkheimer and Theodor W. Adorno (1988: 62), that contemporary readers identify much more closely with Odysseus because he is an Enlightenment figure whose heroic journey is "an exact representation of the risks which mark out the road to success." What's more, in no small part the reason for preferring the tale of Odysseus to that of Achilles is that he seems to be the one who triumphs in the end. The *Odyssey* ends with the *nostos* [νόστος; homecoming] that Odysseus has worked to achieve for so long, whereas the *Iliad* concludes on a more ambiguous note with regard to the *kléos* [κλέος; glory] for which Achilles has chosen to fight and to die. The former has clearly accomplished his end, but, with the Trojan War still ongoing, the latter seems to have a good deal of unfinished business to handle in addition to his own death still to confront.

Perhaps most importantly, Odysseus seems to confront and overcome a series of challenges and enemies on a difficult journey to be reunited with his family. Achilles, by contrast, seems to confront only his own bad attitude and his displeasure with the heroic lifestyle as he struggles with the decision to maintain his glorious name. In other words, the *Iliad* is meant to be the tale of a warrior who does impressive or outsize deeds, but it is the *Odyssey* that actually seems to be filled with many more such deeds. And yet, as I have already argued, it is not Odysseus' deeds that are meant to impress the reader of the *Odyssey* so much as it is his endurance of the terrible suffering meted out to him. On this score, Odysseus cuts a much more sympathetic figure than Achilles—who is, after all, a demigod—and his survival encourages readers to hope that, in a similarly difficult situation, they would be able to endure some hardship and come through it in order to achieve their goals. Of course, a careful reader will note that none of the characteristics that make Odysseus a hero who is preferable to Achilles touch on the concept of caring for or helping others that stands at the center of Socrates' heroism.

Indeed, I argued in the previous chapter that Socrates sought his own elevation by comparing himself favorably to Achilles while, at the same time, he attempted to bring the great hero down to earth both by denigrating some of his accomplishments and by challenging the virtue of some of his behavior. In this chapter, I claim that the same is true of the comparisons that Socrates draws between himself and Odysseus. And yet making this case is considerably more challenging than it was with regard to Achilles, in no small part because Socrates' criticisms of Odysseus seem almost nonexistent when compared with his critique of Achilles. Indeed, while Socrates famously argues in favor of censoring much of Homer's presentation of Achilles in order to make the warrior seem more properly heroic, he seems to celebrate Odysseus in the closing myth of the *Republic* as the only hero wise enough to choose a life that is nearest to the philosopher's. I begin by looking at arguments that Plato seeks to positively compare Odysseus to either the just man or the philosopher of the *Republic*, or even to Socrates himself. I then turn to an analysis of the *Lesser Hippias*, in which Socrates elevates Odysseus above Achilles as the best of the Homeric heroes. Finally, I turn to the several implicit Socratic criticisms of Odysseus in the Platonic corpus to make the case that, despite any perceived superiority to Achilles, Odysseus cannot compare favorably with Socrates, whose other-regarding heroism far surpasses that of the suffering of the Homeric hero.

ODYSSEUS IN PLATO'S *REPUBLIC*

Unlike the discussion of Achilles—which takes center stage in the section of the *Republic* devoted to the education of the guardian class—the Platonic treatment of Odysseus is far more circumspect. Homer's treatment of Achilles in both the *Iliad* and the *Odyssey* is in need of some revision, according to Socrates, because he is presented in a way that seems less than heroic and also because he behaves in a manner unbefitting a great warrior. It is, of course, this perceived endorsement of the censorship of the poets that touches off the millennia-old quarrel between poetry and philosophy. And while I argued in the previous chapter that this quarrel ought not to be ignored or minimized—insofar as it goes as deep as Plato's desire to ultimately unseat Homer as the principal educator of the Greeks—it is important to recognize that only one of Homer's great heroes receives this negative treatment from Socrates. Of course, a great deal of Socrates' most virulent criticism of Achilles stems from Homer's portrayal of the hero's shade in the *Odyssey*, rather than the living hero's behavior in the *Iliad*, but it is noteworthy that Socrates does not similarly turn to the *Iliad* to critique the way Homer portrays Odysseus as a man who never speaks plainly and who seems a good deal less invested in making war than in making sure his bodily needs are met.

Odysseus barely appears in the *Republic* at all, in fact, or at least not in the immediately obvious way in which Achilles is featured. And yet Socrates' allusion to Odysseus and to his heroic journey plays a role in Plato's dialogue, however much under the surface it remains, that is undoubtedly as important as the one played by Socrates' critique of Achilles. Indeed, Dennis J. Schmidt (2001: 23) points out the central role played by at least one part of Homer's *Odyssey*: "The first word of the *Republic*, *kateben*, echoes what Odysseus says to Penelope when he describes how he went down to the realm of the dead." In this way, Plato begins what is generally regarded as his defense of Socrates against the charges leveled against him by Athens with a direct comparison between his mentor and Odysseus, the archetypical suffering hero.

Nor is this, of course, the only time in the *Republic* when Socrates makes an implicit comparison between the philosopher—a character who remains something of a mystery, since Socrates does not ever name himself as one of the characters in book 7's Allegory of the Cave—and Odysseus. Just as Socrates descends to the Piraeus in order to converse about justice with the group of young men and then returns to Athens after the discussion has come to an end—though the latter takes place outside the action of the *Republic*—so too does the unnamed philosopher descend into the Cave in order to attempt to free the captives from their bonds. This second descent, which is Socrates' method of setting out his argument for the necessity of philosophers to rule the ideal city, recalls Odysseus' descent into Hades to converse with the shades. Once again, the allusion is not at all explicit; nowhere does Socrates say that either he or the philosopher resembles Odysseus in these descents. But given the prominence of Homer's epic poetry in Athens at this time, it is likely that Plato's readers would have drawn the connection to Odysseus and likely would not have seen these references as coincidental (cf. Voegelin 1966: 52–62).

Indeed, Patrick J. Deneen has made much of the comparison between the various accounts of ascending and descending in the *Republic* and the *Odyssey*. After highlighting each of the three journeys in a series of figures, he notes that

> Socrates' descent, as well as the philosopher's ascent, mimics the motion of Odysseus's several ascents and descents to and from Hades. Odysseus, like Socrates, initially descends (one to Hades, the other to the Piraeus) and reascends; like the philosopher, Odysseus both ascends and descends

(one from and to Hades, the other from and to the Cave). Odysseus's motions contain both versions of the ascent and descent; moreover, in a mixture of the motives of the philosopher, who must be compelled in both directions, and of the motives of Socrates, who goes and returns freely (after being compelled to stay in the middle), Odysseus's journey is composed of both compulsion and choice. (Deneen 2000: 128)

Somewhat strangely, he concludes his discussion of these journeys by claiming that "Odysseus proves more a model for Socrates, as Achilles appears as a model for the 'philosopher'" (Deneen 2000: 128). This is unusual both because he does not mention Achilles anywhere else in this lengthy explanatory note and because he does not offer any further explanation for the way in which Achilles might be seen as a model for the philosopher of the Allegory of the Cave, especially insofar as Achilles is not traditionally seen as a hero who descends or ascends in the way that Odysseus, Socrates, and the philosopher do. Instead, Deneen (2000: 114, 116) argues that the most important comparison is not in the journey itself but in the motivation for the undertaking; in this, the philosopher better resembles Achilles, who must be compelled to return to battle, than Odysseus or Socrates, whose descents are voluntary. The much more straightforward reading would be one that sees the journeys of both Socrates and the philosopher as modeled on Odysseus' journey at the center of the *Odyssey*. This is where Deneen (2000: 115) begins but not where he concludes, in large part because he wants to preserve the strongest possible connection between Plato's Socrates and Homer's Odysseus even at the expense of a connection between Socrates and the unnamed philosopher of the Allegory of the Cave.

Because the philosopher's motivation for descending into the cave might not line up with Socrates' own motivation for descending to the Piraeus, then, Deneen (2000: 115) suggests that "Socrates appears at first to identify himself (here as the philosopher) with Achilles, only to distance that identification from himself. Recalling the initial descent of Socrates to the Piraeus, we find by comparison that his journey is quite voluntary: he seeks to instruct the young gentleman Glaucon." My sense is that Deneen goes too far in attempting to untangle Socrates from the philosopher here, as it seems quite clear that Plato wants to highlight that connection through the series of descents he includes in the *Republic* rather than in just the specifics of one or another of them. More than just that impression, however, Deneen—who wants to focus on the motivation of the descent—is less forthcoming than he ought to be when it comes to both Odysseus' descent into Hades *and* Socrates' descent to the Piraeus. Indeed, it seems to me to be a mistake to claim that either Odysseus or Socrates act in a way that can be described as entirely or perfectly voluntary. With regard to Odysseus, it seems clear that he chooses to sail to Hades and to converse with the shades he encounters there. But it is equally clear that neither he nor his crew is particularly enthusiastic about the journey. There are seemingly no other options available if *nostos* is the true prize that he and his men claim it is. Indeed, he is told by Circe that he *must* speak to Tiresias, the famed blind seer whose shade now resides in Hades, in order to find his way home. The descent of Socrates is a bit more complex, however. He voluntarily goes down from Athens to the Piraeus in order to see a festival that is scheduled to take place there, but he does not willingly remain there for the discussion about justice at the house of Cephalus. As is well known, Socrates fully intends to return to Athens but is instead compelled to remain by Polemarchus and a group of young men, who argue that he must "either prove stronger than these men or stay here" (Plato 1991: 327c). In both cases, then, the story of the descent is far less straightforward than Deneen suggests; Socrates is effectively press-ganged into the *Republic's* philosophical discussion, and Odysseus has no other option but to descend to Hades if he wants to achieve the homecoming for which he is celebrated and through which he achieves *kléos*. On my reading, then, Odysseus and Socrates are not really so different from the philosopher of the Allegory of the Cave as Deneen suggests. The circumstances and the full weight of the project at the heart of their journeys—into Hades to converse with shades, to the house of Cephalus for a lengthy and controversial discussion, into the cave where danger might await at the hands of the captives—make it difficult to embrace these descents in a completely voluntary manner.

All of this, of course, is bound up with my own claims about the relationship between Socrates and the philosopher at the heart of the Allegory of the Cave, some of which were discussed briefly in the previous chapter. While it remains unclear whether Socrates is meant to be the philosopher or the mysterious (and unmentioned) figure who first freed the philosopher and dragged him from the cave,[1] my argument is that the hesitation evinced by the philosopher, Socrates, and the Homeric heroes to undertake their difficult journeys is not so much a character flaw as it is the thoughtful—and, ultimately, the heroic—engagement with their own mortality. After all, in each case, the descending hero faces clear and mortal danger that might be avoided by simply choosing otherwise. And though Deneen wants to connect the philosopher to Achilles, the connection ultimately does not hold up. The philosopher who would not return to the cave is directly compared by Socrates to the ghost of Achilles in Hades, and, although his feeling might be perfectly understandable, it is still judged to be incorrect. The philosopher, Socrates concludes, must descend into the cave, just as Odysseus descended into Hades, rather than remaining in the sunlight above—as Achilles in Hades says he desires—"to be on the soil, a serf to another, to a portionless man" (Plato 1991: 516d). In this way, Socrates connects himself directly to the philosopher of the Allegory of the Cave and to Odysseus as well—as he descended to the Piraeus, endangering himself in the process—while ultimately rejecting the comparison to Achilles' shade in Hades.

While my position contra Deneen is fairly clear on this point, his position is an intelligible one at which, I think, he arrives as a consequence of his broader project, just as my position is an outgrowth of my own argument about the relationship between Socrates and the Homeric heroes. That said, and regardless of whether the philosopher is meant to be regarded as Socrates, it is certainly quite clear that Plato puts a direct comparison between his mentor and a great Homeric hero in Socrates' mouth. He does so—here in the *Republic* just as with his reference to Achilles in the *Crito*—in a way that might not hit his reader over the head in the way that he does in the *Apology*, where Socrates claims to be exactly like Achilles in his behavior.[2] The reader is undoubtedly meant to connect Socrates' descent with that of Odysseus and to consider that connection from the very outset of the *Republic*. What's more, the connection is reinforced—at least on my reading—by the Allegory of the Cave. And then, to make the matter even more straightforward, Plato concludes the *Republic* with the Myth of Er, wherein Socrates makes both an indirect and a direct reference to Odysseus. As Schmidt (2001: 23) notes, Plato frames the entire discussion of justice contained in the *Republic* by beginning and ending with either an allusion or a direct comparison to Odysseus' descent into Hades in the central chapter of the *Odyssey*: "as the opening and ending of the dialogue make abundantly evident, the question put to us by death fundamentally shapes the course of the entire dialogue." In this way, Plato seems quite clearly to be instructing his reader to keep in mind the intimate connection between human mortality and the good life that Socrates extols both in word and in deed throughout the dialogues.

Of course, both Achilles and Odysseus devoted a great deal of time to pondering the interaction between their mortality and the kind of life they ultimately chose to live, as Socrates here instructs. But the *Republic* seems unequivocal in preferring Odysseus to Achilles, even if the former appears only briefly in the dialogue. After all, when he does appear, he seems not to be subjected to anywhere near the same level of scrutiny and negativity as Achilles. Or, to put a finer point on it, Socrates sees a need to censor only a single passage that Homer writes about Odysseus. Homer has erred, Socrates asserts, in claiming that Odysseus would have approved of immoderation:

> And what about making the wisest of men say that, in his opinion, the finest of all things is when
>
> The tables are full of bread and meat
> And the wine bearer draws wine from the bowl
> And brings it to pour in the goblets?
>
> Do you think that's fit for a young man to hear for his self-mastery? (Plato 1991: 390a–b)

As Deneen (2000: 91–92) notes, "Socrates accuses this passage of encouraging the physical and erotic appetites of the guardians, in opposition to the moderation that must be instilled in the excessive, unhealthy regime." But Deneen (2000: 92) also argues that the passage, like many of the others

Socrates censors here, is pretty clearly taken out of context: "the passage cited is not so much a celebration of food and wine as a celebration of fellowship."[3] Whether you read into the passage a tacit appreciation for Odysseus here or a more straightforward critique of one component of his character, it is clear that this is a fairly minor quibble with Homer's hero, especially in comparison with the treatment Socrates reserves for Achilles.

Considering that all of the other passages to be excised from the *Odyssey* are spoken by or about others, many readers have taken the *Republic* to be evincing something of an endorsement of Odysseus as a hero. Indeed, in the discussion of the education of the guardians, when Socrates censors Homer's portrayal of Achilles in both the *Odyssey* and the *Iliad*, he actually refers favorably to a critically important description of Odysseus:

> "But," I said, "if there are any speeches and deeds of endurance by famous men in the face of everything, surely they must be seen and heard, such as,
> Smiting his breast, he reproached his heart with word.
> Endure, heart; you have endured worse before.
> "That's entirely certain," he said. (Plato 1991: 390d)

Socrates here recalls Odysseus' reproach of his heart's desire to murder the suitors and servants in his house immediately upon his return. In this, he celebrates the hero's endurance of great suffering and his ability to delay the gratification he has awaited for so long in order to assure the success of the project he has been planning. As Deneen (2000: 93) notes, "This is the only *positive* example of instructive poetry offered by Socrates in his discussion of poetic education (against his stated intention not to offer one); thus the importance of the virtue being recommended here is stressed." Of course, this is only the smallest snippet of text on which Socrates barely comments at all. Much more obviously, at the conclusion of the *Republic*, Socrates retells the Myth of Er and puts his thoughts on Odysseus seemingly at center stage when a truly impressive group of shades—with Odysseus receiving pride of place among them—make an appearance, but Achilles is notably absent.

As is well known, the myth is the story told by Er of Pamphylia, a warrior who died in battle, was afforded a glimpse of the afterlife, and then was restored to health before his funeral pyre was lit. He proceeds to recount the manner in which the souls of the dead come to be reincarnated and thus take up new lives on Earth. Central to the process is, of course, the ability of each soul to select for itself the next life that it will lead. Deneen (2000: 103) sets out the circumstances of the choice nicely:

> As the "spokesman" (*prophētēs*) relates, there are many more "patterns" of lives than souls who will choose them; thus, in theory we all have the same possibility of choosing wisely (618a). Our equality is finally most fundamental, not our inequality, because even those most disadvantaged

by previous habit and life-circumstances can still exercise wise choice if they can achieve "the capacity and knowledge to distinguish the good from the bad life, and so everywhere, and always to choose the better from among those that are possible." (618c)

Thus, each soul chooses and, having made the choice, drinks a measure of water from the river of Carelessness and so forgets the knowledge obtained through the previous life before returning to Earth and starting the new life just selected (Plato 1991: 621a).

The description of the choices made by all of the souls prior to Odysseus' own choice is used to demonstrate the particular virtue of the Homeric hero. After all, the majority of the souls reflect but a little on the enormity of the choice before them, and thus some of them choose poorly, or at least they make choices that are almost wholly informed by the experiences of their previous lives. The very first soul to choose, famously, selects the life of the tyrant, having failed to "notice that eating his own children and other evils were fated to be a part of that life. When he considered it at his leisure, he beat his breast and lamented the choice" (Plato 1991: 619c). The majority of the souls, of course, are not as rash when they choose as this one who made the first selection—"because they themselves had labored and had seen the labors of others" (Plato 1991: 619d)—and so the choices generally go more smoothly. But, at bottom, the choices they make are not philosophical ones; they are the choices of those who reflect only on their previous go-round on Earth rather than on what the best life would entail. As Er narrates the choices of two Homeric heroes, "The soul that got the twentieth lot chose the life of a lion; it was the soul of Ajax, son of Telamon, who shunned becoming a human being, remembering the judgment of the arms. And after him was the soul of Agamemnon; it too hated humankind as a result of its sufferings and therefore changed to the life of an eagle" (Plato 1991: 620a–b).

Finally, the tale describes the soul of Odysseus—in just a few more sentences than are given to any of the others—and, not surprisingly, this final choice takes on great meaning for readers of the *Republic*. As Rosen (2005: 386) notes, "It is Odysseus's lot to choose last. He is said to have recovered from his love of honor because of the labors of his former life, and so spends considerable time in looking for the life of 'a private man who is not a busybody' (*andros idiōtou apragmonos*: 620c6–7). Odysseus says that this would have been his choice even if he had chosen first." Strangely, what this choice tells the careful reader of the *Republic* has been regarded as generally unimportant by virtually everyone who writes about Socrates.[4] For Deneen (2000: 106), however, Odysseus' choice could not be more important, and he nicely sets out why it also presents something of a puzzle:

> If we are to note that Odysseus's is among the only souls to act out of more than mere habituation from his last life, what is admirable about the particular life that the soul of Odysseus chooses is not altogether obvious.

Socrates does not explicitly say that the soul of Odysseus chooses the life of the philosopher or that his choice will lead to the institution of the just city in speech. Rather, it is simply the fact that he chooses the life of "the private man who minds his own business" that is intended to elicit our admiration. If the method of Odysseus's soul's choice is notable for its singular reflection, the choice itself remains perplexing.

I agree with Deneen in both his assessment of the importance of Odysseus' choice and the fact that it needs some elucidation. Deneen (2000: 108) begins by noting that "to prefer the life of one who 'minds his own business' seems in the first instance to mean that Odysseus's soul prefers the life of the just man, one who has properly ordered his soul to 'mind its own business,' thereby charging 'the calculating part to rule, since it is wise and has forethought about all our soul, and for the spirited part to be obedient to it and its ally' (441d)." In this, Deneen is clearly correct: the connection between the choice made by Odysseus' soul and the life of the just man as set out by Socrates earlier in the *Republic* is unmistakable.[5] Perhaps the paucity of writing on the choice is explained by how seemingly obvious the connection appears to be.

And yet Deneen proceeds in his thorough analysis, noting that Odysseus' choice might be meant to imply more than his wisdom in selecting the life of the just man. As he argues, Odysseus might be choosing the life not simply of the just man but also of the philosopher who is the proposed ruler of the city in speech but desires not to rule. He claims that "internally, the various parts of the philosopher's soul are said to 'mind their own business' (hence indicating that perhaps only the philosopher can have the truly just soul); externally, the philosopher seeks to weather the violent storm of his polity by remaining apart from the violence of others" (Deneen 2000: 108). Rather than delving too deeply into this possible reading, Deneen instead turns to its most extreme form, the conclusion put forward by Bloom, who argues that Odysseus' choice is meant to recall the life of not only the philosopher but also a specific philosopher: Socrates. As Allan Bloom (1991: 436) argues, "The wise voyager Odysseus gains higher status. All he needed was to be cured of love of honor (a form of spiritedness), and he could live the obscure but happy life of Socrates. In this Socrates also gets his inspiration from Homer, and thus he lets us know that there may be another side to Homer's poetry than that which the tradition had popularized." It is not immediately obvious what leads Bloom to this conclusion about Odysseus and Socrates, nor is it clear exactly what Bloom has in mind when he intimates that Socrates might be putting forward some sort of defense of Homeric poetry.[6]

And indeed, Deneen seems less certain about this conclusion, and my sense is that he would do well to distance his argument from Bloom's on this point, as it is markedly less clear that Plato intends the reader to recognize the life of Socrates in the choice of Odysseus' soul. As Deneen (2000: 107) rightly notes, "While the choice of a 'private man' (i.e., one not actively involved in politics) hits the mark, one can hardly conclude from the description of Socrates' activities in the Platonic corpus that he is a man who 'minds his own business.'" But this is not the sum total of Deneen's conclusion about the lesson to be drawn from the Myth of Er. He hedges his bets quite a bit toward the end:

> Rather than unwisely choosing, either a soul that is not well governed or one that too fully anticipates the situation in which his life will unfold, Odysseus's soul chooses a life that will likely retain the ordering of his soul. Whether he becomes a philosopher or a "busybody" or even a Socrates will depend in large part on the situation into which he will be born. (111)

Ultimately, he concludes with the following observation: "In effect, he chooses to remain a man 'of many ways,' but one, in all events, whose soul will be justly ordered" (Deneen 2000: 111).[7] But if Deneen is persuasive in this, it is likely to his detriment, because if Odysseus remains a man characterized principally as *polytropos* [πολύτροπος; of many ways], then he is likely not choosing the life of *either* the just man or the philosopher. The man of many ways—as I have argued in previous chapters—is one who is able to deceive others when it suits his own, largely private purposes; the philosopher, by contrast, finds such dissembling to be odious. Indeed, this is the central critique of Odysseus leveled by Socrates in the *Lesser Hippias*, to which we now turn.

ODYSSEUS: SHAMEFUL AND UNJUST

While it is very clear, then, that Odysseus receives better treatment at Socrates' hand in the *Republic* than Achilles, it is important to note that this is not the only discussion of the second of the great Homeric heroes in the Platonic dialogues. Indeed, whereas Odysseus is alluded to a handful of times in the *Republic* and likely receives no more than a paragraph of direct discussion, his heroism is a central component of another, lesser-known dialogue: the *Lesser Hippias*. Indeed, in this dialogue, Socrates makes the precise argument that most scholars assume when they read the allusions to a Socratic preference for Odysseus in the *Republic*—namely, that Odysseus is certainly the better hero when compared against Achilles. And yet very few scholars make reference to the *Lesser Hippias* when they discuss the role that the *Odyssey* plays in the Platonic dialogues. The reason for the dearth of references to this Socratic argument is likely the way that Socrates makes his case and, specifically, the conclusion that he draws with regard to Odysseus' heroism: "he who voluntarily goes wrong and does what is shameful and unjust, Hippias, if indeed there is any such person, would be no one else than the good man" (Plato 1997c: 376b). This conclusion is abhorrent to Hippias and even to Socrates himself.[8]

In considering the way in which Socrates arrives at this conclusion, praising one who voluntarily acts unjustly, we will arrive at the first of two major critiques of the idea that Plato envisions Socrates as the Athenian incarnation of Odysseus, or even as a hero cut from that cloth. The *Lesser Hippias* is one of the earliest Platonic dialogues, and, due in part to the strange argument, it has generally received substantially less discussion than the rest of Plato's work. But Socrates' argument will receive a good deal of scrutiny here, as it clearly speaks directly to the topic at hand. The setting of the dialogue, as Laurence Lampert (2002: 233–235) highlights, is every bit as important as in other Platonic dialogues: it most likely takes place in 420 BCE, the same year as both the nineteenth Olympiad and Alcibiades' victory in the diplomatic conference for which Hippias was likely visiting Athens from Elis.[9] With regard to the former momentous event, the dialogue mimics the Olympic celebration by suggesting

> that the contest between Hippias and Socrates is a pre-Olympic trial between the acknowledged Olympic champion of wisdom and the local favorite (*Lesser Hippias* 363c–364a; 368b). In his first speeches in the *Lesser Hippias* Hippias boasts of being an undefeated Olympic victor who takes on all comers at the temple of Zeus in Olympia during the games and has "never yet met anyone better than I am in anything" (364a). Yet Socrates proves better than Hippias in this pre-Olympic trial on the question, Who is better, Achilles or Odysseus? (Lampert 2002: 234)

With regard to the latter, which Lampert (2002: 234–235) rightly regards as the more important scene-setting component, "Alcibiades won the diplomatic battle in 420 by perpetuating an outrageous trick on the Spartan ambassadors, persuading them to lie to the Athenian assembly about their power to finalize a treaty. Unscrupulous Alcibiades then immediately denounced them to the assembly as unscrupulous liars, inciting the assembly into a frenzy of outrage against the Spartans and turning it toward his own policy." Thus, the dialogue concerns the question of whether acting deceitfully can ever be lauded as a virtue, played against the backdrop of the victory of the masterfully deceitful former student of Socrates.

Of course, the *Lesser Hippias* also proceeds in the shadow of the *Greater Hippias*, a private conversation between Hippias and Socrates in which the former invites the latter to hear him speak on the question of "what sorts of pursuits were beautiful, pursuits that would make a young man who practiced them most highly reputed" (Plato 1997a: 286b). This is, as Hippias imagines the scene, the question that Achilles' son, Neoptolemus, asks of Nestor, whom Hippias asserts is the wisest of all who sailed against Troy. And it is, to be sure, a question of great interest to Plato, as it touches directly on the matter of instructing young men about the best sort of life to live. This speech has just been delivered publicly, and now, in a more private setting, Socrates seeks to challenge Hippias, who has cast himself as a latter-day Nestor by defending the virtues of the life of Achilles. What Socrates now desires to know is whether Hippias believes that Achilles is the better of the two great Homeric heroes (Plato 1997c: 363b–c, 364b). Hippias begins his answer by asserting that there are three distinct types of men who sailed against Troy and that Achilles, Odysseus, and Nestor are the pinnacles of each type: "I say that Homer made Achilles the 'best and bravest' man of those who went to Troy, and Nestor the wisest, and Odysseus the wiliest" (Plato 1997c: 364c). This answer bewilders Socrates, or at least he claims that it does, for wiliness is not necessarily a praiseworthy characteristic.

As noted in the earlier chapter on Odysseus, the translation of the word in question—*polytropos* [πολύτροπος]—has occasioned all sorts of debate with regard to the information it provides the reader about the Homeric hero. I have used "of many ways" throughout in order to convey two things: first, the many twists and turns that Odysseus must take before returning home to Ithaca, and second, his personality trait of being strategic or wily. Thus, I have chosen to use wiliness as the adjective here, even though, as Hoerber (1962: 125) argues, "The adjective . . . may be ambiguous, in that it appears in Greek literature also in the sense of 'crafty,' 'shifty,' 'clever,' 'versatile.'" Hoerber concludes that Hippias intends versatility "by equating πολύτροπος with ψευδής (365b)." But it is not at all clear why such a connection ought to imply versatility any more than wiliness, as ψευδής [*pseudēs*] is generally translated as lying, false, or untrue. As Weiss (1981: 291) claims, "For Hippias, πολύτροπος is from the first a pejorative word. Hence, Howett's and Fowler's 'wily' is a suitable translation of πολύτροπος when Hippias says it. Were this not so, it would be difficult to see why Hippias regards it as obvious that Homer's characterization of Odysseus as πολύτροπος makes Odysseus the lesser of the two heroes." Mulhern (1968: 284n2) disagrees with me and also, to some extent, with Hoerber:

> The rendering must suggest no more than that an ability is possessed; it must not give the reader to believe that the ability in question receives any typical or regular employment. "Wiles" and "wily" are unsuitable candidates because, according to the *Shorter Oxford English Dictionary*, they suggest craft, cunning, and deceit; that is to say, they suggest τρόπος-concepts. The interpretation of craft, cunning, or deceit does not appear in the dialogue until πολυτροπία and ψευδής are coupled in 365B 4–5.[10]

For Weiss (1981: 291n15), however, "'wily' is a suitable translation of πολύτροπος because (*a*) it suggests the cleverness which is essential, and (*b*) it is a word which, while having an appropriately pejorative taint, does not go so far as to become a *tropos*-adjective like, say, 'wicked' or 'treacherous.'" In this sense, what has typically been regarded as Odysseus' characteristic cleverness might also be regarded as a skill.

All of this debate over language actually matters because the way that we understand Hippias and Socrates to be using *polytropos* in their descriptions of Odysseus will determine whether we ultimately consider the first of the two conclusions of the *Lesser Hippias* to be a paradoxical one. That conclusion, famously, is that the truthful man—Achilles—and the false man—Odysseus—cannot actually be distinguished from one another. Thus, as far as Socrates is concerned, it makes little sense to praise the one while criticizing the other, as Hippias has done. As far as Mulhern (1968: 286) is concerned, the conclusion represents a clear paradox

> because it is true in one sense and false in another: it is true that the same man is able to be both false and true, in cases wherein the prerequisite for either τρόπος is acquaintance with some department of knowledge; yet it is false that the same man must both lie regularly and tell the truth regularly, even though acquaintance with some department of knowledge may enable him to do either with success.

What's more, "the paradox is of use to Socrates in this dialogue because it provides him with a decisive objection against the mixture of δύναμις-concepts and τρόπος-concepts employed by Hippias in his attempt to distinguish Odysseus from Achilles" (Mulhern 1968: 286). That said, there is another interpretation that does not rely on paradoxes. As Weiss (1981: 292) points out,

> The difference between the positions of Socrates and Hippias is not the difference between *tropos*-concepts and *dunamis*-concepts, between terms indicating typical behaviour and terms indicating skill, but rather the difference between two kinds of *dunamis*-concept, one of which is neutral and the other of which is negative. . . . Thus, by introducing ψευδής as a synonym for πολύτροπος, Hippias, though indeed aiming at giving πολύτροπος a negative sense, was not substituting a *tropos*-adjective for a *dunamis*-adjective.

When read this way, she points out, "it means: The man skilled at speaking truthfully and the man skilled at speaking falsely are the same man; the paradox vanishes" (Weiss 1981: 290). On this reading, the man who can voluntarily speak falsely when it serves his interests, rather than the man who habitually speaks falsely, is the good man, and, with regard to this ability, neither Achilles nor Odysseus should be seen to be better or worse than the other.

And yet this also seriously impacts the way in which the remainder of the dialogue unfolds because, on this reading, Achilles ought not to have this ability to voluntarily speak falsely. In contrast to Odysseus, who is heralded by Homer as a man of many ways, he is ἁπλοῦς [*haploús*; simple, straightforward]. Indeed, it is Achilles himself who charges that Odysseus speaks in a duplicitous manner while he is always straightforward in speech. If this is the case, perhaps Achilles—who claims never to speak falsely—ought not to be celebrated as the greater hero when compared to Odysseus, who is always characterized as *polytropos*. It might be the case, then, that Achilles and Odysseus ought to be differentiated in some other manner, or else it could be that *polytropos* should be thought of differently (i.e., not directly connected to lying). This is especially the case insofar as Hippias maintains his preference for Achilles over Odysseus and insofar as Socrates contends that, in actuality, Achilles is depicted by Homer as the one who lies.[11] And thus the remainder of the *Lesser Hippias* is devoted to the question of whether the lies of Achilles are voluntary or involuntary ones.

Once Socrates demonstrates that Achilles is shown telling lies in the *Iliad*, Hippias must argue that the lies he tells are surely unintentional ones; this defense, however, is not particularly useful to Hippias' overall argument, since the two agree that the man who acts voluntarily is better than the one who acts involuntarily.[12] As Weiss (1981: 297) nicely summarizes the argument, Socrates compares

> (*a*) one who intentionally does poorly with one who does poorly unintentionally in all forms of bodily exercise requiring strength and/or grace, for example, running and wrestling; (*b*) organs which are intentionally defective with organs which are unintentionally defective—voices, feet, eyes, ears, etc.; (*c*) instruments with which one does poorly intentionally with those with which one does poorly unintentionally, for example, rudders, musical instruments, horses, and dogs (here regarded as instruments for man's use); and (*d*) ψυχαί which intentionally exercise their skills badly with those which exercise their skills badly unintentionally, such as the ψυχαί of archers, users of the bow, physicians, flute-players, lute-players, and slaves. In each instance, Hippias agrees that the first in the pair is preferable to the second.

Thus, when Socrates and Hippias arrive back at the discussion of Achilles and Odysseus, Hippias must conclude that the latter is the better of the two Homeric heroes insofar as he *intends* to speak falsely when he does so. Weiss (1981: 303) argues, after all, that it is the intention of the actor with regard to a particular act or skill, not the action itself, that is at issue throughout the dialogue: "There is no suggestion anywhere that, for example, the intentional *lie* is better than the unintentional, but rather that the intentional *liar* is better because more skilled." On this reading, Weiss (1981: 304) argues, Socrates is simply putting forward the logical conclusion to the argument that Odysseus is better than Achilles insofar as the voluntary nature of his actions demonstrates his superior skill, rather than arguing in favor of the immoral conclusion that lying somehow equates with justice or goodness: "ὁ ἀγαθός of the *Hippias Minor* is thus not the standard ἀγαθός who is judged on the basis of his actions. Since the agent in this dialogue is judged solely on the basis of his skill, things may be said with impunity about this man that could not be said so freely about the ordinary ὁ ἀγαθός. We need only bear in mind that ὁ ἀγαθός here is 'the man *skilled* at justice'—not 'the just man.'" In other words, the better man—the one who is better skilled—is able to lie when he so chooses regardless of whether one *ought* to do so. And yet, as every scholar who writes on this dialogue notes, Hippias and Socrates are both horrified by this conclusion:

SOCRATES: So the one who voluntarily misses the mark and does what is shameful and unjust, Hippias—that is, if there is such a person—would be no other than the good man.

HIPPIAS: I can't agree with you in that, Socrates.

SOCRATES: Nor I with myself, Hippias. But given the argument, we can't help having it look that way to us, now, at any rate. (Plato 1997c: 376b–c)

These lines have led the majority of scholars to conclude—wrongly, to my mind—that Socrates must either be making a scandalous moral claim here—namely, that the just or good man is the one who lies voluntarily, or else—more plausibly—that he does not personally believe what he says here.

Lampert, for example, concludes that Socrates is taking the part of Homer in the dialogue in order to argue a preference for Odysseus and, specifically, his unique sort of wisdom. Specifically, he suggests that "in arguing for the superiority of Odysseus while refusing Hippias's offer to consider Nestor the 'wisest,' Socrates will imply that Homer himself held Odysseus to be a better man than Achilles and that he purposely veiled his judgment of Odysseus's superiority by the glory in which he wrapped Achilles" (Lampert 2002: 239). But Lampert goes beyond simply this claim that Socrates speaks for Homer in celebrating Odysseus at the expense of Achilles; in the end, his claim—like that of Allan Bloom noted earlier—is that Socrates actually takes the position of Odysseus. His argument follows that of Mulhern (1986: 287–288)—namely, that Socrates equivocates in his final statement on the matter, voicing qualified agreement with Hippias that "it would be terrible . . . if those doing injustice voluntarily are to be better than those doing so involuntarily" (Plato 1997c: 375d). For Lampert (2002: 255), this demonstrates that

> Plato shows Socrates vacillating as the wise must vacillate. Plato makes it possible to see that Hippias may well be a fitting Nestor to almost all the sons of Achilles, whereas Socrates, student of an ancient wisdom deeper than Hippias knows, could be Odysseus to the rarest of those sons, a truly wise teacher who may be of help to the best offspring of the apparently best, those who can be cured of the need to be most highly reputed.

Of course, both arguments—that Socrates is committed to the logical conclusion he sets out and that he is troubled by its immorality—are actually in evidence at the end of the *Lesser Hippias*.

On these dual possibilities and the reason that Plato allowed for this seeming lack of clarity on a matter of such importance, Weiss is somewhat strangely silent. Instead of attempting to tackle the puzzle represented by the conclusion of the *Lesser Hippias*, she simply agrees that the problem exists and that it remains a very challenging one:

> Having come this far, we face the problem of determining what Plato's purpose could possibly have been in having Socrates reach a paradoxical-sounding conclusion about a non-standard ἀγαθός And, of course, if this conclusion is valid based on the premises [sic] elicited by Socrates himself, we must wonder why he is dissatisfied with it. If Plato claims no more than that the good man is wise and able and hence does wrong only intentionally, why does he have Socrates wonder if there are any such men (εἴπερ τίς ἔστιν οὗτος—376b5–6)? These difficulties, as stated at the outset, are beyond the scope of this paper, which has attempted only to lay the groundwork for the inquiry into them. (Weiss 1981: 304)

But while Weiss' conclusion leaves much to be desired, my sense is that her analysis of the linguistic turns of the *Lesser Hippias* actually enables us to think carefully about Plato's own intentions. Although Weiss avoids a reliance on the linguistic vacillations proposed by Mulhern and Hoerber, her argument leaves open the possibility of concluding that Socrates does not actually hold the position to which he has led Hippias. The same cannot be said of Lampert's conclusion: though it is likely to be compelling to those who already see Socrates as someone who saves his true teaching on any subject for the next generation of philosophers—in other words, those who are already committed to the idea that Socrates is polytropic like Odysseus—it would require ignoring one of Socrates' central arguments in a wide variety of subsequent dialogues. As Hoerber (1962: 128) notes, "It was well-known that Socrates (and Plato) consistently held to a theory directly opposed to the second proposition of the Lesser Hippias; namely, according to Socrates and Plato no one commits injustice voluntarily." This position (cf. Plato 1984a: 25d–26a; Plato 1997b: 860d, 731c, 734b)—or one closely connected to it, that no one desires what is wrong or bad (cf. Plato 1991: 589c; Plato 1996b: 345d–e, 358c–d; Plato 1997d: 86d–e; Plato 1999a: 77b–78b)—is consistently put forward by Socrates. Thus, we might take Weiss' argument about linguistics to be accurate and so note that Socrates' conclusion is that the better man is the one who is skilled at speaking falsely, insofar as it means only that he *can* lie rather than that he *ought* to do so, while also holding the opposite conclusion to Weiss'—namely, that Socrates simply seeks to lead Hippias down the path of an argument he does not himself believe to be correct. This position, I think, is evidenced by the very last sentence of the dialogue: "However, as I said before, on these matters I waver back and forth and never believe the same thing. And it's not surprising at all that I or any other ordinary person *should* waver. But if you wise men are going to do it, too—that means something terrible for us, if we can't stop our wavering even after we've put ourselves in your company" (Plato 1997c: 376c). In other words, it would be quite plausible to argue that Socrates is simply taking Hippias down a peg here—as he does with each of the presumably wise men he encounters in the dialogues—rather than actually grappling with the question at hand about Achilles, Odysseus, and the morality or skill of speaking falsely.[13]

In either case—whether the dialogue advances an argument about the skill of lying in order to elevate Odysseus or simply "is a legitimate, valid attack on Hippias" (Zembaty 1989: 64)—it seems clear that Socrates' concluding position in the *Lesser Hippias* does not correspond particularly well to the image, described in the preceding section, of Odysseus as either the just man or the philosopher. After all, while Odysseus is here described as the just man, even more directly than in the *Republic*'s Myth of Er, the argument is either that the just man is the one who lies voluntarily or that the just man is the one who is skilled at lying.[14] Either way, the image of the just man here—and of Odysseus, certainly—is not so much one who minds his own business, as in the *Republic*, but one who speaks falsely. As Odysseus' most notable characteristic is being polytropic—identified here with speaking falsely when it suits his purposes—and as Socrates voices his disapproval that this is somehow just (here and elsewhere), it is very difficult to read this dialogue as any sort of endorsement of the life of Odysseus. In other words, in the dialogue where Socrates argues that Odysseus should be understood as the better hero when compared to Achilles, he damns Odysseus with the absolute faintest of praise: he is the better hero—or the good, or the just—insofar as it is his distinct skill to tell voluntary lies as opposed to those, like Achilles it seems, who can tell only involuntary ones.

While this conclusion would be just as shocking to those who read the Myth of Er as Plato's straightforward and authoritative statement of praise for Odysseus as the straightforward conclusion that the *Lesser Hippias* advances an immoral argument has been to many scholars, my argument is that no one ought to be puzzled or surprised. In the case of the conclusion of the *Lesser Hippias*, I agree with Weiss that the arguments put forward by Socrates are simply not the presumed immoral ones that scholars have suggested. And neither, to my mind, should the Myth of Er be read as Socrates' true teaching about either the afterlife or about Odysseus' as the best and most choice-worthy heroic life; thus the conclusions that scholars like Deneen, Benardette, and Bloom read into Odysseus' choice in the *Republic* ought to be taken with a substantial grain of salt.

THE MYTH OF ER AS IRONY

The mythical conclusion to Plato's *Republic* seems designed as a reply to Homer's treatment of a similar descent by a living warrior into the underworld (cf. Schmidt 2001: 40–41). But what sort of reply is Plato setting out here? As Deneen (2000: 101) rightly notes, "The Myth of Er is perhaps the most curiously placed myth in the whole of the Platonic corpus: it effectively contradicts a major argument that has preceded it." If so much of the *Republic* is devoted to privileging reason over myth and to the censorship of poetry in favor of philosophy, then concluding with the retelling of a myth is unusual indeed, especially if the reader is meant to take seriously its message.

Nevertheless, some eminent scholars argue that the myth is meant to be taken at face value, that Socrates hopes to convince his young interlocutors either of the virtue of the philosophic life through his retelling of the story of Er, of the existence of the afterlife and the immortality of the soul, or some combination thereof (cf. Annas 1981; Thayer 1988; Rosen 2005; Voegelin 1966). Others—and I fall into this camp—argue that the myth ought to be read with a fairly liberal dash of irony. The reasoning behind opting for such a reading, rather than a more straightforward one, is nicely explained by John Evan Seery (1988: 243):

> The answer cannot be that, in telling us a myth, Plato is hoping that we believe *what it says* on a literal level (namely, that this character Er saw some souls judged, etc.). Second, that the myth is deliberately presented as fifth-order myth (as opposed to a *straight* presentation of a myth, myth not embedded in layers of ironic relief) forecloses the interpretation that Plato is hoping for us merely to accept the simplest *message* of the myth, that he is sharing with us a difficult and esoteric vision of an *afterlife.* . . . Third, if, following the reasoning of the dialogue on representation, the point of the myth (as *pseudos*) is to convey the true (*aletheia*) message of pursuing justice, then it still needs to be explained why the myth is presented at fifth remove from the truth. Straight myth would have sufficed, and Plato would not have needed to add on the ironies involved in mimicking Homer.[15]

In other words, the manner in which Plato sets out the myth and, of course, the fact that the story is presented as a myth in the first place both suggest that one ought to delve a bit deeper in order to determine whether the character of Socrates is setting out his actual position through the myth. After all, if we take the teaching of the myth at face value, we are told that our souls are reincarnated and that Odysseus' soul makes the wisest choice. This choice is notable because Odysseus makes it after a lengthy, deliberate search and because he seems to choose the life that Socrates has previously ascribed to the just man. Neither of these conclusions necessarily needs to be considered surprising or out of place; as outlined in an earlier chapter, Socrates argues in favor of the immortality of the soul in the *Phaedo*, and, as outlined just earlier, he also argues that Odysseus should be considered the just man. In both cases, of course, I have noted that understanding either of these arguments in a straightforward manner is problematic. It remains to discuss, then, what it would mean to take the Myth of Er as ironic or, at the very least, less than the straightforward teaching about the afterlife and the choice of Odysseus' soul.

Regardless of whether a scholar chooses to consider the Myth of Er as straightforward or ironic, virtually everyone reads it as a response to Homer. With regard to the first—and, I think, simplest—issue, the myth's central conceit, that of descending to Hades to observe the souls of the deceased, mirrors exactly Odysseus' own descent to Hades at the heart of the *Odyssey*. But the lesson about the status of the souls in the afterlife is very different: in the *Odyssey*, Homer presents the orthodox account of shades in permanent residence in Hades, bemoaning the loss of their lives and the specific causes of their deaths. In the *Republic*'s conclusion, Plato presents a heterodox account of the afterlife, in which souls are only briefly below the earth, choose new lives, and then quickly ascend again to begin life anew. In the orthodox understanding of the afterlife, the dead are permanently identified with the lives they led; it is in this way that Odysseus and Achilles have their brief discussion that begins with Odysseus' celebration of Achilles' great deeds at Troy, which have surely earned him enduring glory even in Hades. In Socrates' heterodox account, however, the only connection between a soul in Hades and his or her former life on earth revolves around the choice of a new life, which is heavily influenced by the circumstances of the soul's former life. We might, then, take Plato to be challenging the most common or generally accepted thinking about religion, using the Myth of Er to press a very different—and far more dynamic—understanding of death and the afterlife. Or, what is more likely given Socrates' continual disavowal of any knowledge of the afterlife, Plato might simply be challenging *Homer's* authority on matters of belief, as I have argued he wants to do with regard to the poet's authority in every aspect of Greek life.

This is, of course, directly tied to the second Platonic challenge to Homer presented by the myth. As noted earlier, the straightforward reading of the myth suggests simply that Odysseus finally chooses the life of either the just man or the philosopher. This leads to the conclusion that he is the more thoughtful of the two great Homeric heroes and therefore the one who is ultimately preferred by Socrates. But thinking a bit more deeply about the choice made by Odysseus' soul leads one to recognize that the reason Odysseus chooses the life of the man who minds his own business is because he repudiates the labors of his previous life. In other words, Odysseus—having lived the life of the Homeric hero who endures great suffering—chooses a life that is the *exact opposite* of the heroic life he led. In this, he is like all of the other souls, if a bit more careful than the others in making his selection. And thus the Homeric hero who is supposedly preferred by Socrates turns out to be preferred only because he has decided that the heroic life he led is not one he would care to live again. As Schmidt (2001: 42–43) argues, "It is a curious and significant choice: the supreme Homeric hero chooses a reconciled life, a life that is measured only against itself. It is a choice made on the basis of what was learned from his life as it was presented by Homer; in other words, here the hero of the Homeric tragedy shows that he has learned, on the basis of a tragic life, not to choose such a life once again." In this, Odysseus seems to echo the words of Achilles from the *Odyssey*, when he tells Odysseus that he would rather live any sort of life—even that of the meanest laborer—instead of the life that led him to his predicament as a shade in Hades. The suggestion, then, is that after they died, both of the great Homeric heroes ultimately renounced the decisions they made in the heroic lives they led.

There are two interesting points about this repudiation of classical heroism that require some further elucidation. Achilles' rejection of the heroic lifestyle takes place in Homer's own writing—first, briefly, in book 9 of the *Iliad* and then again in book 11 of the *Odyssey*—while Odysseus is made to reject the hardships that led to his elevation as a hero in a myth told by Socrates. We might conclude that in this way Homer expresses a preference for the heroism of Odysseus over the heroism of Achilles by letting stand the choices of the former while the latter's are openly questioned. And while that might be a compelling reading of Homer, we cannot—as many scholars have done—make the same case with regard to Plato's position on the Homeric heroes. After all, *Plato* here puts forward the repudiation of the choices that made Odysseus a hero not found in Homer. Further, Odysseus' soul actually carries out the rejection of his former heroic life that Achilles' shade tells him he wishes he could undertake, choosing a new life on the earth that will allow him to avoid repeating any of the challenges imposed on him by his former life. While we might conclude that this is simply another example of Odysseus finding a way to improve on the life of Achilles, and thus lend some support to the argument that Plato preferred the former to the latter, it is noteworthy that Odysseus' action—and, indeed, the actions of all of the souls in the myth—is one that Socrates censors when Achilles voices it. More specifically, Socrates argues that it would be improper to allow the guardians to believe that a hero like Achilles—in addition to several other Homeric characters—would lament death or express any unhappiness at trading away life in exchange for glory. And yet, in specifically choosing a life that will allow him to avoid the hardships that made him a hero, Odysseus' soul ensures that his next life will not be a heroic one. It seems counterintuitive that Socrates would censor such a repudiation of the heroic preference for glorious deeds when voiced as a wish by Achilles' shade but celebrate it when Odysseus' soul actually makes good on that wish.

What, then, are we to make of such a choice? In particular, what should the myth tell us, finally, about Socrates' complicated relationship with Odysseus? Considering the life that Odysseus' soul chooses, Schmidt (2001: 42–43) argues

> It is, one should also note, a life which the community described in the *Republic* might render difficult since that community, which relentlessly politicizes everything (and so always has the shape of a totalitarian regime), does not leave much room for a life apart from others. It is also, quite obviously, the life that Socrates expressed as his wish for himself at the

very outset of the *Republic* when he suggested that he simply wanted to return home after having witnessed the religious celebrations. Of course, the life that Socrates led, the life of a gadfly who could never completely "mind his own business," was itself far removed from such a choice.

As noted earlier, it seems clear that the choice of Odysseus' soul is not meant to represent the life of Socrates, but it does clearly call to mind the life of the just man set out earlier in the *Republic*. As I have suggested here, however, this choice says just as much about the life of the just man—the virtues of which Socrates has been tasked with extolling by Glaucon and Adeimantus—as it does about Odysseus who chooses it. For although Odysseus is elsewhere in the *Republic* given the epithet "the wisest of men" (Plato 1991: 390a), it seems clear that he is deserving of it only insofar as he is the most skilled in speaking falsely—as demonstrated in the *Lesser Hippias*—or as he makes the most carefully considered choice to repudiate his heroic lifestyle in the Myth of Er. In this way, Socrates is able to signal his disapproval of the heroic life of Odysseus even as he seems to straightforwardly suggest that Odysseus is the best of the Homeric heroes. And either a straightforward or an ironic reading of the myth will ultimately yield the same conclusion: Socrates' vision of Odysseus always repudiates the life that Homer celebrates as heroic. Or, to put it somewhat differently, the only version of Odysseus that Socrates finds worthy of any praise is the one who recognizes that the life of Odysseus is not a choice-worthy life.

There is little doubt, then, that the Myth of Er has much to offer anyone who seeks to analyze Socrates' opinion of Odysseus, though most scholars have chosen not to spend a great deal of time dissecting the few sentences devoted to the choice of Odysseus' soul. In particular, it seems to confirm the position that I set out at the beginning of this chapter: Plato seeks to elevate Odysseus throughout both the *Republic* and the *Lesser Hippias*, especially in comparison with Achilles, only to finally demonstrate that neither Achilles nor Odysseus can compare favorably with the life of his own hero, Socrates. While I have tended to adopt ironic readings of Plato's dialogues throughout, it seems clear that Socrates is not expressing a preference for the life of Odysseus in either the *Lesser Hippias* or the *Republic*; even if one reads these dialogues in the most straightforward manner, it would be challenging indeed to arrive at the conclusion that Plato was expressing admiration for Odysseus or suggesting that the Homeric hero ought to be viewed as a model of excellence by the Athenians. As Rosen (2005: 386), in an example of a straightforward interpretation, writes,

> Socrates thus closes the myth with one final rebuke of Homer, and in this way with the whole Greek tradition of justice. The praise of the quiet life is of course to be found elsewhere among the Greek writers, for example, in Herodotus, but it goes counter to the Greek love of glory, for which Homer is the most fluent spokesman, and which even

Socrates ranks second to the pursuit of wisdom. As it turns out, the happiest life for the wise man is philosophy together with the quiet of the private life in which one minds one's own business.

What we ought to glean from the myth—even a straightforward reading of it—is that the deliberative nature of Odysseus' soul's choice is instructive; he ends up choosing a good life, or at least a life that is far better than the one that he had previously lived as Odysseus the Homeric hero.

Indeed, Seery's ultimate conclusion is that the myth is meant to give notice to the reader that the entirety of the *Republic* should be read in a profoundly ironic way. At bottom, he suggests that the true lesson of the dialogue is that one ought to question everything. He argues,

> The book cannot just tell us what it is trying to tell us—for in a sense, an imitated thought is no thought at all. . . . Irony requires an active involvement by the reader, to the extent that to recognize a phrase as ironic (without yet knowing the point of the irony), the reader must be able to question the validity of the literal text. The reader, then, *participates* in a kind of dialogue with the author as he or she faces the written text, doubting it and making guesses about when the author is being serious or literal with his words and when not. . . . Put in other terms, one can say that irony is a "sense of the difference and yet the relation between the realms of the actual and the ideal". . . . But this *sense* is a thought process; put briefly, irony presupposes, and cultivates, a capacity for open-ended, critical thinking. (Seery 1988: 243–245)

In this way, reading the myth—and, indeed, the *Republic* itself—ironically, we might argue that the choice made by Odysseus' soul is not necessarily the best possible choice, even if the myth suggests that it certainly is. And yet the process by which Odysseus makes his choice—and the rejection of his previous life, the life of the hero—is quite possibly the concept that Plato wants to hold out to his reader. To put it another way, it is not necessarily the case that the best life is the one that involves minding one's own business, even though Socrates suggests in the *Republic* that it is the just man's life and the choice made most carefully by Odysseus' soul; after all, this is not the life that Socrates himself has chosen to live. This might simply be the life that Odysseus—reflecting on the many and various labors of his previous, heroic life—has sought out above all of the other available possibilities because it seems the most likely to allow him to avoid the suffering and humiliation of his previous life. In this way, Plato sets out a scene wherein Odysseus both rejects the life portrayed by Homer as distinctly heroic and points—through the manner in which he chooses his next life—to the central lesson of the *Republic* and, indeed, of the Platonic corpus.

Of course, it is not particularly surprising that the Myth of Er revolves around a good deal more than just a simple rejection of the second of

Homer's two great heroes; though that would be sufficient for our purposes in this chapter, it likely was not the only idea that Plato hoped to get across to his reader given that so little about Odysseus is actually written there. Instead, the central lesson of the myth points toward my argument in the concluding chapter by providing an answer as to why Socrates—rather than Odysseus or Achilles—ought to be the preferred model of heroic behavior and why Plato, rather than Homer, ought to be regarded as the principal educator of the Greeks. The best life, on this reading, is the one dedicated both to the good of others and to the sort of deliberativeness employed in this one instance by Odysseus' soul; this, of course, is the life of Socrates.

7 The Shifting Sands of Contemporary Heroism

The dying Socrates became the new ideal, never seen before, of noble Greek youths. (Nietzsche 1992a: 89)

At the heart of this concluding chapter is the argument that the Platonic brand of heroism outlined in the previous chapters—and instantiated in the character of Socrates—has today effectively replaced the Homeric heroes exemplified by Achilles and Odysseus. As I have argued from the outset, one of the central projects of Plato's dialogues was to remake the heroic ideal in the image of the philosopher, undermining and finally replacing the Homeric ideals of the great warrior or wily survivor. But what accounts for Plato's success is more than his ability to twist the examples of Achilles and Odysseus so that they shine less brightly in our estimation once Socrates gets his rhetorical hooks into them.

By the time that Plato carefully crafted the character of the Socratic hero in memory of his deceased mentor, Athens had undergone changes that directly impacted the way in which both of the Homeric heroes were perceived. Though every educated young man had a very detailed knowledge of the outsized feats of Achilles and Odysseus, the days of the great heroes had passed and Athenians knew it. As Seth Benardete (2005: 71) argues,

> No matter how well he is described, unless we have seen him beforehand in action, and know what kind of man he is, the poetic hero will ever remain alien to us. Unless we are in immediate sympathy with Achilles, and regard not his submission but his apostasy as the sign of his greatness, the *Iliad* will never seem real. His submission, which his humanity imposes upon him, signifies his tragedy: but his greatness lies in his disregard of all civility.

One might still continue to daydream about the towering giants of Homeric epic poetry, but—faced with the grim realities of the Peloponnesian War—the time was ripe for a far more human example of the best or most choice-worthy life. That said, while the Athenians might have learned that the experience of warfare no longer resembled the heady days described by Homer, this is only part of the explanation for the transformation of the heroic ideal. After all, it was this same group of Athenians, fresh from the experience of the Peloponnesian War, who sentenced Socrates to death rather than celebrating both his excellent achievement of orderly retreat from battle and his public questioning of the leading lights of the city.

As I have argued throughout, the other important part of this change can be attributed to the presentation of the character of Socrates by Plato, especially in the dialogues devoted to Socrates' trial, imprisonment, and execution. In other words, it seems more likely than not that Socrates himself was not single-handedly responsible—or perhaps not really responsible at all—for his elevation from social pariah to heroic archetype. I have already spent a great many pages detailing the ways in which Plato accomplished this elevation of his mentor—and, indeed, of philosophy more generally—through the favorable comparisons between Socrates and the larger-than-life Homeric heroes. But it remains to me to look closely at the way in which the distinctions I've pointed out between Socrates and the Homeric heroes actually impact our thinking about heroic behavior today. To that end, I will explore the way in which heroic actions define those who perish as a result of undertaking them, as well as the premium we have placed on heroes who make other-regarding choices over self-interested ones.

The majority of this chapter revolves around four contemporary cases. First, I look closely at the stories of John Kerry and John McCain with which this project began in order to consider both the shadow of classical heroism that covers all of our contemporary heroes and the privileging of other-regarding heroism over the Homeric exemplars. I follow these stories with two examples that speak directly to the question of how we might choose to live when confronted by our own mortality. The first case—of Janusz Korczak, who was murdered by the Nazis at Treblinka in 1942—illustrates the way in which the exemplary deeds of other-regarding heroes can outlive those who perform them, confirming the point made by Socrates in giving up his life for the good of others. The second example—of Father Wenceslas Munyeshyaka, a Catholic priest at the Church of Sainte Famille in Kigali, Rwanda, in 1994—highlights the legacy of failure that attends a decision to make one's life as comfortable as possible within an immoral social order. While there are, unquestionably, many hundreds of cases of both virtuous and appalling behavior during the Holocaust and the Rwandan genocide, I focus on these two cases at present because of their conclusions: the first achieved heroic status after his death while the second lives in exile today as an indicted war criminal.

As the examples of Achilles, Odysseus, and Socrates powerfully illustrate, the actions that one takes (and the stories that are told about them) are ultimately all that will remain of this fleeting existence; if we can combine critical thinking about our mortality with an expansive imagination about those who need our assistance, then the kind of lives that we lead takes on an incredible importance and we are able to open a space for the sort of other-regarding heroic action that has become the defining feature of our contemporary discourse on the topic of heroism.

INSUFFICIENTLY HEROIC OR HEROIC IN THE WRONG WAY

The examples of John Kerry and John McCain speak directly to the question of how we think about our heroes today. In both cases, these contemporary politicians acted heroically while serving in the U.S. Armed Forces during the Vietnam War. Kerry—the recipient of a Bronze Star, a Silver Star, and three Purple Hearts—took decisive action after coming under enemy fire, thereby preserving his own life and taking the lives of enemy combatants. Upon his return from Vietnam, however, Kerry both testified before Congress in opposition to the war and led the Vietnam Veterans Against the War in a protest in Washington.[1] Famously, or perhaps infamously, he was seen—along with many other veterans—throwing medals and ribbons over the fence separating the protesters from the U.S. Capitol. In taking these actions, Kerry both effectively launched his political career and provided his political opponents with cannon fodder for decades to come. Indeed, for more than thirty years Kerry has been dogged by questions about whose medals and ribbons he threw, whether he actually kept his own medals despite claiming that he threw them, and—of course—what exactly he meant by throwing them. Due to heightened scrutiny of both Kerry's Vietnam record and his later opposition to the war, he was even forced to address the question of the medals on his 2004 presidential campaign website.[2] Of course, the issues of the medals and his antiwar stance stuck with Kerry because of their public nature and visibility. But underneath the critique of Kerry's medal-throwing behavior was always the argument that he ought not to have been made such a prominent veteran in the first place; the medals, in other words, should never have been Kerry's to throw away because he was not really much of a hero in the first place. A *real* hero would never take the position that Kerry took or throw away medals that were so hard-earned. This, of course, is the position made famous in 2004 by the so-called Swift Boat Veterans for Truth, who alleged that Kerry's actions really were not so heroic and that his wounds were not at all serious ones.

Since Kerry's actions are, on their face, heroic insofar as they were recognized as such by his commanding officers and insofar as they went above and beyond what he was required to do as a soldier, I will move past the debate about whether Kerry deserved his medals. What is really at issue, to my mind, is whether Kerry's heroism ought to be diminished by the antiwar position that he adopted in the aftermath of his battlefield actions. That it has been so diminished is not really at issue; even a cursory look at the various attacks on Kerry's service record over the years makes clear that his critics have focused on his antiwar efforts to argue against the traditional view of Kerry as a war hero. But is this a valid criticism? A look at my argument about Achilles should make clear the crux of my argument that Kerry's postwar behavior ought not to have any bearing on public perception of his wartime heroism. That is, Achilles is well known to both Achaeans and Trojans for his many great and terrible deeds on the battlefield prior to the action that is chronicled in Homer's *Iliad*: he is a killer of men and a sacker of cities, a warrior without peer. And yet, for the majority of the *Iliad*, Achilles stays away from battle because his pride is wounded by Agamemnon. But not only does Achilles sit idly by his ships while his comrades are killed in droves, he—like John Kerry—also takes the opportunity to offer a passionate critique of Agamemnon's leadership, of the mission to Troy in general, and even of the heroic culture that heaps trophies on warriors for killing one another.

Achilles, of course, eventually returns to the battlefield and acquits himself with characteristic martial skill; Kerry never fought again, and thus he opens the door to a remembrance that focuses more on his antiwar activities than on his battlefield heroics. That said, I have argued that Achilles is remembered as a great hero only because of the return to the community of men and the values of his time that he accomplishes through his engagement with Priam, his enemy. If the *Iliad* ended with Achilles dragging Hector's corpse around Patroclus' funeral pyre rather than with the shared meal between Achilles and Priam, readers would have a much different impression of the great warrior. It matters, then, that Achilles chooses to fight and do the great deeds of which he is capable, but it also matters that he is ultimately restored to the value system of his society. To do the former without also accomplishing the latter would jeopardize the *kléos* [κλέος; glory] for which he chooses to court death. The warrior hero, then, must accomplish distinctly impressive deeds on the battlefield, and he must also take care not to undermine those deeds through excessive questioning of the cause for which he fights. Like Achilles, Kerry meets the first of these requirements in a fairly clear and straightforward manner; the second requirement, however, is where Kerry falls down, in no small part because he does not return to the battlefield after he presents a powerful critique of the war in which he earned such acclaim. Unlike Achilles—who fights, criticizes the war effort, fights again, and then reconnects with his society's value system—Kerry fights and then broadly criticizes his society's war effort. Achilles, in other words, ends up the preeminent warrior, one who is also complicated and sympathetic despite the savagery of his deeds. Kerry—for all of his heroic deeds—does not manage to sustain the warrior image and leaves us with nothing but the complicated critic of warfare.

Thus, the timing of one's heroic deeds clearly matters. If Kerry had returned to the battlefield and earned more medals despite his reservations about the war's motivations, he might have been recognized as a warrior first and foremost. That said, it might still be the case that some detractors would attempt to run down his accomplishments. Alternatively, if Kerry had been killed in action it would have been substantially more difficult to dispute his heroic bona fides. But, given the number of young men killed in Vietnam, the bar would have been set considerably higher for Kerry to earn any sort of lasting glory through a battlefield death. Achilles, after all, is remembered for his heroic deeds in battle, not for his battlefield death; indeed, we might even go so far as to say that Achilles remains the preeminent warrior hero *despite* his battlefield death at the hands of Paris. Thus, I want to suggest two possible scenarios in which a warrior hero might earn acclaim today: one might almost single-handedly turn the tide of war through one's deeds or one might give one's life in the service of others. The former is, in essence, the story of Achilles: in killing Hector, he sets the stage for the eventual destruction of Troy. And it is, to my mind, simply not an option that is readily available to contemporary warriors. None of us today can be like Achilles—in no small part because of his status as a demigod—and so the latter option is the only one by which battlefield heroism can be attained. Indeed, I want to argue that it has become the norm in our society today to think about a soldier's heroism as arising entirely from a willingness to set aside personal safety in order to assist comrades or to ensure the safety of a larger group. A look at newspaper accounts of heroism from America's wars in Iraq and Afghanistan should make this clear, but one might also dig deeper and read through accounts of the heroic deeds performed by the past decade's recipients of the Congressional Medal of Honor (U.S. Army Center of Military History 2010a, 2010b).[3]

Kerry, of course, was assailed on both the timing of his heroism—as described just earlier—and its content. That is, many have alleged that his exploits were insufficient to earn him the plaudits he received. The Silver Star medal citation, for example, details Kerry's bravery, but there is no mention of sacrificing himself for others in doing so. Kerry might have put himself in harm's way by his actions, but it is never explicitly spelled out. Nor is there any mention of keeping others safe from danger, though the citation at least makes clear that Kerry managed not to get anyone injured by his actions (cf. Zumwalt 1969). None of this was a problem for Achilles, or for any warrior in his day, but it has become a clear expectation we have for our battlefield heroes today, in part because our warriors cannot measure up with Achilles but also because we have a much more complicated relationship with killing, even in war, than did the Greeks of either Homer's or Plato's day. In other words, we want our warriors to do valiant deeds but, insofar as they must kill in doing those deeds, we also want those killings to be justified because they result in lives saved.

On this point, consider the argument between Polemarchus and Socrates in Plato's *Republic* on the question of whether justice can ever entail harming enemies. Offering the common understanding of justice—and quoting Simonides, the famous lyric poet—the former argues that justice involves giving to friends and enemies "just what's owed to them. And I suppose that an enemy owes his enemy the very thing which is also fitting: some harm" (Plato 1991: 332a). Socrates' response challenges this understanding of justice and complicates our understanding of whether we might ever legitimately harm others; he says, "If someone asserts that it's just to give what is owed to each man—and he understands by this that harm is owed to enemies by the just man and help to friends—the man who said it was not wise. For he wasn't telling the truth. For it has become apparent to us that it is never just to harm anyone" (Plato 1991: 335d–e). Perhaps the best example that Socrates' argument has seeped into the public consciousness today can be seen in the fact that many people—including some relatively prominent public figures—have gone so far as to debate the justice of killing of Osama bin Laden (cf. Dorman 2011; Mustich 2011; Sefton 2011). In what many would consider one of the most clear-cut cases of justifiable harm done to an enemy, the ongoing debates about both the ethics and the legality of the killing speak volumes.

At bottom, then, Kerry runs into the problem of being a warrior whose heroism is simply not heroic enough. On the other side of the coin is John McCain, who is simply the wrong sort of hero. Like both Achilles and Kerry, McCain interacted with his enemy, both while imprisoned in Hanoi and long afterward, as he worked toward normalizing relations between the United States and Vietnam. Of course, his first set of interactions were clearly coerced; nonetheless, the famed hospital-bed interview, his call for normalized relations, and his trips to Vietnam have drawn the ire of his critics across a series of campaigns for higher office (cf. Sampley 1992). Indeed, the fact that McCain could find a way to work with and support the aspirations of people who formerly imprisoned and tortured him suggested to some Americans that he must not have been treated quite as badly as had so often been suggested. It was, in short, confirmation of the suspicion that McCain was not really so heroic after all and that all the talk of his heroism is actually the central component of a self-serving narrative designed to further his political career.

There is one line of argumentation, then, that puts McCain's wartime record on trial, and there are three different ways to proceed with this critique of his heroism. The first is to argue that there was nothing particularly heroic about McCain's service record because he simply did not excel with regard to warfare; in a straightforward comparison with John Kerry, for example, it is clear that we should be extremely skeptical of his skill as a warrior. Whereas Kerry received numerous commendations for gallantry—jumping out of boats and shooting enemy soldiers, for example—the majority of McCain's commendations came as a result of his imprisonment rather than his fighting acumen. To put a finer point on it, it would not be out of bounds to claim that McCain simply was not a good pilot; four planes under his control crashed—three in training flights and the fourth during the incident that resulted in his capture by the Vietnamese—and a fifth plane was destroyed in an explosion that occurred on the aircraft carrier deck. At the heart of this critique is the viewpoint that McCain was more reckless and impulsive than a good warrior ought to be:

"Three mishaps are unusual," said Michael L. Barr, a former Air Force pilot with 137 combat missions in Vietnam and an internationally known aviation safety expert who teaches in USC's Aviation Safety and Security Program. "After the third accident, you would say: Is there a trend here in terms of his flying skills and his judgment?" (Vartabedian and Serrano 2008)

If we follow this point to its conclusion, we likely run into the argument that a more skilled warrior would not have found himself in McCain's position. He would, instead, have earned his renown through valorous actions on the battlefield.

This, of course, ties in directly with the second way to proceed with this line of argumentation—namely, making the case that McCain's style or method of engaging the enemy—which largely involved dropping ordnance on the Vietnamese from high above them—is simply not the sort of thing that comes to the minds of most people when they imagine heroism in warfare (cf. Raphael 2002; Segura 2008). Indeed, Senator Jay Rockefeller was famously quoted as saying, "McCain was a fighter pilot, who dropped laser-guided missiles from 35,000 feet. He was long gone when they hit. What happened when they [the missiles] get to the ground? He doesn't know. You have to care about the lives of people. McCain never gets into those issues" (Phillips 2008). This is, of course, quite clearly related to the age-old argument in favor of Achilles' military prowess in comparison to Odysseus': the former, after all, fights in close quarters with sword and spear, while the latter is best known for killing his enemies from afar with bow and arrow.[4] This argument rests on the proposition that some methods of engaging an enemy afford opportunities for heroism and some others simply do not. Members of certain branches of the contemporary armed forces, then, are just less likely to be viewed as heroes by the citizens on whose behalf they are fighting because of the remove from which they fight; in other words, it is far more difficult to do something heroic on a submarine or in a fighter jet than it is to act heroically in the trenches or while storming the beaches.

Finally, the third way is to note that even when McCain did something to merit commendation, it was not really so impressive. This is to argue that, while McCain was imprisoned in the infamous Hoa Lo Prison and elsewhere, his treatment was actually far better than that of the average American prisoner of war held captive there, owing in no small part to the fact that his captors knew that he was a prisoner with some value to them. In other words, as soon as the Vietnamese became aware that McCain's father was a high-ranking officer—an admiral, in fact, and soon to become the commander-in-chief of the United States Pacific Command—they recognized that their prisoner presented them with both military and public relations opportunities.[5] While the question of whether McCain received better treatment than other American POWs remains a difficult, if not impossible, one to answer, there is no debate about the fact that his family name afforded him both medical attention and the opportunity for release from captivity; the former he desperately needed and the latter he would not accept because he felt it violated the military code of conduct. With regard to the life-saving medical attention that McCain received shortly after his imprisonment, it is clear that his father's rank had a life-or-death impact and that some other injured pilot would not have received the necessary medical care:

> Fearful of blood poisoning that would lead to death, McCain told his captors he would talk if they took him to a hospital.
>
> "They brought in this doctor we called Zorba, and he examined me, took my pulse and turned to this other guy we called The Bug and said something in Vietnamese. And The Bug said, 'It's too late, it's too late,'" McCain said.
>
> "I said, 'If you take me to the hospital, I'll get well.' Zorba took my pulse again and shook his head, and The Bug said, 'It's too late.' And they took me back to my cell."
>
> About two hours later, McCain's cell door burst open, and The Bug rushed in, saying, "Your father is a big admiral. Now we take you to the hospital."
>
> It had taken some time, but the North Vietnamese figured out that McCain's father, Jack, was a major U.S. Naval commander.
>
> They started calling McCain "The Crown Prince." (Nowicki and Muller 2007b)

Of course, McCain's description of his situation—corroborated by some others who were imprisoned with him—makes clear that no matter how much better his treatment, he still suffered, both as a result of his injuries and due to physical and psychological torture. He is also clear on the reason that the offer of an early release came to him rather than to some other POW:

> McCain knew the real reason the North Vietnamese wanted to release him. Adm. Jack McCain, his father, was an important U.S. military figure. In July he would assume command of all U.S. forces in the Pacific. McCain's release would help the North Vietnamese propaganda machine.
>
> McCain realized that the Code of Conduct gave him no choice. Alvarez, who was being held elsewhere, was supposed to be the first man released.
>
> "I just knew it wasn't the right thing to do," he said. "I knew that they wouldn't have offered it to me if I hadn't been the son of an admiral." (Nowicki and Muller 2007b)

McCain, of course, refused the early release each time that it was offered to him by his captors, and this, in part, is what many people believe makes him a hero. It is also, conversely, one of the quintessential examples that detractors cite when they explain that McCain's treatment was clearly better than most POWs and thus that his endurance of terrible conditions might not be so very heroic.

To answer these detractors, it is useful to recall the argument, earlier, that Kerry could only approximate the heroism of Achilles. This is not to argue, of course, that McCain is simply an even worse approximation of the archetypical battlefield hero. Instead, it is to remind ourselves that the battlefield hero is not the only classical archetype and that McCain's military service lines up substantially better with the experiences of Odysseus, the second of the Homeric heroes, than it does with the first. Thus, rather than accomplishing particularly impressive deeds on the battlefield, McCain's heroism lies in his endurance of terrible conditions, much like Odysseus.[6] In other words, we ought not to hold McCain to the standard of Achilles, or even to the standard of John Kerry. McCain will necessarily pale in comparison to those who distinguish themselves on the battlefield because, like Odysseus, he earned his plaudits from a very different sort of wartime activity—namely, enduring a great deal of suffering and surviving the many dangers that attend fighting a war and then attempting to return home at its conclusion.

Of course, as noted earlier, many might fault McCain for enduring conditions and challenges that are far easier to endure than those confronted by Odysseus, just as Kerry was faulted for being less impressive as a warrior when compared with Achilles. It is certainly true that Odysseus endured far more hardship than did McCain and for a far longer period of time too. But, of course, this critique misses the mark, just as the same critique about Kerry and Achilles misses the mark; McCain is not a new or modern Odysseus so much as he is a contemporary example of someone whose heroism fits the classical heroic archetype embodied in Odysseus. There are, of course, a great many compelling similarities, and that is why McCain draws one's attention back to the heroism of Odysseus: both are better known for their endurance of hardship than for their fighting acumen (or, put a different way, neither one is a conventional warrior), both consider suicide during their respective ordeals,[7] and both are generally considered to be more wily or crafty than they are straightforwardly heroic. Despite these similarities, McCain's reputation cannot compare with that of Odysseus, and not simply because the latter is a character in an ancient epic poem whose heroism seems to be designed by Homer to contrast—perhaps favorably—with Achilles. While both Odysseus and McCain return home from the destructive wars that claimed so many of their comrades' lives, Odysseus' story essentially concludes with his homecoming and is preserved in amber. McCain's story does not similarly conclude with his triumphant return; instead, he enters professional public service soon thereafter and all of the attendant idiosyncrasies that result from running for and securing an elected office become a matter of public record.

These foibles have drawn a great deal of attention, of course. In the late 1980s and early 1990s, most famously, McCain became embroiled in a national scandal as one of the so-called Keating Five, senators who acted improperly on behalf of Charles Keating by meeting with federal bank regulators in what might have been an attempt to discourage too much unwanted attention from being paid to Keating's banking practices. After several years of negative press, a prison stint for Keating, and a cost to taxpayers of $2.6 billion for the bailout of Lincoln Savings & Loan, a Senate Ethics Committee investigation ultimately found McCain to be "guilty of nothing more than 'poor judgment,' . . . and declared his actions were not 'improper nor attended with gross negligence'" (Suellentrop 2000).[8] While McCain considered himself to be fully exonerated at the end of the investigation—and devoted an entire chapter to the affair in his memoir (McCain and Salter 2003)—his political opponents continued to bring back the specter of the Keating scandal as late as 2008 in order to link McCain's name to questionable decision making, especially with regard to the financial sector (cf. Allen 2008; Abramowitz 2008; Bacon 2008). As an Obama campaign staff member argued, "While John McCain may want to turn the page on his erratic response to the current economic crisis, we think voters will find his involvement in a similar crisis to be particularly interesting. His involvement with Keating is a window into McCain's economic past, present, and future" (Allen 2008).

Interestingly, McCain overcame the Keating Five scandal in large part by making himself available to the media to discuss the role he played and the mistakes he made (Nowicki and Muller 2007a). It was at this time that McCain first became something of a press darling, buying a great deal of good will with the media strategy that would hold him in very good stead when he decided to make his first presidential run:

> McCain's hobnobbing with the press had an unexpected side effect. Reporters started to like him.
>
> McCain always returned phone calls. He showed up for his television appearances. He was willing to go off the record to help reporters unearth certain stories. He answered questions bluntly, without much political tap dancing.
>
> For Beltway reporters bored with bureaucrats, McCain was fresh, new and different. (Nowicki and Muller 2007a)

For several years thereafter, McCain displayed a rare ability to charm reporters by seeming to let down his guard, bantering with them, and giving them a greater level of access than most other politicians would comfortably allow. This access culminated in the Straight Talk Express, the campaign bus tour on which McCain built legitimacy as a presidential hopeful and cemented his reputation as a political maverick; as a CNN article notes, "In an era where candidates restrict their appearances before the press and stagecraft their every move, McCain has opted for a different media strategy: All McCain, all of the time" (Ferullu 2000).[9]

But while this unprecedented access endeared McCain to those who covered his campaigns, it also meant that the politician was almost completely on display almost all of the time. And this, of course, led to a particularly high level of scrutiny of all of McCain's personal and political flaws. The range was impressive, from possible ethics violations involving a lobbyist (Rutenberg et al. 2008) to Cindy McCain's plagiarized "family recipes" (Shear 2008). But the single biggest problem for McCain was the fact that his political positions on major issues—like immigration reform (Martinez 2008), gays and lesbians in the military (Shear 2010), and abortion (Neal 1999; Davenport 2007)— seemed to change as the political winds shifted. It is clear, from a quick look at these issues, that McCain changed from one policy position to another— shifting to a more conservative stance each time—when it became clear that his original position put him at odds with an important part of his constituency. In making these moves, McCain was quick to shed his reputation as a maverick in favor of a more standard right-wing position, and, while he was critiqued for each move by journalists who seemed to cherish McCain the maverick, he made these moves work for him, winning the Republican presidential nomination in 2008 and reelection to his Senate seat in 2010 (Montopoli 2010).

While changing his position on these issues earned him a substantial amount of fairly scathing criticism, then, McCain also managed to remain connected to people in Arizona, many of whom seemed to be continually moving to the extreme right of the political spectrum, and to enough of the Republican base that he bested several serious challengers for the presidential nomination. But none of this should be particularly surprising, as a careful understanding of McCain's character would easily explain this sort of flip-flopping as the careful maneuvering of a politician who knows that what ultimately matters most is setting one's sail with—rather than against—the blowing of the political winds. Deep down, what matters most to McCain—at least as a politician—is not friendship, wealth, or acclaim; instead, McCain seems to be driven almost entirely by the desire to survive. In Vietnam this desire served him in particularly good stead, as he suffered and bent but ultimately did not break under the terrible conditions he faced in captivity. And, as a politician over the past thirty years, the same has been true: McCain has weathered each political storm he has faced because he "has been willing to do all that it takes to get whatever it is he wants" (Purdum 2010). This is *precisely* what allowed McCain to accomplish his heroic feats of endurance in Vietnam. It is simply a mistake to assume that McCain's endurance would somehow *not* be connected to the way he has long conducted himself in the political arena and the way he lives his life even now. That is not to say that we should avoid criticizing John McCain as a politician because he is related to John McCain the hero, who endured a great deal of hardship and suffering in Vietnam. It is, instead, to say that we ought to realize that those things that allowed for his heroism might not make him the noblest politician in all of our eyes.

Of course, this ties in directly to the second completely distinct line of argumentation against McCain (and also against Odysseus)—namely, one that suggests that we ought not to see the endurance of some ordeal or other as distinctly heroic at all. This critique is often brought up by those who find certain character traits of the survivor to skirt the boundaries of conventional morality, though it might also be leveled by those who argue that such heroism is not so much a choice as it is a result of not having a choice. Both of these critiques have been discussed in some detail earlier, and so it remains to me to turn to the final—and perhaps the deepest—argument in this second line of argumentation. At bottom, this critique ultimately rests on the argument put forward by Max Horkheimer and Theodor W. Adorno (1988: 43) that Odysseus is "a prototype of the bourgeois individual." On their reading, the *Odyssey* should properly be considered the first Enlightenment tale insofar as it celebrates the battle of man against nature and the suppression of desire. At bottom, they argue, all of the problems inherent in the Enlightenment can be summarized in a single critique of Odysseus: he is just like all the rest of us, and the epic poem that Homer devotes to him can, thus, "be read as a morality tale for the modern world" (Dant 2003: 26). Without delving too deeply into Horkheimer and Adorno's critique of work and of the modern class-based society, it is clear that their argument against seeing Odysseus' journey as heroic ties directly into the notion that the world in which we live today is one devoid of heroism:

> This focus on the self and its capacity for preservation is a theme of the Odysseus myth and also a theme of modernity. The idea that one is responsible for one's own destiny and doesn't have to give oneself up to what fate has in store comes with a form of reason in which planning and forethought are used instrumentally to dominate and overcome the natural world. Adorno and Horkheimer see Odysseus as the prototype bourgeois individual who is 'compelled to wander' (1979: 43)—our wandering is not across Greek seas but along the paths of what we call 'careers'. He engages in a form of sacrifice as his men are eaten by the Cyclops, lost to the monster Scylla and perish in a shipwreck. The sacrifice is of the collective for the project of the journey, which in modernity means that the individual identity is sacrificed to keep the system going. (Dant 2003: 27)

All of Odysseus' suffering—and, by extension, John McCain's suffering—does not really seem to be heroic because, despite its apparent break with society's conventional rules and norms, it ultimately only reinforces the dominant power structure in the end (Horkheimer and Adorno 1988: 36, 61, 71–73). But, to go beyond the Horkheimer and Adorno critique, it is also the case that the ultimate conclusion to Odysseus' wandering—and the suffering that attends it—is, in fact, no conclusion at all: we learn halfway through the *Odyssey* that he will set off from Ithaca on another journey before the end of his life.[10] Thus, all of his suffering—which was made meaningful by his prizing of *nostos* [νόστος; homecoming]—is, in the end, ultimately meaningless insofar as his homecoming is a radically incomplete one. The same, as I have noted earlier, holds true about McCain; his heroic return is, in some very real sense, seen to have been spoiled by his actions thereafter. In the end, our suffering heroes need to be seen to be suffering *for* something, and, on this reading, both McCain and Odysseus fall down in this respect. Of course, even if their suffering had helped them to achieve some goal they valued above all others or if the principle for which they suffered was one that seemed to matter a great deal, the way that most people now view their lives very well might not be any different.

Indeed, as I have argued throughout, there is a further problem facing classical heroes and those who wear their mantles today. In considering the example of John Kerry, I claimed that we want our warriors to do valiant deeds but, to gain our full admiration, we insist that any killing they do must result in lives saved. It is also the case that heroes who endure great hardships fail to gain our full admiration—even when their suffering has clearly been awful and in the service of some important principle or goal—because these heroes' actions are seen as purely self-serving. What most people today have in mind when they think about heroic behavior is *other-regarding* heroism, what I have described throughout as a third classical form of heroism. I have argued that not only is Socrates meant to stand alongside Achilles and Odysseus insofar as he possesses many of the same classically heroic qualities, but also that the philosopher is meant to surpass the skilled warrior and the scheming survivor by giving his life on behalf of others rather than in pursuit of his own *kléos* or *nostos*. And from our perspective, Plato has certainly succeeded: it is not simply that many of us today prefer other-regarding heroic actions to those of the skilled warrior or the wily survivor; we actually have a difficult time recognizing as heroic any action today that does not seem to have been undertaken in the service of others, and we seem to require other-regarding behavior from our warriors and our survivors in order for them to qualify as heroes. Having now looked at Kerry and McCain in detail, especially in contrast with the great Homeric heroes, it is clear that, no matter how well they might have compared with Achilles and Odysseus, neither of these heroes would have been celebrated fully. Kerry might have been seen as a great American warrior, and McCain might have been lauded as a wily survivor, but neither would have been seen to act on behalf of others. And this, as I have been arguing, is the crucial difference between the Homeric heroes and the Platonic hero who eclipsed them.

CONTEMPORARY CONFRONTATIONS WITH MORTALITY

To make complete sense of the way in which Socrates was able to accomplish his usurpation of the heroic mantle from Achilles and Odysseus, it is important to remember that Socrates' willingness to sacrifice himself is not his defining character trait. It is, instead, the logical conclusion to a life lived philosophically. Having committed himself to the claim that "the unexamined life is not worth living for a human being" (Plato 1984a: 38a) and thus to the critical investigation of every argument, Socrates is afforded the opportunity near the end of his life to put into action his claim that the kind of life one lives—rather than its duration—is of primary importance. Indeed, confronted by the fact of his mortality and then presented with the option of escaping his fate, Socrates recognizes that his claims about the good life now necessitate his death. Thus, he demonstrates his dedication to the pursuit of justice and wisdom above even his own life and sacrifices himself so that others, even those who see themselves as his enemies, might reap the benefits of philosophy in the future.

One consequence of choosing to live life on one's own terms—doing impressive deeds in the face of one's mortality—is that one might achieve the only sort of permanence available to mortals—namely, having one's actions recalled by others, as discovered by Greece's classical heroes. In this section, I examine two contemporary examples that speak to this question of how we might choose to live when confronted by our own mortality. The case of Janusz Korczak illustrates the way in which exemplary deeds often outlive the heroes who perform them and highlights the fact that a successful life is not best measured by its length. The second, of Father Wenceslas Munyeshyaka, highlights the legacy of failure that attends a decision to live as comfortably as possible within an immoral social order, bargaining away one's beliefs in exchange for a longer life. The defining moments in the lives of Korczak and Munyeshyaka nicely highlight the ways in which Socratic other-regarding heroism has become the dominant answer to the question of what we ought to do when faced with situations that compel us to make the most difficult decisions.

Korczak and the Children

The man at the center of the first case, Janusz Korczak, is celebrated today as one of the heroes who went to his death in Nazi-occupied Poland. Born Henryk Goldszmit in the late 1870s to Jozef and Cecylia Goldszmit, assimilated Polish Jews, he first took up the pseudonym of Janusz Korczak as a young medical student in 1898 (cf. Lifton 1988). This was not a name chosen at random; instead, it seems to have been a misprinting of Janasz Korczak, the fictional hero of Jozef Ignacy Kraszewski's *The Story of Janasz Korczak and the Swordbearer's Daughter*. Betty Jean Lifton (1988: 31–32) suggests that

> the noble character and courage of the fictional Janasz Korczak, a poor orphan of gentry lineage, must have appealed to Henryk, if not the contrived plot. A broken leg prevents Janasz from serving in the Battle of Vienna in 1863, but he does not let it prevent him from rescuing his beloved cousin, Jadwiga, and his uncle, the King's swordbearer, from the enemy. Denied Jadwiga's hand in marriage because he is only a poor relative, Janasz turns his fate around by patience, honesty, and self control, eventually winning Jadwiga and a place in the king's court.

While he continued to use his given name, especially in the scholarly work he published in medical journals, the Korczak pseudonym gradually found its way into his more literary work. It was as Janusz Korczak that he became famous as an author and educator, although he was a trained physician and began his career working in a hospital, for Korczak found himself drawn to the plight of children and specifically orphans.

At the age of thirty-three, he helped to found and operate an orphanage for Jewish children in Warsaw. It was in these years that Korczak became quite well known in Poland, both as an author and a radio personality; his most famous literary character, King Matt, was created in the early 1920s, in the immediate aftermath of the Polish-Soviet War, and the story was first read to the children in the orphanage. *King Matt the First* earned Korczak a literary following in Poland, especially among children, but the plot is ultimately a tragic one. The youthful king is eventually drawn into a war and fights valiantly before being captured and sentenced to death. But, like his creator, "Matt holds his head high to prove that he has more strength of character than the enemy. 'True heroes show themselves in adversity,' he tells himself. He refuses the blindfold: to die 'beautifully' is still his only wish" (Lifton 1988: 110). In the end, the king is granted a reprieve and finally exiled to a deserted island, setting up the sequel, *King Matt on the Desert Island*. In addition to these works of literature and his scholarly publications, Korczak adopted a second pseudonym for his radio program. He did so, according to Lifton (1988: 207), "to placate higher officials who did not want to be accused of allowing a Jewish educator to shape the minds of Polish children. (It was already common knowledge by then that Janusz Korczak was a pseudonym for Henryk Goldszmit.)" As the "Old Doctor," Korczak now earned a loyal following among Polish adults, who regularly tuned in to his program until anti-Semitism put an end to his broadcasting career in the mid-1930s.

Though he visited Palestine and wrote frequently to his friends there about the possibility of emigration from Poland, the timing for such a move never seemed right for Korczak, despite the storm clouds of war that were unmistakably darkening over Warsaw. He was finally scheduled to depart in 1937, but wrote that "conscience did not permit him to leave the children at that moment" (Lifton 1988: 221). Of course, it would be precisely this devotion to the children of his orphanage that truly cemented his legacy. Even after the Jews of Warsaw were confined to a ghetto, Korczak tended to his charges in the orphanage with the same diligence, if not more. In addition to his usual pedagogical activities with the children, he now spent a great deal of time each day attempting to secure additional funds or supplies for them. When rumors intensified that Jews were being murdered en masse and the Germans began to empty Warsaw's ghetto, Korczak even talked about setting up a factory in the orphanage "to sew German uniforms or whatever was needed. He was hoping that if the children could prove themselves useful they would be allowed to remain where they were" (Lifton 1988: 335).

Of course, Korczak never had an opportunity to put this idea into practice, as the closing of the orphanage occurred within days.

Despite his inability to prevent the deportation of his young charges to the Treblinka concentration camp, Korczak serves as a powerful example of heroism because he remained devoted to their comfort and care even in the face of death. Because he was quite famous and very well regarded, numerous non-Jewish friends went to extraordinary lengths in their attempts to rescue him from the ghetto before it was too late. According to Lifton (1988: 323), "Maryna Falska, who was still hiding Jewish children under her roof, found a safe room for Korczak near her orphanage." And then, Igor Newerly, his former secretary, "who had managed to obtain an identity card with an assumed name for Korczak, went to the ghetto disguised as a water and sewer inspector, carrying papers to bring out a 'locksmith' who was working there" (Lifton 1988: 323). But, despite their tremendous actions on his behalf, Korczak refused to leave the ghetto and abandon the children; according to Newerly, "He looked at me as though I had proposed a betrayal or an embezzlement" (Lifton 1988: 323). Even at the end, as they awaited deportation from Warsaw's Umschlagplatz, Korczak would not be separated from his children for even a moment. Nahum Remba, a Judenrat official who ran a first-aid station there, thought it might be possible to delay the deportation of the orphans for a day or two. In his memoirs, he recalls that he "took Korczak aside and urged him to go with him to the Judenrat to ask them to intervene. But Korczak wouldn't consider it; if he left the children even for a moment in this terrifying place, they might panic. He couldn't risk that. And there was always the danger that they might be taken away in his absence" (Lifton 1988: 344). The final such story, though perhaps apocryphal, is nonetheless very much in keeping with Korczak's character. When the order was given for the orphans to be loaded onto the waiting trains, some report that "a German officer made his way through the crowd and handed Korczak a piece of paper . . . [offering him] permission to return home—but not the children. Korczak is said to have shaken his head and waved the German away" (Lifton 1988: 345).

This decision, to accompany the children onto the trains rather than accept the assistance of others for himself, meant certain death for Korczak. But the alternative, abandoning children when they surely needed him the most, was not something he could do. Although he undoubtedly could have saved himself from the horrors of the ghetto and then Treblinka, Korczak was far less concerned with the length of his life and far more concerned with its quality. Indeed, as life in the ghetto got progressively worse, Korczak thought and wrote about death with increasing frequency. The topics of suicide and euthanasia are frequent ones in his *Ghetto Diary*, including an entire section that provides a detailed program for allowing people to choose when to end their own lives (cf. Korczak 2003: 86–90). Further, as he wrote about his family and his childhood, he recognized that he was approaching death and seemed not to be overly concerned. "It is a difficult thing to be born and to learn to live," Korczak (2003: 101) writes. "Ahead of me is a much easier task: to die. After death it may be difficult again, but I am not bothering about that."

The greatest concern about his death involved the orphans, and Korczak's emphasis, here, is on making one's own choices. On this point, he writes, "I don't know what I should say to the children by way of farewell. I should want to make clear to them only this—that the road is theirs to choose, freely" (Korczak 2003: 101). And, indeed, Korczak seems to have instilled this lesson in his young charges. When the orphanage was closed, 192 children followed the doctor to the Umschlagplatz; Lifton (1988: 340) writes that "one of the older boys carried the green flag of King Matt, the blue Star of David set against a field of white on one side. The older children took turns carrying the flag during the course of their two-mile walk, perhaps remembering how King Matt had held his head high that day he was forced to march through the streets of his city to what he thought was to be his execution." And when the time came for the children to board the trains, "unlike the usual chaotic mass of people shrieking hysterically as they were prodded along with whips, the orphans walked in rows of four with quiet dignity. . . . As Korczak led his children calmly toward the cattle cars, the Jewish police cordoning off a path for them saluted instinctively" (Lifton 1988: 345). This final image that we have of Korczak is a poignant one, to say the least, and it highlights the ways in which we might make our own choices even under terrible constraints: "This was no march to the train cars, but rather a mute protest against this murderous regime . . . a procession the like of which no human eye has ever witnessed" (Lifton 1988: 345). With regard to his own life and to its limits, Korczak wrote, "The road I have chosen toward my goal is neither the shortest nor the most convenient. But it is the best for me—because it is my own. I found it not without effort or pain, and only when I had come to understand that all the books I read, and all the experiences and opinions of others, were misleading" (Lifton 1988: 61–62).

It is precisely because Korczak was more concerned about living well than about simply living that he has become a legendary figure today. There is a Janusz Korczak International Society, devoted to his educational ideas, schools and streets are named after him all over Europe, and "UNESCO declared 1978–79 the Year of Korczak, to coincide with the Year of the Child and the centenary of his birth" (Lifton 1988: 350). In Poland, writes Lifton (1988: 350), he is considered "a martyr who, had he been born a Catholic, would have been canonized by now." And in Israel, Korczak is venerated as "one of the Thirty-six Just Men whose pure souls, according to ancient Jewish tradition, make possible the world's salvation" (Lifton 1988: 350). Finally, one of the most powerful monuments to Korczak can be found at the site of his murder. Although Treblinka was destroyed by the Nazis toward the end of the war, memorials now stand where the concentration camp once did; there are stone tracks where the railroad tracks once existed, for example, and a monument honors those from Warsaw who perished at the camp. And, as Lifton (1988: 352) notes, "Sometime after the war, the violated space that had once been Treblinka was transformed into a vast stone garden. Seventeen thousand rocks were brought in from Polish quarries to represent the villages, towns, and countries of the million men, women, and children who died there." While these rocks themselves are an impressive memorial to all of the murdered innocents, it is especially noteworthy that only one bears a personal name; it reads, "Janusz Korczak (Henryk Goldszmit) And The Children" (Lifton 2003: *xxx*).

The Priest with a Pistol

The second case, that of Father Wenceslas Munyeshyaka, provides quite the opposite example. Unlike Korczak, who refused to compromise his values to save his life, there is significant evidence that Munyeshyaka, a Catholic priest, chose to sacrifice some of the Tutsis who sought refuge in his church from the genocidal militias that roamed Rwanda in 1994. In doing so, he was able to protect himself and also some selected others from the killers. As Philip Gourevitch (1998: 124) points out,

> Because of its prominence, and its consequent visibility to the few international observers who were still circulating in Kigali, Sainte Famille was one of half a dozen places in the city—and fewer than a dozen in all of Rwanda—where Tutsis who sought refuge in 1994 were never exterminated en masse. Instead, the killing in such places was incremental, and for those who were spared the terror was constant.

Of course, the fact that massacres were carried out in an incomplete way does little to mitigate the horrors faced by those who survived the genocide by hiding in the church. Indeed, the list of offenses that are alleged against Munyeshyaka is a long one, and it includes "providing killers with lists of Tutsi refugees at his church, flushing refugees out of hiding to be killed, attending massacres without interfering," and more (Gourevitch 1998: 136). That said, at the time of this writing, the priest, who currently resides in France, has succeeded in evading punishment of any kind.[11]

While it still remains unclear whether Munyeshyaka participated in the violence or simply stood by while it occurred—largely because he has not answered to any of these charges in court—he is certainly "blamed for colluding with the killers" (Walke 2004: 1). During the periodic massacres that occurred at Sainte Famille, the priest is frequently described as absent or unwilling to prevent the killings. One of the survivors, Bonaventure Nyibizi, said of Munyeshyaka that "he was not actually denouncing anybody at first, but he would do nothing for the people" (Gourevitch 1998: 125). Indeed, during the first massacre on April 15, when more than one hundred Tutsi men and boys were taken from the church and killed, "Fr. Munyeshyaka witnessed the abductions, but although he had a phone, refugees say he made no effort to call for help" (Matthews 1999: 2). On June 16, when nearly one hundred more Tutsi men and boys were killed, survivors note that "although Fr. Munyeshyaka disappeared during the massacre, he came back at midday, when it had ended. . . . He simply said that: 'all these Tutsis had killed themselves'" (Matthews 1999: 3). This issue of failing to call for help was also noted by Paul Rusesabagina, who was the hotel manager at the Mille Collines, only a few hundred yards from Sainte Famille. According to Gourevitch (1998: 135), "When Paul recalled how he had used his telephone at the Mille Collines to focus international attention on the plight of his guests, he said, 'But, you know, Sainte Famille also had a working phone line, and that priest, Father Wenceslas, never used it. My goodness!'"[12]

Irrespective of his guilt or innocence on these charges, it is instructive that every account of the priest from that time mentions his unusual choice of wardrobe: "The survivors of Ste. Famille all expressed their shock at the appearance and attitude of Fr. Munyeshyaka. . . . Clad in a flak jacket, and armed with a pistol, Munyeshyaka was an intimidating figure who, from the beginning, did nothing to make the refugees feel welcome" (Matthews 1999: 2). And Rusesabagina notes that "Wenceslas himself wore a pistol, yet he was a priest. I can't say that he killed anyone. I never saw him killing. But I saw him with a pistol" (Gourevitch 1998: 124, 135). The hotel manager had plenty of opportunities to see the priest, who kept his elderly mother, a Tutsi, safely hidden at the Mille Collines: "And he was so arrogant that when he brought her, he told me, 'Paul, I bring you my cockroach.' Do you understand? He was talking about his mother. She was a Tutsi" (Gourevitch 1998: 141).[13] Far worse, however, are the allegations that Munyeshyaka was often to be found at the Mille Collines because, in the words of survivor Valentine Gahonzire, "he had a room there, and would go in with his girls, then return to St. Famille" (Matthews 1999: 4). Almost all those who were killed at the church were men and boys, and survivors claim that this was no coincidence. The priest, many claim, protected Tutsi women from the militias only if they agreed to sleep with him; Matthews (1999: 4) argues that "these women were given special treatment: food, water and accommodation which he withheld from the rest." Rusesabagina (2006: 129) seems to confirm this, introducing his brief discussion of the priest by saying, "I also sheltered some questionable guests." He might simply be referring to the fact that he gave a room to Munyeshyaka's mother, but that seems much less likely since her status as a guest at the Mille Collines would not be regarded as questionable.

During one of Munyeshyaka's visits to the hotel, Rusesabagina's wife, Tatiana, pointedly asked him, "Priest, instead of carrying your Bible, why do you carry a pistol? Why don't you put this pistol down and take up your Bible? A priest should not be seen in blue jeans and a T-shirt with a pistol" (Gourevitch 1998: 135). Munyeshyaka's response, remembered differently by Odette Nyiramilimo and Rusesabagina, is particularly instructive. Nyiramilimo remembers the priest replying that "everything has its time. This is the time for a pistol, not a Bible" (Gourevitch 1998: 136). This is certainly a plausible response, given the allegations that have been levied against Munyeshyaka by survivors of the genocide. But Rusesabagina "remembered the exchange differently. By his account, Father Wenceslas had said, 'They've already killed fifty-nine priests. I don't want to be the sixtieth'" (Gourevitch 1998: 136).[14] Here, if Rusesabagina's memory is correct, is a clear statement of Munyeshyaka's intentions with regard both to the Tutsi refugees at Sainte Famille and the Hutu militias who wanted to kill them. For the priest, the refugees seemed to serve as a bargaining chip that allowed him to live unmolested by the militias during the worst of the genocidal violence. Of course, Munyeshyaka would not express his position in such terms; however, in an interview from France in 1995, he argued that "it was necessary to appear pro-militia. If I had had a different attitude, we would have all disappeared" (Gourevitch 1998: 136). The actions of which he stands charged, I argue, are the result of precisely this sort of thinking—namely, that other human beings can be used as a means with which to preserve one's own life.

Although the Rwandan government regularly demanded his extradition from France to stand trial for the crimes he allegedly committed during the genocide, the French authorities chose not to comply. And indeed, in June 2004, France found itself at the center of this controversy, convicted by the European Court of Human Rights for the failure to prosecute Munyeshyaka in a timely manner (Grellier 2004: 1). Meanwhile, the next year in Rwanda, the priest was finally formally charged with "genocide, conspiracy to commit Genocide, incitement of the public to commit genocide, war crimes, rape and other crimes against humanity in 1994" (Bungingo 2006: 1). After more than ten years in exile, he was ordered—in May 2006—to be tried in absentia by the same Rwandan Military Tribunal that presided over the trial of his codefendant, Major General Laurent Munyakazi (Kimenyi 2006: 1; Asser Institute Centre for International & European Law 2011). Unsurprisingly, Munyeshyaka failed to appear to answer the charges leveled against him, and—equally unsurprisingly—he was found guilty and sentenced to life imprisonment in November 2006. As noted earlier, he remains a free man in France and has avoided censure by the Catholic Church. Regardless of whether the priest will ever face the charges leveled against him by the International Criminal Tribunal for Rwanda—and, increasingly, it appears that he will not—it is fair to say that he is considered to be guilty by those who study the Rwandan genocide and those who hear these stories. His legacy, in Rwanda and around the world, is as one of those "members of the Church [who] failed in their mission, they contradicted what they stood for" (Walke 2004: 1).

CONCLUSION

Just as Korczak and Munyeshyaka could not seem any more dissimilar from one another, especially in the choices they made, so too do the examples of Korczak and Munyeshyaka seem as different as possible from the examples of

Kerry and McCain with which this chapter began. In one sense, they clearly are very different: the former are ordinary civilians who simply found themselves in desperate straits while the latter are trained soldiers who earned some measure of glory by fighting or surviving a battlefield experience. But it is also the case that there are some clear similarities, at least when it comes to the lessons that we can learn about heroic behavior from considering them together.

Taken all together, the lives of these four individuals highlight the distinction between the three classical heroic archetypes and make plain our preference today for the other-regarding hero.

There are two possibilities for people who come face-to-face with their own mortality, as Achilles' destiny highlights: "if on the one hand I remain to fight / around Troy town, I lose all hope of home / but gain unfading glory; on the other, / if I sail back to my own land my glory / fails—but a long life ahead for me" (Homer 1974: IX.502–506). Odysseus, as is well known, faces something of a similar choice: he can remain with the nymph Calypso on her island and share in her immortality or, facing a great deal of additional humiliation and mortal peril, he can attempt to return home to his family and to a mortal life (Homer 1990: 87). While Socrates certainly never receives an offer of immortality, he too is confronted by a choice that echoes those of Achilles and Odysseus: either remain in prison and face the fate decreed by the Athenian jury or, with the assistance of his friends, escape from prison and live out the remainder of his life in exile. In each case, the hero rejects a longer life—or immortality, for Odysseus—and embraces his mortality. The lesson—best encapsulated in Socrates' phrase, "Not life, but a good life, is to be chiefly valued" (Plato 1984b: 106)—is one that can be seen clearly in the cases of Korczak and Munyeshyaka.

When Munyeshyaka found himself facing the very real possibility of his own death, at best he chose not to assist those who came to him in need; at worst, he decided to actively collaborate with the militia members in their violence against Tutsis. No matter his motivation, it is clear that he opted not to risk his own life in an attempt to assist others, even those who had specifically come to him because they thought he—a Catholic priest— would help them in some way. For Korczak, however, the kind of life he led was more important than its length. While he might have saved himself, as Munyeshyaka did, he chose instead to embrace his fate and remain with the children who had no one else to comfort them as they faced certain death at the hands of the Nazis. While Munyeshyaka survived the Rwandan genocide, he did so at the cost of his reputation and his ability to live a normal life; he is known around the world as a priest who failed dramatically in his calling such that he has been living for more than a decade as an indicted war criminal, who is wanted to stand trial by an international prosecutor and has already been convicted in absentia by a Rwandan court. Indeed, his failure to offer assistance during the genocide is emblematic of the general failure of the Catholic Church in Rwanda in 1994, a dark stain on the worldwide religious institution. On the other hand, Korczak, who did not survive the Holocaust, is well known and well regarded around the world precisely because he is seen as having made what virtually everyone today considers to be the incredibly difficult but morally correct decision.

In considering these two lives, the most challenging question is not about which life is more choice-worthy, for that seems obvious; it is, instead, whether we could possibly make the choices that Korczak did. And this, of course, is what makes Janusz Korczak's a life that is both challenging to us and worthy of our emulation. Indeed, he writes that in his younger days he asked God to "give me a hard life but let it be beautiful, rich and aspiring" (Korczak 2003: 90). Could we—would we—ask for the same sort of life? Although many people today are fortunate to live in unprecedented safety and comfort, there are parts of the world—as well as of our own countries—where the majority of people cannot say the same. Should we involve ourselves in those lives, different as they are from our own, or should we simply be thankful that we cannot be held accountable for what happens to them? Should we, in other words, act like Korczak or like Munyeshyaka? While our choices do not seem nearly as pressing to us—largely because the situations in which they found themselves were extreme and because we have the ability to create a gulf between ourselves and those who require our assistance as they could not—those choices are no less serious ones, especially to those who are suffering today.

And, of course, while the contemporary situation for most of us is far less intense, it is important to remember that the most basic fact of our existence remains the same as it was for Korczak and Munyeshyaka, for, as Shakespeare (1992: 5.5.27–29) pointed out, "Life's but a walking shadow, a poor player / That struts and frets his hour upon the stage / And then is heard no more." Macbeth, into whose mouth Shakespeare puts these words, is nearing his own death and is correct that the most basic fact about human beings is that their lives are brief. But he is wrong, I have argued here, about the very next line that he utters, for life is not necessarily "a tale / Told by an idiot, full of sound and fury, / Signifying nothing" (Shakespeare 1992: 5.5.29–31). Macbeth would likely desire this conclusion; he has done terrible things to others in his pursuit of power so that his life has turned out to be one that has been lived badly. But each life, however brief, can have great significance if lived well. This is the lesson we can take away from a careful reading of the Homeric epic poems, especially when read through the lens of the Platonic dialogues. As Korczak wrote, "The lives of great men are like legends—difficult but beautiful" (Lifton: 1988: 3).

The idea that the best lives are filled with hardships whose navigation or endurance contributes substantially to their virtue nicely ties together the lives of the characters who have populated the preceding chapters. As we have seen, Achilles must embrace his mortality before accomplishing his battlefield heroics to avenge Patroclus, and Odysseus must turn his back on Calypso's offer of immortality in order to continue his arduous journey home to Ithaca. In doing so, both men are ultimately able to achieve a glorious name and thereby to set the standard for either battlefield heroism or heroic endurance. At the heart of these two classical heroic epics is a clear recognition of human finitude; only when human beings give up all hope for a permanent existence are they able to think most clearly about the sort of life they want to have lived. The same is true about the life (and death) of the archetypical other-regarding hero: Socrates chooses to give up his life rather than to pay a fine, live under house arrest, or escape to Thessaly. In this way, Plato aligns his hero with those of the great Homeric epics.

But, of course, I have been arguing that Plato does a good deal more throughout the dialogues than simply elevating Socrates to the same level as Achilles and Odysseus. In sacrificing himself on behalf of both his friends and enemies, rather than in the name of some personal good like *kléos* or *nostos*, Socrates demonstrates that the philosophical life is distinctly choice-worthy because its practitioners are principally devoted to the pursuit of wisdom and to assisting others. Plato's rehabilitation of the life of the philosopher, now cast as the other-regarding hero, has been so successful that anyone who undertakes the hero's journey today is necessarily measured against the Socratic model rather than either Achilles or Odysseus. This is good news, insofar as the life of Socrates is unmistakably a life that any one of us might live, whereas the outsized lives of Homer's heroes are not. It is not clear that any people alive today are capable of the sort of heroism found in the epics devoted to Achilles and Odysseus; as the cases of John Kerry and John McCain highlight, even our most impressive deeds seem to pale in comparison, in no small part because the Homeric heroes so clearly stand above us in both the size and scope of their actions. But anyone might, given the proper conditions, make the Socratic choice of putting the greater good or the good of others above one's own and, in so doing, achieve the acclaim we afford other-regarding heroes.

This acclaim is not misplaced, nor do I want to argue that we would do better to once again give pride of place in our heroic pantheon, for example, to the warrior. There are some obvious reasons for us to prefer the other-regarding hero over the hero who behaves amorally or even immorally, as both Achilles and Odysseus seem to us to do, not the least of which is that a society in which other-regarding heroism is prized is one in which we might experience substantially less human suffering than we see in the Homeric epics. And yet, insofar as we have pushed to the side all sorts of distinctly impressive people who would have been considered heroes in a different time and place, my argument is that we have impoverished the contemporary discourse about heroism even as we have raised the profile of those heroes who seem to us to fit the model we prefer today. This is not to say that we ought to do more to encourage battlefield heroes or that we need to celebrate the survivor who has only his own good in mind when he acts; it is, instead, to recognize that not all heroes will be cut from the same cloth. In insisting that heroism can mean only one thing—sacrificing oneself in order to benefit others—we minimize the terribly difficult choices made by a great many people who have, on my reading, undertaken heroic action. And, of course, disentangling one heroic archetype from another as I have attempted to do with this project can help us to understand exactly what it is about *other-regarding* heroism that we find so compelling. Thus we might be in a better position to encourage people to act on behalf of others if and when they are presented with the sort of difficult choice that faced Korczak or Munyeshyaka.

In the end, then, the lesson learned from a careful examination of Socrates' elevation over the Homeric heroes is that we ought to assign more weight to living a good life—one devoted to the pursuit of wisdom and virtue—than we do to living a long life. And when we can combine critical thinking about our mortality with an expansive imagination about those who are suffering, then the kind of life that we lead takes on an incredible importance and we are able to open a space for the sort of other-regarding heroic action that has become the defining feature of our contemporary discourse on the topic of heroism.

Notes

CHAPTER 1

1. In 2007, Autrey—a construction worker and veteran of the Navy—jumped from a Manhattan subway platform to rescue another man who had suffered a seizure and fallen onto the tracks as a train approached (cf. Buckley 2007). In 2009, Sullenberger averted catastrophe for the 155 passengers on board the plane he was piloting by safely landing US Airways 1549 in the Hudson River after losing power in both engines (cf. McFadden 2009).
2. According to the Silver Star medal citation, signed by Vice Admiral Zumwalt, "KERRY expertly directed the fire of his craft at the fleeing enemy while simultaneously coordinating the insertion of the embarked troops. . . . Patrol Craft Fast 94 then beached in the center of the enemy positions and an enemy soldier sprang up from his position not ten feet from Patrol Craft Fast 94 and fled. Without hesitation, Lieutenant (junior grade) KERRY leaped ashore, pursued the man behind a hootch and killed him, capturing a B-40 rocket launcher with a round in the chamber. . . . As a result of this operation, ten Viet Cong were killed and one wounded with no friendly casualties."
3. It is important to note that a central component of McCain's heroism surely involves his decision not to accept the early release offered to him by the North Vietnamese and instead to insist on the principle that POWs should be released in the order of their capture (cf. Timberg 1996: 133, 137, 172). At least part of the heroism of McCain's decision turns on his reasoning for refusing early release, which continues to be debated:

    > A September 13, 1968, cable from Averell Harriman, U.S. ambassador-at-large, to the State Department confirmed that McCain's captors had offered him early release, but that he had refused. The cable reported that, according to the Vietnamese, "Commander McCain feared that if he was released before the war is over, President [Lyndon] Johnson might 'cause difficulties' for his father because people will wonder if McCain had been brainwashed." Harriman speculated that instead, McCain was abiding by the Code of Conduct. (Silverman 1999)

4. In all that follows, I translate *kléos* as "glory" even though it might also be translated as "fame" or "renown." What I have in mind by "glory" is a more enduring, everlasting, or long-standing sort of fame that comes from the chronicling of one's deeds even after one's time on Earth has passed. Bruce Lincoln (1991: 15) nicely highlights the reason for my chosen translation in his discussion of the Proto-Indo-European origins of *kléos*:

Those who hoped for some continuation of their own individual, egotistical existence had only one recourse, summed up again in a poetic formula of P-I-E origin: "the fame that does not decay" (*klewos *ndhgʷhitom,* on which see Schmitt 1967, 61–102). In a universe where impersonal matter endured forever but the personal self was extinguished at death, the most which could survive of that self was a rumor, a reputation. For this, the person craving immortality—a condition proper only to the gods and antithetical to human existence—was totally reliant on poets and poetry. P-I-E warrior heroes—like their later I-E reflexes Siegfried, Achilles, Arjuna, and the like—desperately hoped to amass in their lifetimes a body of deeds so awesome as to move poets to sing of them forever.

Achilles, in other words, is concerned with a glorious name, one that transcends his particular time, rather than with the fame or renown he might get from his comrades-in-arms. Robert L. Oprisko (2012: 101–104) spends a great deal of time carefully setting out the distinction between fame, celebrity, and glory, ultimately reaching the same conclusion: "To be famous, then, is to be capable of individuality and to have a name in the mass of society. . . . Celebrity extends beyond reputation—beyond the direct impact of the individual's geographic or professional stomping grounds. However, it is encapsulated by temporality. . . . Celebrity can transcend the situated position of the individuals being celebrated such that they experience a level of renown that extends beyond direct impact in time and space. . . . I call this transcendent form 'glory.'"

5. I have chosen to refer to Socrates' heroism as other-regarding because, while it might not roll off the tongue quite like the battlefield hero or the suffering hero, it captures the nature of his heroism without falling victim to the various difficulties that arise from words like altruistic or moral. Those loaded terms take our own view of Socrates today, as someone who behaved altruistically and thus morally by our lights, and seem to suggest that Athenians ought to have held a similar view of morality. Other-regarding to my mind is not fraught with the same sort of backward-looking issues; instead, it seems simply descriptive of the addressees of Socrates' sacrifice—namely, the many others (both future philosophers and the Athenians at large) for whom Socrates chooses to give his life.

6. In discussing the Platonic critique of Homer and the poets, Dean Hammer (2002: 5) notes that the "distinction between the epistemological status of poetry and philosophy persists in our understanding of the epic. The first task of philosophy, Havelock reminds us, was 'escaping from' the 'narrative flux' of the Homeric language, a flux revealing of 'error of thought.'" And with regard to the enduring nature of Plato's critique, Hammer (2002: 5) argues that "what has often emerged is a distinction, made both implicitly and explicitly, between political theories—which are depicted as systematic, reasoned, reflective, and critical accounts of the political world—and the epic—which is often characterized as an uncritical appropriation of myths, legends, stories, and superstitions."

CHAPTER 2

1. Throughout this chapter, I have changed the spelling of proper names for people and places found in Robert Fitzgerald's translation of Homer (1974) from the Greek to the more standard Latin, mostly by removing pronunciation marks and changing "k" to "c." Thus, "Patroklos" is here rendered "Patroclus" and "Heracles" is the more common "Hercules." Generally, the variation is so minor as not to cause any problems for the reader; I have, however, maintained the Greek spelling in any quoted material.

2. While I put a great deal of stock in the choice(s) that Achilles makes, and in his ultimate decision to embrace the brief life of the mortal hero, Eric Voegelin (1953: 499) argues that I go much too far in celebrating it as a choice at all: "The alternative of fate, therefore, does not offer a true choice to Achilles any more than to the other lords—though for a different reason. The other princes are bound to their station by their oath and duty; they cannot return as long as victory has not become obviously hopeless in military terms. Achilles is bound to the war, and can never return, because he is a warrior (perhaps even killer would not be too strong a word) who would fit into the order at home even less than into the order of the army." In all that follows, I will argue, against Voegelin, that Achilles recognizes these divergent destinies as possibilities that are worthy of serious consideration and then actively chooses one over the other. In agreement, here, is John Alvis (1995: 4), who notes that "the more prominent of the heroes enjoy moments when their feats seem to lift them above human limits. They can imagine being honored as gods or at least achieving a kind of immortality through fame. The alternative is namelessness, the oblivion suffered by ordinary human beings who hoard their lives and who are subject like the lower animals to ignoble compulsions of self-preservation and appetite."

3. Katherine Callen King (1987: 3) argues that Achilles is "the swiftest, the most beautiful, the youngest, and very importantly, the most complex of heroes who fight at Troy." For additional discussion of each one of Achilles' distinguishing features, see King (1987: 2–13).

4. It is important to note, of course, that the source of the quarrel between Achilles and Agamemnon that leads to Achilles' curse is Agamemnon's public mistreatment of Achilles after Achilles attempts to find a solution to the communal plague brought on by Agamemnon's impious behavior.

5. Gilgamesh is most often compared to Odysseus, in large part because of the centrality of a great voyage to his heroic story (cf. Campbell 1972: 49–58, 185–188; West 1999: 402–417). That said, Schein (1984: 17) is persuasive on the comparison to Achilles, noting that "Gilgamesh strives to achieve immortality for Enkidu and himself, but in the end learns that heroic deeds and the memory of them are the only immortality possible for human beings, however great." Patrick J. Deneen (2000) has an excellent discussion of Odysseus as a model of heroic behavior quite distinct from that of Achilles, to which I will turn in later chapters. While Achilles is not specifically mentioned in Joseph Campbell's seminal *The Hero with a Thousand Faces*, the Homeric epics clearly fit very comfortably within the framework of the monomyth that Campbell (1972) sets out in the first part of that book, especially in the ways that Schein notes with regard to Achilles and that scholars routinely reference with regard to Odysseus.

6. Voegelin (1953: 496) makes a forceful case for reading Achilles' behavior, especially his public discussion of the certainty of his fate, as decidedly unheroic: "The injection of his predicted fate as an argument in the debate is a display of poor taste which the other lords are well-bred enough quietly to ignore." He goes on to argue, more broadly, that "the *cholos* [χόλος; anger] of Achilles has a highly improper complexion" because it "is not a finite reaction against a finite threat, with the purpose of repairing the momentary breach of order; it rather is an outburst of the deep-seated anxiety that has grown in him through the preoccupation with his fate; it is caused by an emotional short-circuit between the diminution of his honor and the anticipation of his death" (Voegelin 1953: 500). Indeed, the overall picture put forward in Voegelin's (1953: 517) essay is that Achilles "emerges from Homer's description as a splendid warrior, useful to have on your side in an emergency, but otherwise as a not very appealing figure, almost a pathological case."

7. The status of Agamemnon's apology remains an open question, of course. After detailing the long and impressive list of gifts that he will present to Achilles, he continues: "So let Achilles bow to me, / considering that I hold higher rank / and claim the precedence of age" (Homer 1974: IX.193–195). It might well be the case that, in fact, Agamemnon's hope is to pay for his insult with treasure rather than apologize to Achilles for the offense he committed in taking Briseis from him. In this case, Achilles' response is unsurprising, as his timê [τιμή; honor, prestige] is not properly restored by this quasi-apology from Agamemnon.

8. Bonnie MacLachlan (1993: 19n10) raises an interesting disagreement with Schein's reading of this important scene, as she argues that Achilles' position might instead be recalling his quasi-divinity rather than noting his divorce from the heroic values of his community: "The Trojan War itself was fought to compensate for the shame that two goddesses had received at the hands of a Trojan. Hera and Athena make it clear throughout the epic that they will not be satisfied until their τιμή is restored, with the destruction of Troy." While this is certainly true, I follow Schein's reading throughout because it seems both to follow the text of the *Iliad* a bit more closely and to resonate with the Platonic critique of Achilles in the *Republic*, to which I will turn in later chapters.

9. Schein's (1984: 129–130) translation reads as follows: "a dark cloud of grief covered him; / with both hands he grasped the grimy dust / and poured it over his head, and disfigured his lovely face; / and the dark ashes settled on his tunic which was as fragrant as nectar. / He himself, great in his greatness, stretched out in the dust / lay, and he disfigured his hair, tearing it with his hands."

10. Dean Hammer puts forward something of a different reading of the central role played by Patroclus' death in Achilles' decision to return to battle, though one that clearly has connections to my own. For Hammer (2002: 174), "the death of Patroklos . . . recasts Achilles' experience of pain since he becomes implicated in the suffering of another." In other words, rather than seeing more clearly his own death when confronted with the death of Patroclus, Achilles here recognizes his obligations as a result of Patroclus' death. Arlene W. Saxonhouse (1988: 36) makes a similar point, though without reaching the same conclusion about personal obligation as Hammer, arguing that "the death of Patroclus shows that Achilles cannot easily discard the warrior ethic; while death is the fate of all, he learns that his own actions can precipitate the death of those he loves." My own reading ultimately casts Achilles' decision in a somewhat more selfish light than does Hammer's, as I want to argue that his restoration to the community happens only after his battlefield exploits are completed; Hammer, conversely, sees them as of a piece.

11. Homer's portrayal of the mortal Hercules, in the *Iliad*, is a conscious choice that serves the purpose of connecting Herculean and Achillean heroism. Schein (1984: 134) notes that "in accordance with the themes of his poem, Homer ignores, and makes Achilles ignore, the alternate tradition that Heracles achieved deification for his heroism." Anthony T. Edwards (1985) has a great deal more on the hero cult and on alternatives to the Homeric portrayal of the mortality of Achilles.

12. Odysseus also expresses this sentiment in the *Odyssey*—in word and deed—by ultimately rejecting Calypso's offer of immortality, even after he sees the fate of his dead comrades in Hades, in order to achieve his νόστος [*nostos*; homecoming].

13. Achilles is a hero Nietzsche (1992a: 344) could admire, both because he chose his own way in the world and because he embodied the proper spirit of hardness: "In man *creature* and *creator* are united: in man there is material, fragment, excess, clay, dirt, nonsense, chaos; but in man there is also creator, form-giver, hammer hardness." That this hardness is a necessity in order to create oneself can have unpleasant consequences for others, just as Achilles' hardness

meant the deaths of weaker men and the eventual destruction of Troy. Indeed, the metaphors that Nietzsche (1982: 326) chooses when he emphasizes the importance of hardness sound particularly violent:

> And if your hardness does not wish to flash and cut and cut through, how can you one day create with me?
> For creators are hard. And it must seem blessedness to you to impress your hand on millennia as on wax,
> Blessedness to write on the will of millennia as on bronze—harder than bronze, nobler than bronze. Only the noblest is altogether hard.
> This new tablet, O my brothers, I place over you: *become hard!*

14. Saxonhouse (1988: 37) makes a similar point: "The psychological motives and the physical necessities that govern the Achaeans are irrelevant for Achilles. His thymos no longer sets him within the structure of human society. The vengeance he seeks goes beyond the boundaries of the laws of camp and body."

15. Though Achilles himself is portrayed as godlike and even—on several occasions—as a force of nature (cf. Homer 1974: XX.420–421, 567–570; XXI.14–19, 606–609; XXII.30–38, 161–162), it is clear that he does not actually have the kind of power that is reserved for the gods. Despite being mortal and less powerful, however, Achilles can still behave like a god, largely because of the powerful forces working on his behalf.

16. The only other times that cannibalism is mentioned are at the very beginning and very end of the poem. In the first instance, Zeus chides his wife for her seeming desire to "breach the gates / and the great walls yourself and feed on Priam / with all his sons, and all the other Trojans, / dished up raw" (Homer 1974: IV.40–43). In the second case, Priam's wife—Hecuba—expresses her overwhelming anger at Achilles for killing and then dishonoring her son: "*I could devour the vitals of that man, / leeching into his living flesh!*" (Homer 1974: XXIV.255–256).

17. In one noteworthy exception, Diomedes manages a slight wound to Aphrodite as she is attempting to protect Aeneas, her son, from him: "He knew her to be weak, not one of those / divine mistresses of the wars of men . . . therefore he dared assail her / through a great ruck of battle. When in range / he leaped high after her and with his point / wounded her trailing hand: the brazen lancehead / slashed her heavenly robe, worked by the Graces, / and cut the tender skin upon her palm" (Homer 1974: V.383–391). Unlike Hera and Hades, wounded by Hercules, Aphrodite is portrayed as weak, here, and Diomedes has no further success against Apollo, who protects Aeneas after Aphrodite returns to Olympus to be healed. Homer (1974: V.495–501) says that "Diomedes, lord of the warcry, charged Aeneas / though he knew well Apollo has sustained him. / He feared not even the great god himself, / but meant to kill Aeneas and take his armor. / Three times he made his killing thrust; three times / the Lord Apollo buffeted his shield, / throwing him back."

18. Interestingly, King (1987: 14) argues that it is at this moment, when Achilles is most unlike himself, that he is most like Agamemnon: "When Achilles' slayings go beyond Agamemnon's both in number and in grimness of detail, there is a dreadful sense that the man has crossed the bounds of his own nature, has gone to the level of his opposite." In this argument, she builds on the work of Fenik (1968), who compares the Homeric descriptions of the two Achaean champions' *aristeía* [αριστεία; martial prowess].

19. In Achilles' rejection of suppliants, the comparison with Agamemnon is an apt one once again. King (1987: 13–14) notes that Achilles' "past behavior provides the only instances mentioned in the *Iliad* of prisoners being taken or released for

ransom . . . and this behavior stands in sharp contrast to that of the Greek leader Agamemnon, who thrice rejects the suppliant. Homer, it seems, has deliberately led us to expect that Achilles . . . will be more humane than Agamemnon and most of the other warriors, whose fighting has become increasingly savage as the Battle Books progress. Instead, he is the most violent, most terrible warrior of them all."

20. Jinyo Kim (2000) focuses on Achilles' recognition of his shared mortality even with his enemies, casting it in a positive light with regard to his eventual reconciliation with Priam. He argues that "Achilles' pity toward Priam as a fellow mortal, a φίλος, signals his reconciliation with his own mortality. With the rupture of his φιλότης toward Agamemnon, Achilles reexamines the conventional definition among the heroes that his φίλοι are the Achaians and his enemy the Trojans. In the end, he comes to redefine all mortals as his φίλοι: all humans alike are bound by death (cf. 'the same allotment', ἴση μοῖρα) and suffering (κήδεα)" (Kim 2000: 182). On my reading, however, Achilles' sympathy never fully extends to his battlefield enemies, only to those—like Priam—with whom he personally identifies. I arrive at what I take to be a more nuanced position on this matter in considering other moments when he does not challenge the common understanding of friends and enemies, such as his rejection of Lycaon's supplication even as he recognizes their shared mortality and his unwillingness to treat Hector's corpse with the respect commonly understood to be required. Thus, I argue that his sympathy toward Priam has less to do with their common humanity and more to do with Achilles' specific identification of Priam with Peleus.

21. It is important to note that praise for Coriolanus is never meted out privately; when Menenius and Cominius praise him, they do so publicly and in order to encourage others to aspire to martial greatness (cf. Shakespeare 1967: 1.9). Of course, this idea of instructing the youth to virtue is strikingly similar to that found in Plato's *Republic*, where two distinct classes (artisans and warriors) exist and the city's children are almost immediately separated into their appropriate class to begin their training for a productive life. This type of division, however, requires the complete supervision of a third class: the enlightened philosopher-kings. Rome, clearly lacking in this third class, is forced to leave class stratification to chance.

22. Interestingly, Coriolanus does not—at this point—conceive of himself as a god. Rather, the patricians and plebeians elevate him to that state. Only later, leaving the city, will Coriolanus attempt to realize his power, but by then he will be the only one who believes in his godlike status.

23. Coriolanus is classically aristocratic in his hatred of the plebeians, that "common cry of curs, whose breath I hate / As reek o'th'rotten fens" (Shakespeare 1967: 3.3.120–121). This aristocratic detachment from the masses is a point particularly celebrated by Nietzsche (1992: 243), who argues that "one must shed the bad taste of wanting to agree with many. 'Good' is no longer good when one's neighbor mouths it. And how should there be a 'common good'! The term contradicts itself: whatever can be common always has little value."

24. One of the most noteworthy elements of Shakespeare's *Julius Caesar* is the politics of appearance. Caesar's concern about his image above all else is a testament to Coriolanus' astute observations about the state of Roman affairs. If the only difference between Coriolanus and Caesar is that the former was unwilling to sacrifice honor to rule, it seems easy to argue that Coriolanus' republic, though only in its infancy, was ripe for take-over by any military hero with a greater love of ruling than of honor.

25. Seth Benardete (2005: 75) sets out several similarities between the two warriors:

> Achilles' attack on Agamemnon's authority corresponds to Coriolanus' refusal to acknowledge the tribune's office; his loss of Briseis to the loss of the consulate; the ingratitude of Agamemnon to that of the people; his

withdrawal from the battle to the other's banishment; the fulfillment of his wish that Zeus avenge his wrongs to Coriolanus' invasion of Rome; his rejection of the embassy of Ajax and Odysseus to the other's denial of Comunius and Menenius; and his acceptance of his duty, after Patroclus' death, corresponds to Coriolanus' sparing of Rome after his family's petition.

That said, Benardete (2005: 76) reaches quite a different conclusion from my own about the concluding acts in the lives of these two warriors: "[Achilles'] ties to the world are more attenuated than Coriolanus'; and as it is easier for him to break them, so it is harder to renew them. Drained of all human substance, isolated from other men, but unable to become divine, Achilles cracks, becomes monstrous, and dies."

26. Hammer (2002: 185) argues that Achilles is able to sympathize with Priam because of his seemingly unusual "ability to imagine himself in the position of another, an imagination that grows out of his experience of suffering-with another." He goes on to note that "Achilles first experiences this vulnerability when the death of Patroklos precipitates a corresponding loss of himself. The appearance of Priam now calls to mind Achilles' own vulnerability to the suffering of Peleus, as well. Whereas the vulnerability experienced through the death of Patroklos is immediate, the vulnerability to Peleus's suffering is both immediate, as Achilles experiences Peleus's absence, and more distant, as Achilles imagines the experience of Peleus" (Hammer 2002: 185).

27. On two occasions, Apollo intervenes to save Trojan warriors who face Achilles in battle. A third time, the god leads the great warrior away from the battle so that the Trojans can escape. This third time, Achilles attempts to catch Apollo—disguised as a Trojan warrior—but is finally reminded of his place by the god: "Why run so hard, Achilles, / mortal as you are, after a god? / Can you not comprehend it? I am immortal. / You are so hot to catch me, you no longer / think of finishing off the men you routed. / They are all in the town by now, packed in / while you were being diverted here. And yet / you cannot kill me; I am no man's quarry" (Homer 1974: XXII.9–16).

28. The centrality of pity, which I refer to throughout this project as sympathy or fellow feeling, to the dramatic unity of the *Iliad* is explored in extremely careful detail by Kim (2000). As he argues,

> 'Achilles' pity and pitilessness' is evidently not just an incidental motif but rather an important theme. First, the idea is underlined through formulaic expressions and their variants which occur no more than four times for a given formula and in connection exclusively with Achilles. . . . Second, the motif occurs in connection with events that are of central importance to the plot of the *Iliad*: the embassy, Patroklos' return, Achilles' own return (as is implicit in Lykaon's supplication and his plea ἐλέησον), the funeral games and Priam's supplication. Third, the motif is developed in a musical pattern, so to speak, which informs the structure of the poem: the motif of Achilles' being νηλεής to his friends yields to the motif of his pity toward Patroklos; the motif of his pitilessness toward the Trojans yields to the motif of his pity toward Priam. Thus the motif of his pitilessness is twice resolved, as it were, in the motif of his pity. . . . The formal evidence of the theme of Achilles' pity indicates that his pity toward Priam, far from being an anomaly in the *Iliad*, complements the poem's thematic structure. Achilles' pity toward Priam, therefore, must in an essential way be connected to the theme of Achilles' *mēnis*. (Kim 2000: 32–33)

Saxonhouse (1988: 44) also makes mention of the role that pity plays in Achilles' restoration to the community: "In the agreement to hold off battle, he also acknowledges his commitment to battle, to reenter the world of imperfect justice and bodily mortality. It is here that pity must take precedence over the principles of distribution. It is pity for the lot of all men in this world without purpose that lifts man above fame in song and that shows us the necessary limits to our spirit."

29. The fellowship found in the relationship between guest and host—which involves ceremonial gift giving and, often, a shared meal—is a theme that is featured prominently in the *Iliad*—as well as in the *Odyssey*—and with good reason. While the clearest example can be found in the battlefield conversation between Diomedes and Glaucus (Homer 1974: VI.253–275), who choose not to fight because their ancestors exchanged gifts with one another and broke bread together, it is noteworthy that a particularly egregious example of broken fellowship—Paris' stealing of Helen from the house of Menelaus after the former receives the latter's hospitality—provides the context in which all of the poem's action takes place.

CHAPTER 3

1. As in the preceding chapter, I have, throughout this chapter, changed the spelling of proper names for people and places found in Robert Fitzgerald's translation of Homer (1990) from the Greek to the more standard Latin, mostly by removing pronunciation marks and changing "k" to "c." Thus, "Ithaka" is here rendered "Ithaca" and "Kyklops" is the more common "Cyclops." Generally, the variation is so minor as not to cause any problems for the reader; I have, however, maintained the Greek spelling in any quoted material.

2. Indeed, Odysseus' lies serve to bind him more directly to his maternal grandfather, Autolycus, who "surpassed all men in fraud and ambiguous oaths" (Callaway 1998: 167; cf. Cramer 1973: 2–29 and Callaway 1993: 19 for more on the lies of Odysseus). Of course, Odysseus' willingness to employ lying and trickery also earns him the condemnation of both Pindar (1980: 262), who contends "that Odysseus' fame was far greater than his worth," and Euripides (1954: 99), who portrays him as a "monster of wickedness whose tongue twists straight to crooked, truth to lies, friendship to hate, mocks right and honours wrong!" Plato's treatment of Odysseus' lying will be examined in greater detail in a later chapter.

3. The translation of this term—also applied to Hermes—has met with a great deal of debate. Robert Fagles (Homer 2006: I.1) renders it "of twists and turns," while Fitzgerald opts for the far less literal "skilled in all ways of contending" (Homer 1990: I.2). I have chosen to use the Lattimore translation of *polytropos*, "of many ways" (Homer 1999: I.1), which is both more literal than the Fitzgerald translation and captures the dual meaning of the word better than does the Fagles translation. Apart from this single (though important) departure, I use the Fitzgerald translation throughout for its generally easy-to-read and lyrical rendering of the Greek.

4. Laurence Lampert (2002: 232n2) points out that "it is the defining quality of Odysseus, used in the first line of the *Odyssey* and at 10.330. As used by Hippias with respect to Odysseus (365b) it includes being false or lying and carries the connotations of wily and shifty." Quoting Charles H. Kahn (1996: 121–124), Lampert continues: "Antisthenes, a follower of Socrates who wrote Socratic dialogues, also argued against the claim that Homer meant to blame Odysseus by calling him *polytropos*; Antisthenes claims that it is praise for being 'good at dealing with men . . . being wise, he knows how to associate with men in many ways.'"

5. As the story progresses, Odysseus does credit Zeus with keeping him from the clutches of Scylla, noting that "never could I have passed her / had not

the Father of gods and men, this time, / kept me from her eyes" (Homer 1990: XII.568–570). However, the far more impressive feat that happens just before—of jumping from his drifting wreckage as it is sucked into Charybdis' whirlpool and then plunging back into the sea to retrieve it when it resurfaces—he claims as his own handiwork.

6. It is unclear whether Odysseus is actually aided here by Athena or whether Homer simply suggests that he surely must have been. As Odysseus nears the rocky coast, Homer (1990: V.445–446) writes that "he had been flayed there, and his bones broken, / had not grey-eyed Athena instructed him." And, only a few lines later, Homer (1990: V.455–457) again claims that "now at last Odysseus would have perished, / battered inhumanly, but he had the gift / of self-possession from grey-eyed Athena."

7. Nor is this the only time that Odysseus relies on information from Circe rather than on his own skill to get himself home safely. When he returns from his discussions with the dead at the edge of the world and prepares to launch his ships again, Circe tells him, "Sailing directions, / landmarks, perils, I shall sketch for you, to keep you / from being caught by land or water / in some black sack of trouble" (Homer 1990: XII.30–33).

8. In addition to the fact that Odysseus is known for fighting from a distance with the bow rather than in closer quarters with sword or spear, Homer's description of Odysseus' night raid against the Trojans in the *Iliad* shows the hero slaughtering the enemy in their sleep rather than defeating them in a fair fight. Benardete (2005: 16) uses this example to argue that "Odysseus never did quite fit into the *Iliad* and was an obscure figure (his greatest exploit occurred at night)."

9. Horkheimer and Adorno (1988: 34) argue that Odysseus, as the master, is able to hear the Sirens' song while the workers must do the rowing for him and are not allowed to hear; yet in exchange for the knowledge of the Sirens' art, he must surrender his freedom: "He listens, but while bound impotently to the mast; the greater the temptation the more he has his bonds tightened."

10. Homer notes that Polyphemos eats two more of Odysseus' men before becoming drunk and falling asleep. But earlier that day, "he caught / another brace of men to make his breakfast" (Homer 1990: IX.336–337). How many of Odysseus' men constitute a brace? We might assume that the Cyclops selects two men for each meal and thus conclude that Odysseus loses a total of six men before launching his attack.

11. Seth Benardete (2005: 16) goes a good deal further than I do here, as he argues that the age of heroes—understood only as those warriors with divine lineage who distinguish themselves through impressive battlefield deeds—has come to an end with the conclusion of the Trojan War: "The heroes are survivors in the *Odyssey*; they no longer dominate the stage, they are old-fashioned and out of favor." I argue, by contrast, that Odysseus represents a different sort of hero from the sole archetype that Benardete recognizes and, insofar as Homer attempts to connect him to the heroes who were his comrades-in-arms at Troy, he ought to be understood as moving the conversation about heroism forward into the time that Benardete (2005: 15) suggests is characterized by "the simply human things."

12. This first identification of himself as Nobody [*Outis*; Οὖτις] is particularly clever of Odysseus, and not simply because it allows him to save himself from Polyphemus. As Vernant (1999: 7) notes,

> This *Outis* behind which Odysseus conceals himself reveals in full transparency, through an ironic play on the word, precisely what it is that allows the hero to carry off the trick and disguise himself: *mêtis*, devious shrewdness, that subtle form of sly intelligence that is Odysseus's private possession on this earth, just as it is Athena's among the gods. Laughing from behind the

veil, Odysseus himself will declare it in plain language, asserting that the trickery that has ruined the Cyclops is his false name, *Outis*, and his perfect deceit, *mêtis*. He who is nobody is nobody other than *polumêtis Odusseus*, *poikilomêtis*, Odysseus of many deceits.

Of course, as discussed in more detail ahead, this episode sets the stage for the ten years of invisibility that Odysseus must endure before he can once again reclaim his identity by achieving his desired *nostos*.

13. This should not be read as akin to arguing that Odysseus places no value in the goods that are traditionally bestowed on heroes, such as trophies, women, and ultimately *kléos*. In both the *Iliad* and the *Odyssey*, Homer portrays him as someone who clearly is desirous of these goods and who acts in ways that would make him worthy of them. What I have argued throughout, however, is that Odysseus is distinct insofar as he privileges *nostos* over these more traditional goods and is willing, as few would be, to give up *kléos* if it might prevent his homecoming. Susan Neiman (2009) has quite a different take on Odysseus' namelessness, which she contrasts somewhat with the view put forward by Max Horkheimer and Theodor W. Adorno (1988) that it is a penalty whose price he never fully considers, since disowning his formerly glorious self leaves him with nothing but the abstract, modern self of every subsequent modern man. Neiman (2009: 319) suggests, instead, that "modern heroes like Odysseus are no longer tied to their origins: Anyone can be a hero, and anyone can fail. In an era where human choice begins to matter, why not let go of your name itself, first of all the ways in which your parents fix who you will be?" From Neiman's post-Enlightenment perspective, this sort of question likely makes a good deal of sense, but Odysseus' decision to reject namelessness on each occasion that he embraces it suggests that it is not one that would make much sense to him. As I have argued earlier, while Odysseus does not value *kléos* as much as he values *nostos*, I think it must be viewed as a mistake to suggest that he is a hero who embraces an entirely new order centered on different principles from the heroic order that Achilles embraces, rejects, and then embraces again in the *Iliad*.

14. Indeed, the precise cost to Odysseus of remaining with Calypso [Καλυψώ] is always clear: "like a symbol, her name proclaims what she is and what she does. She is the 'hidden' one and equally 'the one who hides'" (Vernant 1999: 21). Καλυψώ shares the same root with Καλύψαι [*kalupsai*; hidden, covered]. In considering a possible connection between Odysseus' blinding of Polyphemus and his invisibility to the eyes of men while he remains on Ogygia, Seth Benardete (1997: 37) notes that "'Calypso' (Καλυψώ) means 'Concealer.' It looks like an anagram of 'Cyclops' (Κύκλωψ)."

15. In his appreciation of his own mortality, Odysseus seems to be intentionally distinct from the suitors who—as a result of his decision to leave Ogygia—he will dispatch to Hades. As Benardete (1997: 95) notes, "The suitors never speak at all of men as mortals (*thnētoi*), though Odysseus himself uses the word some thirty-one times. The suitors do not believe that men are constituted by the contrariety of the pair immortal (*athanatos*) and mortal (*thnētos*). They therefore do not acknowledge 'mortal' as the marked term of that pair, with 'Hades' and all it entails standing behind it."

16. Alfred Heubeck and Arie Hoekstra (1990: 116) correctly note that Odysseus' "descent into Hades is deliberately mentioned as an example of the ἄεθλοι." They are on less firm footing, however, in stating that Hercules' and Odysseus' descent into the world of shadows is "the most dangerous enterprise undertaken by either." While Hercules' journey almost certainly fits this description—as it culminates in the capture of Cerberus, the three-headed hound of Hades—it is not at all clear that the one undertaken by Odysseus is similarly dangerous.

Indeed, Odysseus seems to have very little difficulty in making the journey, and it is not at all clear that any of the shades he meets have anything but useful information to provide him, even if he must follow careful directions and work diligently to ensure that they speak to him.

17. We might also make the argument that, while the shade of Achilles resides in Hades after his glorious death, the shade of Hercules does not. Indeed, the ghost of Hercules who speaks to Odysseus, Homer (1990: XI.718–719) tells us, is only "a phantom . . . for he himself has gone / feasting amid the gods." Though the text is clear on this point, many suggest that making this case would be going too far in the direction of asserting that one sort of hero is deified while the other resides in Hades. Both Finkelberg (1995: 14) and M. L. West (1985: 130, 134, 169), for example, argue that this bit of text must be an interpolation meant to include the existence of a hero-cult around Hercules that did not exist in Homer's day.

18. Nor is Finkelberg alone in making what I consider to be a critical mistake. Deneen (2000) and Lampert (2002) both put forward the argument not only that Odysseus' type of heroism is preferable to that of Achilles but also that Plato also puts that argument into Socrates' mouth. Interestingly, in the end, I will take the part of Hippias, in Plato's *Hippias Minor*, who rejects Socrates' question about whether Odysseus or Achilles is the better hero and instead "employs three criteria, bravest (*aristos*), wisest, and most polytropic" (Lampert 2002: 240) in evaluating the sort of hero most worthy of emulation. On my reading, which will be discussed in greater detail in subsequent chapters, Socrates' heroism does not reside in his wisdom but in the other-regarding nature of his actions. Nonetheless, I agree with Hippias that there are properly three archetypes of heroism and that it is important to separate them out one from another.

19. Benardete (1997: 98) offers a further note of caution—far more extreme than my own—to anyone who would compare Odysseus with Hercules, arguing that any connections we might notice that exist between them ultimately represent "the low point of Odysseus's narrative": "Odysseus's silence seems to be due to his recalling his friend Iphitus, who gave him the bow with which he kills the suitors, and whom Heracles slew in his own home when Iphitus was a guest-friend (21.11–14). The gods reward injustice with immortality."

20. It is, of course, fascinating to see a reading of the Homeric epics that casts Odysseus as a model of moderation, as he does not often seem to be particularly moderate in any of his actions. Indeed, it is precisely Odysseus' immoderation that causes Socrates to insist on censoring the one passage about his heroic exploits that he feels is not appropriate for the education of the guardian class:

> "And what about making the wisest of men say that, in his opinion, the finest of all things is when
>
> The tables are full of bread and meat
> And the wine bearer draws wine from the bowl
> And brings it to pour in the goblets?
> Do you think that's fit for a young man to hear for his self-mastery? (Plato 1991: 390a–b).

21. Some scholars, in fact, suggest that Odysseus' survival is itself a black mark against him. As Telemachus notes, "If he had died of wounds in Trojan country / or in the arms of friends, after the war. / They would have made a tomb for him, the Akhaians, / and I should have all honor as his son" (Homer 1990: I.284–285). Death in war is straightforwardly heroic, but survival seems to require

some explanation. Ruprecht (1998: 59) clarifies what few others do, however; Odysseus is not the only famed warrior to survive the Trojan War and safely arrive back at home: "These exceptions are Menelaus of Sparta, Diomedes of Tiyrns, Nestor of Pylos, and Idomeneus of Crete."

CHAPTER 4

1. David Leibowitz (2010: 183) nicely sums up: "Plato's Socrates demonstrated, or at least indicated, that clear-sighted pursuit of one's own good is compatible with concern for others and generosity. . . . If we are willing to call such concern and generosity virtue, we may even say that there is a *purity* to Socrates' virtue—a freedom from half-buried hopes of reward—that is absent from 'virtue' as ordinarily practiced and understood."
2. While Socrates is made to look ridiculous rather than dangerous in the *Clouds*, he is also clearly identified as someone who encourages sons to challenge the authority of fathers and who sees no place in the world for the gods of Athens.
3. Hobbs (2000: 170) connects the critiques of Thrasymachus and Callicles in an interesting way, arguing that both represent spiritedness [θυμος: *thumos*] in their respective dialogues: "In Thrasymachus . . . we see what happens when the thumoeidic lion of the *Gorgias* does not manage to break through its social bonds, but remains imprisoned in a society it despises."
4. Later, in book 6, Adeimantus imagines someone who would argue that "of all those who start out on philosophy—not those who take it up for the sake of getting educated when they are young and then drop it, but those who linger in it for a longer time—most become quite queer, not to say completely vicious; while the ones who seem perfectly decent, do nevertheless suffer at least one consequence of the practice you are praising—they become useless to the cities" (Plato 1991: 487d).
5. But see Brickhouse and Smith (1989: 9), who attempt to show "that his principles require Socrates to do everything in his power, consistent with those principles, to gain his acquittal. If we are right, they allow him neither to seek martyrdom nor to scorn the proceedings with indifference."
6. Socrates asks, "What, then, is fitting for a poor man, a benefactor, who needs to have leisure to exhort you?" and then argues that "there is nothing more fitting, men of Athens, than for such a man to be given his meals in the Prytaneum, much more so than if any of you has won a victory at Olympia with a horse or a two- or four-horse chariot. For he makes you seem to be happy, while I make you be so; and he is not in need of sustenance, while I am in need of it" (Plato 1984a: 36d–e). But it is quite clear that the jurors, who have just convicted him of impiety, will not choose to reward Socrates in the way they traditionally reward the city's great champions. In failing to provide an adequate alternative punishment to the one proposed by Meletus, Socrates confirms the position that he advocates throughout his trial—namely, that only his death will put a stop to his philosophizing.
7. Of course, in the immediate aftermath of the Peloponnesian War and the rule of Thirty Tyrants, the Athenians of 399 BCE might have had other reasons to be suspicious of Socrates. As Brickhouse and Smith (1989: 20–21) note,

> A number of his associates were men with extremely unsavory reputations at the time Socrates was indicted. Plato's uncle, Charmides, for example, was one of the Thirty, and was recognized as one of Socrates' admirers. . . . Even worse, Socrates may also have been linked to Critias, whose iron-fisted actions as the leader of the Thirty made his name the emblem of their infamy. . . . Yet another potentially dangerous association may have been the one with Alcibiades [infamous for proposing the ill-fated Sicilian

Expedition in 415–413 bce, he fled to the Spartan side in the face of accusations of sacrilege in Athens]. . . . His damaging association with Socrates . . . may have lingered in the jurors' minds.

8. Socrates seems to concede, in the *Phaedo*, that he might have been, at one time in his life, guilty of one of the Aristophanic charges against him: "When I was a young man, Cebes, I was most amazingly interested in the lore which they call natural philosophy. For I thought it magnificent to know the causes of everything, why it comes into being and why it is destroyed and why it exists. . . . I considered the destructions of these things, and what happens about heaven and earth" (Plato 1999b: 96a–c).

9. There is, of course, much debate about the proximate cause of Socrates' trial, but it seems clear that it could have been avoided had Socrates desired. Crito suggests as much (Plato 1984b: 45e), as does Xenophon (1990: 43, 46). Further, in the *Meno*, Socrates seems determined to make an enemy of Anytus, who would later become one of his principal accusers (Plato 1999a: 92b–94a).

10. This runs counter, once again, to the interpretation of Brickhouse and Smith (1989: 110), who argue that "the arguments Socrates develops during his interrogation of Meletus are designed not merely, as other commentators have claimed, to confuse Meletus, and thus discredit him before the jury, but rather to refute the legal changes themselves by showing that they are based upon incoherent and thus indefensible prejudices." If it is the case that Socrates seeks to successfully refute the charges, it is surprising—given all that I have argued to this point—that he takes the tack he does. Brickhouse and Smith (1989: 127) base their conclusion that Socrates believed in the gods of the city on the fact that "if he did not accept customary religion, his leaving the impression that he did would cause him to run afoul of his mission [to tell the truth]; and there is no compelling reason to suppose that he did not accept it." All of this, of course, requires that Socrates is straightforwardly pious and always says exactly what he means, two points that I challenge throughout.

11. This view is also discussed in some detail by Catherine H. Zuckert (2009: 238) and by Robert Metcalf (2009: 81), whose ultimate conclusion is that "we must appreciate the genuine philosophical significance of Socrates' comparison with Achilles, for it speaks to the vigilant sense of shame, or *aidōs*, at the heart of Socrates' philosophical activity. . . . Seen in this way, Socrates' comparison with Achilles proves to be a defense of the proud and confrontational manner in which he presented his defense."

12. Similarly, Zuckert (2009: 238) argues, "The 'proof' of Socrates' 'strongest' logos was, finally, in his life and death. The 'knowledge' it generated was far from certain or indisputable. The conjunction of the speeches with the deeds or facts was, however, difficult simply to dismiss."

13. I adopt this reading because it is, I think, also confirmed in the *Crito* (cf. Plato 1984b: 43b–c) and the *Phaedo* (cf. Plato 1999b: 58e), where Phaedo tells Echecrates that "the man seemed happy to me . . . in bearing and in speech. How fearlessly and nobly he met his end!" As Greenberg (1965: 48) notes, "Crito is amazed at how easily and tranquilly Socrates conducts himself in a situation which Crito considers to be a calamity. Socrates replies that he is acting as any man of his years should, but Crito (and Plato) points out that most old men do not behave in this manner."

14. David Leibowitz (2010: 142) puts forward a similar argument in the course of his detailed analysis of Plato's *Apology*: "Might Socrates' knowledge, despite its shortcomings, be sufficient to replace apprehension and terror, as well as hope, concerning 'the things in Hades' with resignation to death (35a5–7)? And

isn't the toughness needed to recognize and face up to what cannot be changed, to endure what *must* be endured if we are to enjoy the greatest genuine good, admirable and manly? Socrates helps us to understand his own manliness or toughness by letting us see how he is both like and unlike Achilles."

15. In opposition to this claim is the argument by Hanna (2007: 258) about the superiority of the city and its laws to its citizens. This argument, however, relies on an identification between Socrates and the personified laws that I do not find persuasive:

> The speech of the Laws puts Socrates' arguments on display, temporarily freed from any displeasing association with him, any distracting hint of immorality, arrogance, or self-indulgence, and powerfully drives home to the reader the injustice of the verdict and the moral carelessness and igno-rance of the many who rendered it. . . . Most importantly, perhaps, they are calling on people to exercise political and moral responsibility—to respect the law by obeying it, to morally evaluate the law and work to change it by means of rational argument when they find it lacking, and to justly apply it. (Hanna 2007: 265)

Although this interpretation might fit well with a contemporary understanding of civil disobedience, on my reading it is not the argument made by the laws and it also does not conform to the Superiority Thesis—that citizens must respect all laws because there is no equality of rights between laws and citizens—that Hanna puts forward throughout.

16. Weinrib (1982: 98) also notes, rightly, that Socrates took pains in the *Apology* to prevent Meletus from conflating people and laws (cf. Plato 1984a: 24d–25a); to conflate the two here seems problematic, but Crito makes no mention of the inconsistency.

17. In the *Crito*, the laws say, "Now with regard to your father . . . justice was not equal to you, so that you didn't also do in return whatever you suffered: you didn't contradict him when he spoke badly of you, nor did you beat him in return when you were beaten, or do any other such thing" (Plato 1984b: 50e–51a). And, in the *Clouds*, Pheidippides graduates from Socrates' "thinkery" and then immediately proceeds to beat his father, Strepsiades, while arguing about the justice of doing so:

PHEID: Did you beat me when I was a boy?

STREP: Yes, I did. I was well-intentioned and concerned for you.

PHEID: Then tell me, isn't it also just for me likewise to be well-intentioned toward you and to beat you, since in fact to be well-intentioned is to beat? For why should *your* body be unchastised by blows, but not mine? . . . And it's more appropriate for the old to weep than the young inasmuch as it's less just for them to do wrong.

STREP: But nowhere is it the law that the father suffer this.

PHEID: Wasn't he who first set down this law a man like you and me, and didn't he persuade those of long ago by speaking? Is it any less allowable for me too, then, to set down in turn for the future a novel law for sons to beat their fathers in return? (Aristophanes 1984: 1409–1425)

18. The Myth of Er, which Socrates retells to conclude the *Republic*, centers around a similar presentation of the afterlife and the immortality of souls. I turn to a detailed elucidation of that myth, and specifically the problems that arise from a literal reading of its central message and of the choice made by the soul of Odysseus, in a later chapter.

19. Little is known about Socrates' third accuser, Lycon. He is described as quarreling with Socrates "on behalf of the orators" (Plato 1984a: 24a), and there is some speculation that, like Anytus, his animosity was based on the relationship between Socrates and his son.

20. As Zuckert (1984) notes, his argument about the structure of the *Clouds* owes a great deal to that of Leo Strauss (1966), whose explication of the Aristophanic Socrates is excellent.

21. I say that Socrates only *suggests* his agreement because he does not actually admit to being convinced by the arguments of the laws. Instead, he says, "that these things are what *I* seem to hear, just as the Corybantes seem to hear the flutes, and this echo of these speeches is booming within me and makes me unable to hear the others" (Plato 1984b: 54d). The unusual comparison is noted by Weinrib (1982: 101), who argues that "at the end Socrates indicates that the Laws are not voicing reasoned arguments but are producing the music which accompanies a Corybantic frenzy." After all, Socrates is not in need of the Corybantic flutes, used to treat fear or other emotional disturbances; rather, Crito is the one who is frantic to rescue Socrates, while the philosopher earlier reported calm sleep even in the face of his impending execution.

22. This argument runs counter to the one proposed by Xenophon (1990: 42–43), whose Socrates seeks death in the same manner as the Platonic Socrates but whose motivation is quite different and far less noble. As Gray (1989: 139) suggests, Xenophon's Socrates "had lived a life of perfection so far, an object of admiration for himself and his friends. The future held only the prospect of old age, decay of the senses and the intellect, loss of admiration, lack of repute. If he died easily by hemlock, his reputation would be untarnished in his own eyes and those of his friends, and they would miss him. He decided therefore to use the trial to advertise his perfection and secure that reputation forever." The closest that the Platonic Socrates will come to this position is in noting that he will not flatter his jurors because "I am old and have this name; and whether it is true or false, it is reputed at least that Socrates is distinguished from the many human beings in some way" (Plato 1984a: 34e–35a). While it is a clear allusion to his reputation, something for which he has only contempt in the *Crito*, it is also quite different from the argument that he desires an early death to avoid declining in esteem due to the vagaries of old age.

23. Immediately before he dies Socrates tells Crito, "We owe a cock to Asclepios; pay it without fail" (Plato 1999b: 118a), cryptic last words that have been the subject of an overwhelming amount of debate. Joseph Cropsey (1986: 173–174) suggests that Socrates wanted to thank the god of medicine and healing for a relatively painless death. Nietzsche (1968: 473; 1974: §340), however, takes Socrates to mean that he is weary of life and thus owed thanks to Asclepios for his death. Ahrensdorf (1995: 113, 198) concludes that Socrates was suggesting that he remains uncertain about the fate of his soul and is playing it safe by asking that a sacrifice be performed. A note in the text asserts that this was meant to be a gift to the god of healing on behalf of Plato, who was ill and therefore not present at Socrates' death. I am inclined to agree with this interpretation, as Plato's good health offers the only sort of immortality to Socrates of which he can be certain, one that allows him to live on in the reports of his life and conversations. Ronna Burger (1984: 216) writes, "The Platonic Socrates thus invests his dying words with an appropriate implication of gratitude—Thank god for Plato!"

24. In addition to these examples, Socrates provides an argument against suicide, at the outset of the dialogue, that seems straightforwardly pious—namely, that human beings are the possessions of the gods who care for them (Plato 1999b: 62c–d). As Bolotin (1987: 42) notes, "Just as Cebes would be angry if one of

his slaves were to kill himself, without a sign that Cebes wanted him to die, and would even punish him if he could, so might we be punished after death for trying to run away from our divine masters. And if this is true, Socrates continues, it is reasonable that one must not commit suicide until the god sends some necessity, such as the present one, to do so." Of course, Socrates implies to Cebes that he is, in fact, committing suicide—but that he is doing so with the assistance of the god rather than in opposition to the god's commands.

25. Bolotin (1987: 54) concludes that Socrates might not have believed in the immortality of the soul, but that Plato avoided directly arguing in favor of this conclusion in the interest of encouraging the pious image of the philosopher in the *Phaedo*. Further, he argues that "there may be no better way of helping his friends to think as he did, even on the assumption that he did not believe that his soul was immortal, than the one he actually pursues. By encouraging their desire for an argument that would show the immortality of the soul, Socrates sharpens, at least temporarily, their awareness of their own ignorance regarding this most far-reaching of questions; and he may thereby help awaken, in one or more of them, a desire for knowledge of the whole."

CHAPTER 5

1. Patrick J. Deneen (2000: 87) pays careful attention to the wording of this passage, noting "that the tales are not true 'provided' (or 'if') the guardians are to act in a certain way. The stories of the gods will thus depend on their effect, not their validity."

2. There is much that is unusual about what Socrates says in his response to Cebes. As Peter J. Ahrensdorf (1995: 24–25) notes, in thinking that the dream has been encouraging him to philosophize, Socrates

> does not interpret it according to the ordinary meaning of its words. Instead, he interprets it in the light of his own opinion that philosophy is the greatest music. But how does he know that the god shares his opinion about philosophy? . . . In fact, what he says does not preclude the possibility that the dream does not come from a god at all. For he does not say that he is certain either that it does come from a god or that he has committed an impiety. Yet, given his doubts about the accuracy of his second interpretation of the dream, how does he now know that he is not in truth disobeying the god, and hence committing impiety, despite what might seem to be the most pious intentions?

3. "Take the Trojan side / and roll the Achaians back to the water's edge, / back on the ships with slaughter! All the troops / may savor what their king has won for them, / and he may know his madness, what he lost / when he dishonored me, peerless among Achaians" (Homer 1974: I.470–475).

4. The comparison between Achilles and Hercules—developed in far greater detail in the first chapter—is an important one, as it highlights Achilles' initiation, through his barbaric deeds, into a far more savage world than that of the *Iliad*. Seth L. Schein (1984: 79) notes that Achilles, no longer the relatively humane conqueror, is transformed by his rage into someone existing "beyond a boundary that humans in the *Iliad* normally do not cross."

5. Each of the passages is interesting, and Deneen (2000: 91) spends a considerable amount of time on those taken from the *Odyssey* in his attempt to demonstrate his "conclusion that Socrates begins drawing an elusive positive lesson from the *Odyssey* in the early books of the *Republic*." I am sympathetic to parts of his argument, especially as his analyses of the texts are very thoughtfully and

carefully done. That said, I believe he goes a bit too far in embracing some classically Straussian claims, most notably that the middle quotation in this passage of the *Republic*—about Teiresias—is the most important of the seven citations from Homer. While this passage is certainly the most important for Deneen, I might make the claim that the *first* quotation—directly spoken by Achilles—is far more important than the *fourth*. It is never made precisely clear why one should be preferred to another, apart from the place that one or the other occupies in Deneen's argument or in my own.

6. Deneen (2000: 57) points out, correctly, that Odysseus is offered immortality and chooses to decline it after serious contemplation, as will be discussed in greater detail in the next chapter. But he is incorrect in suggesting that Odysseus' choice resembles Achilles', for the latter is offered only a long life rather than immortality. In the end, regardless of how he chooses at Troy, Achilles will die; thus, as I argued in the first chapter, the choice of the type of life he will live becomes most important for him.

7. In my discussion of the *Republic* in this chapter, I leave aside entirely the question of Plato's true intentions regarding the philosopher-king and the ideal city in speech. Bloom debated this question at length with Dale Hall (1977) in the pages of *Political Theory*, and elsewhere, and that debate is rehearsed nicely by Deneen (2000: 126–127n72). As Deneen (2000: 113) correctly argues, "One's answer to this question finally determines how one interprets the solution offered by the *Republic*: if the philosopher refuses to descend, the solution of the philosopher-king to the problem of justice proves impossible, and the *Republic* is a work about the 'limits of the city'; alternatively, his voluntary descent would at least allow for the possibility of the 'city in speech' to come into being."

8. In the *Posterior Analytics*, Aristotle (1975: 74) describes two different types of *megalopsuchia* [μεγαλοψυχία; greatness of soul] and provides several examples. On the one hand are Alcibiades, Achilles, and Ajax, who cannot tolerate any insult or dishonor; on the other hand are Lysander and Socrates, who are not affected by either good or ill fortune. As Hobbs (2000: 195) points out, "Odysseus is not mentioned by Aristotle, but, though he displays both kinds, it is plain that he is more readily associated with the second." Deneen provides a great many examples to stress Socrates' connection to Odysseus, beyond the obvious comparison of Socrates' descent to the Piraeus in book 1 and the cave in book 7 with Odysseus' descent into Hades. Perhaps the most carefully considered is his discussion of the place of Odysseus in the *Republic*'s Myth of Er:

> Several specific life-paths resulting from the choice of the soul of Odysseus seem possible. . . . Perhaps we are to understand that Odysseus will return to life as a full-blown philosopher but will hang back from his society for fear of his life and philosophy, resembling more the philosopher described in the Allegory of the Cave in Book 7. Or perhaps Allan Bloom is correct that Er's tale leads us to conclude that Odysseus's next life will be that of Socrates, namely that of the private man whose soul is ordered, who does not seek public office, but who nevertheless "does many things." (Deneen 2000: 109)

Regardless of the interpretation—about which I will say much more in the next chapter—it is clear that Socrates portrays Odysseus as making a careful choice, one that will lead him to the just life that has been touted throughout the *Republic*.

9. In the quotation from Homer (1974: XVIII.108–109, 111–119), Thetis says, "You'll be / swift to meet your end, child, as you say: / your doom comes close on the heels of Hektor's own." And Achilles responds, "May it come quickly.

As things were, / I could not help my friend in his extremity. / Far from home he died; he needed me / to shield him or to parry the death stroke. / For me there's no return to my own country. / Not the slightest gleam of hope did I / afford Patroklos or the other men / whom Hektor overpowered. Here I sat, / my weight a useless burden to the earth."

10. By contrast, David Leibowitz (2010: 139) notes that "the principle that Socrates and Achilles share, as Socrates states it, is that 'wherever someone stations himself, holding that it is best, or wherever he is stationed by a ruler, there he must stay and run the risk, as it seems to me, and not take into account death or anything else before what is shameful' (28d6–8). Justice now is not mentioned."

11. Seth Benardete (2005) disconnects ordinary human beings from the heroes in a way that I find quite compelling on every point except for the one that is central to Achilles' story. He says,

> How far apart the Achaeans and Trojans are from ordinary men, the "hero" shows; Homer identifies it with *anêr* (the phrase *hêrôs andres* thrice occurs), and it clearly has nothing to do with *anthrôpoi*, for even we can feel how jarring the union *hêrôs anthrôpoi* would have been. But in what consists the heroic distinction? First, in lineage: the heroes are either sons of gods or can easily find, within a few generations, a divine ancestor; and second, in providence: the gods are concerned with their fate. Zeus is a father to them—"father of men (*andrôn*) and gods"—who pities them and saves them from death, while he is not the father but the king of mortal creations—*hos te theoisi kai anthrôpoisi anassei* ("who is lord over gods and men"). (Benardete 2005: 14)

While it is certainly the case that Zeus pities the heroes (treating them "as Odysseus was said to treat his subjects—'he was gentle as a father'" (Benardete 2005: 14)), his pity stems directly from the humanity of the heroes that is bound up with their mortality (Homer 1974: XVII.500–501). As Benardete (2005: 15) later recognizes, "Even the gods are powerless to change man's fate no matter how many gifts they might lavish on him. Mortality and mortality alone makes for the misery of man." In other words, it is clear that the heroes are particularly special human beings for whom the achievement of *kléos* [κλέος; glory] is an option, but—as the story of Achilles reminds us—even they are mortal.

12. Euben (1990: 222) does a particularly nice job of highlighting the connection between Achilles and Socrates with regard to their rejection of the standards of their communities, arguing that "despite the differences between them, Achilles' relationship to the heroic tradition as interpreted and lived by his fellow Achaeans is similar to Socrates' (and philosophy's) relationship to the Athenian political traditions as interpreted and lived by his fellow citizens. By who they are and what they do, each suggests the precariousness of the tradition that nurtured them."

13. Apart from his failure to act on behalf of his suffering Achaean comrades-in-arms as a result of his dispute with Agamemnon, it is also the case that—once he has returned to battle and then he recognizes his connection to another warrior, this time an enemy—Achilles proceeds to kill him because his grief and anger overwhelm both his solidarity with another warrior and his understanding of what is owed to a supplicant. He tells Lycaon, another of Priam's sons, "Come, friend, face your death, you too, / And why are you so piteous about it? / Patroklos died, and he was a finer man / by far than you. You see, don't you, how large / I am, and how well-made? My father is noble, / a goddess bore me. Yet death waits for me, / for me as well" (Homer 1974: XXI.122–128).

14. Leibowitz (2010: 146), however, suggests that Socrates might be speaking ironically here as well: "The gadfly is a parasite: it feeds off the horse for its

own benefit, not the horse's. Flies need horses, not vice versa. The very image Socrates uses to describe his benefit to others suggests that benefitting himself is his chief concern." Hannah Arendt (2007: 15) sees things very differently and underscores the point I have been making throughout: "Socrates wanted to make the city more truthful by delivering each of the citizens of their truths. The method of doing this is *dialegesthai*, talking something through, but this dialectic brings forth truth *not* by destroying *doxa* or opinion, but on the contrary by revealing *doxa* in its own truthfulness. The role of the philosopher, then, is not to rule the city but to be its 'gadfly,' not to tell philosophical truths but to make citizens more truthful."

CHAPTER 6

1. It would not be a stretch to suggest that Socrates is meant to be regarded as the unmentioned character in the Allegory of the Cave and that his students—Plato, for example—would be the philosophers who have to be compelled to return to the cave. But just as Plato does not ever clarify which characters are meant to represent which historical persons, there is also nothing in the allegory to suggest that the unmentioned character chose without any compulsion to return to the cave to free future philosophers.
2. David Leibowitz (2010: 151), however, suggests that—in addition to the explicit comparison with Achilles—the *Apology* also contains an implicit (and perhaps more apt) comparison of Socrates with Odysseus; as he notes, "in the digression and epilogue Socrates moves from an invocation of Achilles to an invocation of Odysseus, the great survivor (34d2–5)." The same comparison is made, even more clearly, by Leo Strauss (1983: 48): "Socrates could beg for mercy in the customary manner since he too, as was said to and of Odysseus, is not born of an oak or a rock, and has relatives and in particular three male children, but he refuses to comply with the common practice."
3. Deneen (2000: 93) actually goes a good deal further, making the argument that Plato is actually using this snippet of text and the one that follows it to make the opposite argument from the one that Socrates sets out here: "The very act of founding the city, the very dialogue of the *Republic*, would itself be suspect under Socrates' rules of excision; again a paradox arises that succeeds in calling more attention to the curiousness of Socrates' 'censored' passages than their simple rejection would at first indicate."
4. Indeed, the footnote in which Deneen lists all of the scholars who do not comment on the meaning of Odysseus' choice is impressive in its length and in the breadth of scholarship it cites. The takeaway is that the best-known lengthy commentaries on the *Republic* do not address the choice and neither do shorter treatments, even those that are devoted specifically to the Myth of Er. His concluding sentences are particularly noteworthy: "Even Thayer's subtle and informative article analyzing the implications of the souls' choices of lives in the Myth or Er (regrettably) does not examine Odysseus's specific choice. . . . The other studies that emphasize the importance of *choice* elucidated in the myth (e.g., Annas, Reeve, and Lieb) also lack any analysis of what makes Odysseus's choice noteworthy" (Deneen 2000: 125).
5. Deneen (2000: 109) acknowledges the argument of Seth Benardete (1989: 229) on the connection between the life chosen by Odysseus' soul and the life of the just man: "perhaps we are to understand Odysseus's soul's choice to resemble that of the prephilosophic private person with the well-ordered soul who is described in Book 4—a person who avoids rule but does not seem especially likely to pursue the philosophic life of Socrates."

6. Bloom (1991: 436) effectively ends his interpretive essay with this point, though he does also note that "at all events, the teaching of the myth is a strictly human one—man in this life, without being other worldly—can attain self-sufficient happiness in the exercise of his natural powers and only in this way will he partake of eternity to the extent a human being can do so. Otherwise stated, only the philosopher has no need of the myth." In other words, Bloom does little to clarify his comments on the connection between the choice made by Odysseus' soul and the life of Socrates; instead, he concludes his essay by suggesting a quite different point—namely, that the Myth of Er is best understood as a challenge to the conventional understanding of the Greek afterlife.

7. Deneen has still more to say on the matter, however, and this adds a bit of confusion to his ultimate conclusion regarding the choice of Odysseus' soul. Turning away from the Myth of Er and back to the *Odyssey*, he claims that "his exploration of the bestial and the divine parts of the human soul makes him finally the most philosophic and the most wise of the ancient heroes: as such, he prepares the way for the next soul, almost certainly a just soul, and very likely the soul of a philosopher" (Deneen 2000: 111). It is not immediately clear whether Deneen is suggesting that Odysseus' soul has "very likely" chosen the soul of a philosopher or whether he wants to argue that Odysseus' way of life in the *Odyssey* prepares the way for the philosopher. Either way, my sense is that Deneen goes too far in his attempts to make Odysseus seem to be a more philosophical hero rather than simply disconnecting the philosopher from Odysseus entirely, as I believe Socrates suggests is the appropriate reading.

8. As Laurence Lampert (2002: 231) notes, the conclusion is "just as unpalatable to Plato's commentators—'inferior to all the others' judge Edith Hamilton and Huntington Cairns of the *Lesser Hippias*, displeased that Aristotle's discussion of it deprives them of the right to deny its Platonic authorship and strike it from the canon."

9. There remains a good deal of debate about the precise time in which the dialogue unfolds, and, as Hoerber (1962: 121–122) notes, very few scholars have risked staking out a position. Lampert (2002: 233–235), however, proceeds with certainty regarding his assessment of 420 BCE, just prior to the Olympic games of August and September, as the most likely time.

10. Weiss (1981: 288–289) sums up this objection nicely:

> Mulhern, who is representative of the many scholars who charge the *Hippias Minor* with patent equivocation and abuses of language, finds support for his unique characterization of this abuse in a pun on the word πολύτροπος. πολύτροπος, which Hippias regards as the special trait of Odysseus, itself contains the word τρόπος, which for Mulhern signifies the typical behaviour of a person, the way he is, his character. But though it contains the word τρόπος, πολύτροπος is itself not a *tropos*-term but rather a *dunamis*-term; it does not signify a person's typical behaviour but rather an ability or capacity to behave a certain way.

Thus, for Mulhern (1968: 283), the following is clear:

> That Nestor is wisest and Achilles bravest presents no difficulty to him: wisdom and bravery are qualities which indicate what sort of conduct one may expect of the man who possesses them. Because of his wisdom Nestor will give good counsel; because of his bravery Achilles will perform valorous deeds on the field of battle. These qualities distinguish a man. Resourcefulness, however, is not a quality like bravery or wisdom:

resourcefulness does not indicate what sort of conduct one may expect of the man who possesses it.

11. The passages in question are taken from the *Iliad*, where Achilles charges Odysseus with speaking falsely (Homer 1974: IX.308–313) and then, very soon thereafter, he actually speaks falsely himself (Homer 1974: IX.357). This is not to say, of course, that Odysseus is never depicted by Homer as one who speaks falsely; there are many examples in the *Odyssey* of the hero doing just that. And yet Socrates here makes reference only to the *Iliad* and the dialogue proceeds without an objection from Hippias.

12. Socrates further asserts, at this point in the dialogue, that in all things the good man acts intentionally while the bad man acts unintentionally. As Weiss (1981: 298) notes, "Although the argument generally emphasizes better/worse rather than good/evil, this is probably because of the form of the hypothesis it tests, i.e. the intentional wrongdoer is *better than* the unintentional, phrased also in comparative rather than absolute terms. As the argument makes clear, however, the one which is better is better because it is good; the one which is worse is worse because it is bad."

13. On this reading, Jane S. Zembaty (1989: 63) notes, "Since, for Socrates no one does wrong willingly, there is no genuine puzzle and his concluding remarks about 'straying up and down' and '*never* holding the same opinion in these matters' are simply an ironical swipe at Hippias." And, as Zembaty (1989: 68n15) points out, "The long list of scholars who see the key to understanding the dialogue in the phrase '*eiper tis estin houtos*' includes A.E. Taylor, Rosamund Kent Sprague, Paul Shorey, and Terence Irwin."

14. The other possibilities—if Socrates is simply walking Hippias around in circles in order to demonstrate that this supposed wise man is not, in fact, so very wise—are a) that Odysseus is not actually better than Achilles or b) that Socrates' position with regard to Odysseus is not revealed at all by this dialogue. My position is that Socrates intends to confound Hippias but that we ought also to take away something about Socrates' position from this dialogue—like all of the others—rather than simply content ourselves with his demonstration that Hippias is unwise. Since it seems clear that Socrates does not hold Achilles in higher esteem than Odysseus—given their respective treatment in the *Republic*—and since it is also improbable that Socrates holds that the just man is the one who lies voluntary, I argue that he considers Odysseus to be distinctly skilled at voluntarily speaking falsely.

15. The idea that the Myth of Er "is presented at fifth remove from the truth" is explained in greater detail by Seery (1988: 242–243): "According to Plato's own logic, his act of reproducing the Myth of Er is not even a straight example of representational artistry but is a report of Socrates' account of the myth (as told to Socrates by Er). If anyone is counting, that means that Plato's writing constitutes a mode of art at *fifth remove* from the truth."

CHAPTER 7

1. A great many of Kerry's comments from his 1971 testimony sound like they might have come from Americans who have served much more recently in Iraq or Afghanistan, which—combined with his so-called flip-flopping on whether the United States ought to go to war—made his protest record seem at least as important as his service record to many voters in the 2004 presidential election: "We saw Vietnam ravaged equally by American bombs as well as by search and destroy missions, as well as by Vietcong terrorism, and yet we listened while

this country tried to blame all of the havoc on the Viet Cong. We rationalized destroying villages in order to save them. We saw America lose her sense of morality as she accepted very coolly a My Lai and refused to give up the image of American soldiers who hand out chocolate bars and chewing gum. We learned the meaning of free fire zones, shooting anything that moves, and we watched while America placed a cheapness on the lives of orientals."

2. According to Brian Ross and Chris Vlasto (2004), the text on Kerry's website declared that the candidate "is proud of the work he did to end the war. The Nixon Administration made John Kerry one of its targets and Republicans have been smearing him ever since. John Kerry threw his ribbons and the medals of two veterans who could not attend the event, and said, 'I am not doing this for any violent reasons, but for peace and justice, and to try to make this country wake up once and for all.'"

3. The Medal of Honor has been awarded to only two living servicemen for "conspicuous gallantry" in Iraq and Afghanistan; in both cases, the men risked their lives to save the lives of others in a manner that was regarded as distinctly notable (cf. Lee 2010; Dempsey 2011).

4. In addition to the classic depiction of Odysseus with a bow rather than a sword, consider Homer's description of the hero's night raid against the Trojans in the *Iliad* (which shows the hero slaughtering the enemy in their sleep rather than defeating them in a fair fight) and his plan, at the close of the *Odyssey*, to attack Penelope's suitors only once their weapons have been hidden from them. These are not necessarily bad strategic decisions, but it is not immediate obvious that they should be considered to be heroic ones.

5. While we should, of course, be incredibly skeptical of the recollections of McCain's captors, it is interesting to note that Tran Trong Duyet—who was in charge of the so-called Hanoi Hilton at the time of McCain's imprisonment there—refers to McCain as his friend and recalls informal chats with him. He also claims that neither McCain nor any of the American prisoners in his charge were tortured (Harding 2008). Though not in direct contrast to the recollections of Tran Trong Duyet, given that the accounts of violence take place prior to McCain's transfer to Hoa Lo, Nowicki and Muller (2007b) provide details on the torture that McCain claims he (and other POWs) endured.

6. That said, and as mentioned earlier, an important part of McCain's heroism also turns on his decision not to accept the early release offered to him by the North Vietnamese and instead to insist on the principle that POWs should be released in the order of their capture (cf. Timberg 1996: 133, 137, 172).

7. After signing a confession under torture, McCain began a suicide attempt that was foiled by his captors:

> No matter how he tried to sugarcoat his actions, he could not avoid the conclusion that he had dishonored his country, his family, and himself, betrayed his comrades, and besmirched the flag.
>
> The cockiness was gone, replaced by a suffocating despair. He looked at the louvered cell window high above his head, then at the small stool in the room. He took off his dark blue prison shirt, rolled it like a rope, draped one end over his shoulder near his neck, began feeding the other end through the louvers. . . .
>
> A guard burst into the room, pulling McCain away from the window. The guard then administered another beating. For the next few days he was watched day and night. (Timberg 1996: 136)

Odysseus never reaches this level of desperation, though he certainly contemplates it. At the outset of the *Odyssey*, Homer writes that as much as he prizes *nostos*, Odysseus has seemingly given up on the possibility after seven years on Ogygia. What he seems to want now is not to return home—which he has come to regard as impossible—but to put an end to his condition, which he regards as miserable even though the nymph has attempted to bewitch him to think otherwise. In appealing to Zeus to assist Odysseus, Athena says, "She keeps on coaxing him / with her beguiling talk, to turn his mind / from Ithaca. But such desire is in him / merely to see the hearthsmoke leaping upward / from his own island, that he longs to die" (Homer 1990: I.76–80).

8. The connections between McCain and Keating run a good deal deeper than the former first disclosed when he claimed his attendance at meetings on Keating's behalf could be explained by the fact that Keating was a constituent:

> Keating was more than a constituent to McCain—he was a longtime friend and associate. McCain met Keating in 1981 at a Navy League dinner in Arizona where McCain was the speaker. Keating was a former naval aviator himself, and the two men became friends. Keating raised money for McCain's two congressional campaigns in 1982 and 1984, and for McCain's 1986 Senate bid. By 1987, McCain campaigns had received $112,000 from Keating, his relatives, and his employees—the most received by any of the Keating Five. (Keating raised a total of $300,000 for the five senators.)
>
> After McCain's election to the House in 1982, he and his family made at least nine trips at Keating's expense, three of which were to Keating's Bahamas retreat. McCain did not disclose the trips (as he was required to under House rules) until the scandal broke in 1989. At that point, he paid Keating $13,433 for the flights.
>
> And in April 1986, one year before the meeting with the regulators, McCain's wife, Cindy, and her father invested $359,100 in a Keating strip mall. (Suellentrop 2000)

9. One of the most interesting glimpses of McCain's campaign bus tour strategy was written by David Foster Wallace for *Rolling Stone*. In his "Optional Forward," Wallace (2006: 156–157) notes McCain's appeal and the reason that he chose McCain when he was given the option of any of the four best-known presidential candidates: "The only candidate I could see trying to write about was Senator John McCain (R-AZ), whom I'd seen a recent tape of on *Charlie Rose* and had decided was either incredibly honest and forthright or else just insane."

10. Seth Benardete (1997: 93–94) sets out a particularly interesting reading of the symbolism of each step of Odysseus' final journey from Ithaca, connecting it directly to both his experience in Polyphemus' cave and his descent into Hades in the *Odyssey*.

11. The Asser Institute's Centre for International & European Law (2011) describes some of the recent legal wrangling involving Munyeshyaka:

> On 21 June 2007, the International Criminal Tribunal for Rwanda (ICTR) issued arrest warrants against Wenceslas Munyeshyaka and against the former prefet of Gikongoro, Laurent Bucyibaruta, who was also exiled in France. The ICTR Prosecutor filed requests to transfer the cases of Munyeshyaka and Bucyibaruta to the French authorities. Although Wenceslas Munyeshyaka was arrested in July 2007, on 1 August 2007 the Paris Court of Appeals ruled that the arrest warrant was invalid and ordered Munyeshyaka's immediate release. According to this Court, the ICTR arrest warrant was imprecise and an infringement of French law on the presumption of innocence and ordered the immediate release of both men.

The ICTR issued a second revised arrest warrant on 13 August 2007 and the two men were again arrested by the French authorities on 5 September 2007. On 26 September 2007, The Paris Appeals Court requested further information from the ICTR stating that it could not make a decision on the basis of the information provided.

On 20 November 2007, the ICTR decided to decline jurisdiction over this affair in favour of the French judicial authorities according to rule 11 bis of the Rules of Evidence and Procedure of the ICTR. On 20 February 2008, the French authorities agreed to try Wenceslas Munyeshkaya and Bucyibaruta in France. As yet there has been little further progress in the proceedings before French courts.

12. Rusesabagina is himself an example of other-regarding heroic behavior, as he put himself directly in harm's way in an attempt to assist others; as a direct result of his actions, the lives of more than a thousand people were saved during the hundred-day Rwandan genocide in 1994 (cf. Kohen 2010).
13. The term *inyenzi*, cockroach, was first used in Rwanda in the early 1960s to refer to antigovernment guerrilla forces made up of Tutsis who had fled the country after independence from Belgium (Gourevitch 1998: 64). It soon became an abusive term for Tutsis more generally and, after its 1990 invasion, of the Tutsi-led Rwandese Patriotic Front in particular. Munyeshyaka's comment about his mother, however, requires further explanation; in Rwanda, ethnicity was determined patriarchically so the priest, despite having a Tutsi mother, was regarded as a Hutu. Perhaps even stranger, given the importance of being regarded as a Hutu at this time, is the revelation by Rusesabagina that Munyeshyaka was "a bastard. He didn't know his father" (Gourevitch 1998: 141).
14. A number of these conversations with and observations about the priest are repeated in Rusesabagina's own book about the genocide (2006: 129–130). On this particular point, about his mortality, the priest, whose name is spelled differently here (as Wenceslas Munyegeshaka), tells Rusesabagina (2006: 130) that "there have been fifty-nine priests murdered in the Christus Center already. I do not want to become the sixtieth."

Bibliography

Michael Abramowitz. 2008. "McCain Lawyers Push Back on Obama Keating Five Charges." *Washington Post*, October 6. http://voices.washingtonpost.com/44/2008/10/mccain-lawyers-push-back-on-ob.html.

Peter J. Ahrensdorf. 1995. *The Death of Socrates and the Life of Philosophy: An Interpretation of Plato's* Phaedo (Albany: State University of New York Press).

Mike Allen. 2008. "Exclusive: Obama to Hit McCain on Keating Five." *Politico*, October 6. http://www.politico.com/news/stories/1008/14302.html.

R. E. Allen. 1980. *Socrates and Legal Obligation* (Minneapolis: University of Minnesota Press).

John Alvis. 1995. *Divine Purpose and Heroic Response in Homer and Virgil: The Political Plan of Zeus* (Lanham: Rowman & Littlefield).

Julia Annas. 1981. *An Introduction to Plato's* Republic (New York: Oxford University Press).

Hannah Arendt. 2007. *The Promise of Politics* (New York: Schocken Books).

Aristophanes. 1984. *Clouds* in *Four Texts on Socrates*. Translated by Thomas G. West and Grace Starry West (Ithaca: Cornell University Press).

Aristotle. 1975. *Aristotle's* Posterior Analytics. Translated by Jonathan Barnes (Oxford: Clarendon).

———. 1984. *The Politics*. Translated by Carnes Lord (Chicago: University of Chicago Press).

Asser Institute Centre for International & European Law. 2011. "Munyeshyaka, Wenceslas." *The Domestic Case Law on International Criminal Law Database*. http://www.asser.nl/default.aspx?site_id=36&level1=15248&level2=&level3=&textid=39966.

Perry Bacon Jr. 2008. "Dems: Forget Ayers, Remember Keating." *Washington Post*, October 6. http://voices.washingtonpost.com/44/2008/10/06/dems_forget_ayers_remember_kea.html.

Seth Benardete. 1989. *Socrates' Second Sailing: On Plato's* Republic (Chicago: University of Chicago Press).

———. 1997. *The Bow and the Lyre: A Platonic Reading of the* Odyssey (Lanham: Rowman & Littlefield).

———. 2005. *Achilles and Hector: The Homeric Hero*. Edited by Ronna Burger (South Bend: St. Augustine's Press).

Allan Bloom. 1977. "Response to Hall." *5 Political Theory* 3 (August).

———. 1987. *The Closing of the American Mind* (New York: Simon and Schuster).

———. 1991. "Interpretive Essay." In *The Republic of Plato*, translated by Allan Bloom (New York: Basic Books).

David Bolotin. 1987. "The Life of Philosophy and the Immortality of the Soul: An Introduction to Plato's *Phaedo*." *7 Ancient Philosophy*.

Costica Bradatan. 2007. "Philosophy as an Art of Dying." 12 *The European Legacy* 5 (August).

Thomas C. Brickhouse and Nicholas D. Smith. 1989. *Socrates on Trial* (Princeton: Princeton University Press).

Cara Buckley. 2007. "Man Is Rescued by Stranger on Subway Tracks." *New York Times*, January 3. http://www.nytimes.com/2007/01/03/nyregion/03life.html.

Silver Bungingo. 2006. "France Asked to Extradite Catholic Cleric." *New Times*, January 7. http://www.rwandagateway.org/article.php3?id_article = 1472.

Ronna Burger. 1984. *The* Phaedo: *A Platonic Labyrinth* (New Haven: Yale University Press).

Cathy Callaway. 1993. "Perjury and the Unsworn Oath." 123 *Transactions of the American Philological Association.*

———. 1998. "Odysseus' Three Unsworn Oaths." 119 *American Journal of Philology* 2 (Summer).

Joseph Campbell. 1972. *The Hero with a Thousand Faces* (Princeton: Princeton University Press).

Paul A. Cantor. 1976. *Shakespeare's Rome, Republic and Empire* (Ithaca: Cornell University Press).

Diskin Clay. 1972. "Socrates' Mulishness and Heroism." 17 *Phronesis* 1.

O. C. Cramer. 1973. *Odysseus in the* Iliad (PhD diss., University of Texas).

Joseph Cropsey. 1986. "The Dramatic End of Plato's Socrates." 14 *Interpretation* 2&3 (May and September).

Tim Dant. 2003. *Critical Social Theory: Culture, Society and Critique* (London: SAGE).

Jim Davenport. 2007. "McCain: Roe V. Wade Should Be Overturned." *Washington Post*, February 18. http://www.washingtonpost.com/wp-dyn/content/article/2007/02/18/AR2007021801100.html.

LTC Jason Dempsey. 2011. "Our Heroes Are All Around Us." *White House Blog.* http://www.whitehouse.gov/blog/2011/07/12/our-heroes-are-all-around-us.

Patrick J. Deneen. 2000. *The Odyssey of Political Theory: The Politics of Departure and Return* (Lanham: Rowman & Littlefield).

Todd Dorman. 2011. "Paul: Killing bin Laden 'Absolutely Was Not Necessary." *Gazette*, May 12. http://thegazette.com/2011/05/12/paul-killing-bin-laden-absolutely-was-not-necessary/.

Anthony T. Edwards. 1985. "Achilles in the Underworld: *Iliad, Odyssey,* and *Aethiopis.*" 26 *Greek, Roman, and Byzantine Studies* 3 (Autumn).

J. Peter Euben. 1990. *The Tragedy of Political Theory: The Road Not Taken* (Princeton: Princeton University Press).

Euripides. 1954. *The Bacchae and Other Plays.* Translated by Philip Vellacott (London: Penguin Classics).

Bernard Fenik. 1968. *Typical Battle Scenes in the* Iliad: *Studies in the Narrative Technique of Homeric Battle Descriptions* (Wiesbaden: Franz Steiner).

Michael Ferullu. 2000. "Life on the Straight Talk Express: All McCain, All of the Time." *CNN*, March 13. http://articles.cnn.com/2000–02–17/politics/mccain.bus_1_john-mccain-straight-talk-express-media-strategy?_s=PM:ALLPOLITICS.

Margalit Finkelberg. 1995. "Odysseus and the Genus 'Hero.'" 42 *Greece & Rome* 1 (April).

Simon Goldhill. 1991. *The Poet's Voice: Essays on Poetics and Greek Literature* (Cambridge: Cambridge University Press).

Philip Gourevitch. 1998. *We Wish to Inform You That Tomorrow We Will Be Killed with Our Families: Stories from Rwanda* (New York: Picador USA).

Trudy Govier. 2002. *Forgiveness and Revenge* (London: Routledge).

V. J. Gray. 1989. "Xenophon's *Defense of Socrates:* The Rhetorical Background to the Socratic Problem." 39 *Classical Quarterly* 1.

N. A. Greenberg. 1965. "Socrates' Choice in the *Crito*." 70 *Harvard Studies in Classical Philology*.

Arnaud Grellier. 2004. "Five Rwandan Files Kept on the Back Burner." *International Justice Tribune*, July 5. http://www.justicetribune.com/index.php?page=v2_article&id=2703.

Dale Hall. 1977. "The *Republic* and the 'Limits of Politics.'" 5 *Political Theory* 3 (August).

Dean Hammer. 2002. *The* Iliad *as Politics: The Performance of Political Thought* (Norman: University of Oklahoma Press).

Nathan Hanna. 2007. "Socrates and Superiority." 45 *Southern Journal of Philosophy* 2 (Summer).

Andrew Harding. 2008. "When John McCain Was My Captive." *BBC News*, June 23. http://news.bbc.co.uk/2/hi/asia-pacific/7459946.stm.

Alfred Heubeck and Arie Hoekstra, eds. 1990. *A Commentary on Homer's Odyssey: Volume II: Books IX–XVI* (New York: Oxford University Press).

Angela Hobbs. 2000. *Plato and the Hero: Courage, Manliness and the Impersonal Good* (Cambridge: Cambridge University Press).

Robert G. Hoerber. 1962. "Plato's 'Lesser Hippias.'" 7 *Phronesis* 2.

Richard Holway. 1994. "Achilles, Socrates, and Democracy." 22 *Political Theory* 4 (November).

Homer. 1974. *The Iliad*. Translated by Robert Fitzgerald (New York: Anchor Books).

———. 1990. *The Odyssey*. Translated by Robert Fitzgerald (New York: Vintage Books).

———. 1999. *The Odyssey*. Translated by Richmond Lattimore (New York: Harper Perennial Modern Classics).

———. 2006. *The Odyssey*. Edited by Bernard Knox. Translated by Robert Fagles (New York: Penguin Classics).

Max Horkheimer and Theodor W. Adorno. 1988. *Dialectic of Enlightenment*. Translated by John Cumming (New York: Continuum).

David Ignatius. 2004. "Dangers of Defaming a War Hero." *Washington Post*, August 24. http://www.washingtonpost.com/wp-dyn/articles/A27210–2004Aug23.html.

Charles H. Kahn. 1996. *Plato and the Socratic Dialogue* (Cambridge: Cambridge University Press).

John Kerry. 1971. "Testimony to the Senate Foreign Relations Committee," quoted in "John Kerry Then: Hear Kerry's Historic 1971 Testimony against the Vietnam War." *Democracy Now*. http://www.democracynow.org/2004/2/20/john_kerry_then_hear_kerrys_historic.

Jinyo Kim. 2000. *The Pity of Achilles: Oral Style and the Unity of the* Iliad (Lanham: Rowman & Littlefield).

Felly Kimenyi. 2006. "Gen. Munyakazi Trial Re-Adjourned." *New Times*, May 10. http://allafrica.com/stories/200605110385.html.

Katherine Callen King. 1987. *Achilles: Paradigms of the War Hero from Homer to the Middle Ages* (Berkeley: University of California Press).

Bernard M. W. Knox. 1983. *The Heroic Temper: Studies in Sophoclean Tragedy* (Berkeley: University of California Press).

Sarah Kofman. 1998. *Socrates: Fictions of a Philosopher*. Translated by Catherine Porter (Ithaca: Cornell University Press).

Ari Kohen. 2010. "A Case of Moral Heroism: Sympathy, Personal Identification, and Mortality in Rwanda." 11 *Human Rights Review* 1 (March).

Janusz Korczak. 2003. *Ghetto Diary* (New Haven: Yale University Press).

Scott Kramer. 1988. "Socrates' Dream: *Crito* 44a–b." 83 *Classical Journal* 3 (February–March).

Laurence Lampert. 2002. "Socrates' Defense of Polytropic Odysseus: Lying and Wrong-Doing in Plato's *Lesser Hippias*." 64 *Review of Politics* 2 (Spring).

Jesse Lee. 2010. "President Obama Presents the Medal of Honor to Staff Sergeant Salvatore Giunta: 'We're All in Your Debt.'" *White House Blog.* http://www.whitehouse.gov/blog/2010/11/16/president-obama-presents-medal-honor-staff-sergeant-salvatore-giunta-we-re-all-your-.

David Leibowitz. 2010. *The Ironic Defense of Socrates: Plato's* Apology (New York: Cambridge University Press).

Betty Jean Lifton. 1988. *The King of Children: A Biography of Janusz Korczak* (New York: Schocken Books).

———. 2003. "Who Was Janusz Korczak?" In *Ghetto Diary*, edited by Janusz Korczak (New Haven: Yale University Press).

Bruce Lincoln. 1991. *Death, War, and Sacrifice: Studies in Ideology and Practice* (Chicago: University of Chicago Press).

Hugh Lloyd-Jones. 1984. *The Justice of Zeus* (Berkeley: University of California Press).

W. Thomas MacCary. 1982. *Childlike Achilles: Ontogeny and Phylogeny in the* Iliad (New York: Columbia University Press).

Bonnie MacLachlan. 1993. *The Age of Grace:* Charis *in Early Greek Poetry* (Princeton: Princeton University Press).

Avishai Margalit. 2002. *The Ethics of Memory* (Cambridge: Harvard University Press).

Gebe Martinez. 2008. "McCain's Immigration Zigzag." *Politico*, June 20. http://www.politico.com/news/stories/0608/11240.html.

Jenny Matthews. 1999. *Father Wenceslas Munyeshyaka: In the Eyes of the Survivors of Sainte Famille* (London: African Rights). http://www.africanrights.unimondo.org/html/munpres.html.

John McCain and Mark Salter. 2003. *Worth the Fighting For: The Education of an American Maverick and the Heroes Who Inspired Him* (New York: Random House).

Robert D. McFadden. 2009. "Pilot Is Hailed after Jetliner's Icy Plunge." *New York Times*, January 15. http://www.nytimes.com/2009/01/16/nyregion/16crash.html.

Robert Metcalf. 2009. "Socrates and Achilles." In *Reexamining Socrates in the* Apology, edited by Patricia Fagan and John Russon (Evanston: Northwestern University Press).

Brian Montopoli. 2010. "John McCain: I'm Not a Maverick." *CBS News Political Hotsheet*, April 5. http://www.cbsnews.com/8301–503544_162–20001775–503544.html.

Anna Lydia Motto and John R. Clark. 1969. "Isê Dais: The Honor of Achilles," 2 *Arethusa* 2 (Fall).

J.J. Mulhern. 1968. "ΤΡΟΠΟΣ and ΠΟΛΥΤΡΟΠΙΑ in Plato's *Hippias Minor*." 22 *Phoenix* 4 (Winter).

Emma Mustich. 2011. "Bush Torture Architect: Killing Osama Was Wrong!" *Salon*, May 6. http://www.salon.com/news/politics/war_room/2011/05/06/john_yoo_bin_laden.

Terry M. Neal. 1999. "McCain Softens Abortion Stand." *Washington Post*, August 24, A4. http://www.washingtonpost.com/wp-srv/politics/campaigns/wh2000/stories/mccain082499.htm.

Susan Neiman. 2009. *Moral Clarity: A Guide for Grown-Up Idealists* (Princeton: Princeton University Press).

Friedrich Nietzsche. 1968. *Twilight of the Idols* in *The Portable Nietzsche*. Edited and translated by Walter Kaufmann (New York: Viking Press).

———. 1974. *The Gay Science*. Translated by Walter Kaufmann (New York: Random House).

———. 1982. *Thus Spoke Zarathustra* in *The Portable Nietzsche*. Edited and translated by Walter Kaufmann (New York: Penguin Books).

———. 1992a. *Beyond Good and Evil: Prelude to a Philosophy of the Future* in *Basic Writings of Nietzsche*. Edited and translated by Walter Kaufmann (New York: Modern Library).

———. 1992b. *Human, All Too Human* in *Basic Writings of Nietzsche*. Edited and translated by Walter Kaufmann (New York: Modern Library).

———. 1992c. *On the Genealogy of Morals* in *Basic Writings of Nietzsche*. Edited and translated by Walter Kaufmann (New York: Modern Library).

———. 1992d. *The Wanderer and His Shadow* in *Basic Writings of Nietzsche*. Edited and translated by Walter Kaufmann (New York: Modern Library).

Dan Nowicki and Bill Muller. 2007a. "McCain Profile: Overcoming Scandal, Moving On," *Arizona Republic*, March 1. http://www.azcentral.com/news/election/mccain/articles/2007/03/01/20070301mccainbio-chapter8.html.

———. 2007b. "McCain Profile: Prisoner of War." *Arizona Republic*, March 1. http://www.azcentral.com/news/election/mccain/articles/2007/03/01/20070301 mccainbio-chapter3.html.

Robert L. Oprisko. 2012. *Honor: A Phenomenology* (New York: Routledge).

Adam M. Parry. 1989. "The Language of Achilles." In *The Language of Achilles and Other Papers*, edited by P. H. J. Lloyd-Jones (Oxford: Oxford University Press).

Kate Phillips. 2008. "McCain Gets an Apology." *New York Times Caucus Blog*, April 8. http://thecaucus.blogs.nytimes.com/2008/04/08/mccain-gets-an-apology/.

Pindar. 1980. *Victory Songs*. Translated by Frank J. Nisetich (Baltimore: Johns Hopkins University Press).

Plato. 1984a. *Apology of Socrates* in *Four Texts on Socrates*. Translated by Thomas G. West and Grace Starry West (Ithaca: Cornell University Press).

———. 1984b. *Crito* in *Four Texts on Socrates*. Translated by Thomas G. West and Grace Starry West (Ithaca: Cornell University Press).

———. 1991. *The Republic of Plato*. Translated by Allan Bloom (New York: Basic Books).

———. 1996a. *Gorgias* in *Protagoras, Philebus, and Gorgias*. Translated by Benjamin Jowett (New York: Prometheus Books).

———. 1996b. *Protagoras* in *Protagoras, Philebus, and Gorgias*. Translated by Benjamin Jowett (New York: Prometheus Books).

———. 1997a. *Greater Hippias* in *Complete Works*. Edited by John M. Cooper and D. S. Hutchinson (Indianapolis: Hackett).

———. 1997b. *Laws* in *Complete Works*. Edited by John M. Cooper and D. S. Hutchinson (Indianapolis: Hackett).

———. 1997c. *Lesser Hippias* in *Complete Works*. Edited by John M. Cooper and D. S. Hutchinson (Indianapolis: Hackett).

———. 1997d. *Timaeus* in *Complete Works*. Edited by John M. Cooper and D. S. Hutchinson (Indianapolis: Hackett).

———. 1999a. *Meno* in *Great Dialogues of Plato*. Translated by W. H. D. Rouse. Edited by Eric H. Warmington and Philip G. Rouse (New York: Signet Classic).

———. 1999b. *Phaedo* in *Great Dialogues of Plato*. Translated by W. H. D. Rouse. Edited by Eric H. Warmington and Philip G. Rouse (New York: Signet Classic).

———. 1999c. *Symposium* in *Great Dialogues of Plato*. Translated by W. H. D. Rouse. Edited by Eric H. Warmington and Philip G. Rouse (New York: Signet Classic).

———. 2000. *The Trial and Death of Socrates: Euthyphro, Apology, Crito, Death Scene from Phaedo*. Translated by G. M. A. Grube and rev. John M. Cooper (Indianapolis: Hackett).

Todd S. Purdum. 2010. "The Man Who Never Was." *Vanity Fair*, November. http://www.vanityfair.com/politics/features/2010/11/mccain-201011.

Chris Raphael. 2002. "Politically Incorrect: A Eulogy." *Big Story*, June 3. http://thebigstory.org/ov/ov-politicallyincorrect.html.

Walter V. Robinson. 2004. "Bush Fell Short on Duty at Guard: Records Show Pledges Unmet." *Boston Globe*, September 8. http://www.boston.com/news/nation/articles/2004/09/08/bush_fell_short_on_duty_at_guard/.

Richard Rorty. 1998. *Philosophical Papers*. Vol. 3, *Truth and Progress* (Cambridge: Cambridge University Press).

Stanley Rosen. 2005. *Plato's* Republic: *A Study* (New Haven: Yale University Press).

Brian Ross and Chris Vlasto. 2004. "Did Kerry Discard Vietnam Medals?" *ABC News*, April 26. http://abcnews.go.com/Politics/story?id=123495&page=1.

Louis A. Ruprecht Jr. 1998. "Homeric Wisdom and Heroic Friendship." 97 *South Atlantic Quarterly* 1 (Winter).

Paul Rusesabagina. 2006. *An Ordinary Man*, with Tom Zoellner (New York: Viking Penguin).

Jim Rutenberg, Marilyn W. Thompson, David D. Kirkpatrick, and Stephen Labaton. 2008. "For McCain, Self-Confidence on Ethics Poses Its Own Risk." *New York Times*, February 21. http://www.nytimes.com/2008/02/21/us/politics/21mccain.html?pagewanted=all.

William Saletan and Jacob Weisberg. 2004. "Unfriendly Fire: Liar vs. Coward in the Vietnam ad War." *Slate*, August 18. http://www.slate.com/id/2105353/.

Ted Sampley. 1992. "John McCain: The Manchurian Candidate." *U.S. Veteran Dispatch*, December. http://www.usvetdsp.com/manchuan.htm.

Paul C. Santilli and Kristine S. Santilli. 2004. "On the Strange Relation between Heroic Socrates and Wise Achilles." In Mythos *and* Logos: *How to Regain the Love of Wisdom*, edited by Albert A. Anderson, Steven V. Hicks, and Lech Witkowski (Amsterdam: Rodopi).

Arlene W. Saxonhouse. 1988. "*Thymos*, Justice, and Moderation of Anger in the Story of Achilles." In *Understanding the Political Spirit: Philosophical Investigations from Socrates to Nietzsche*, edited by Catherine H. Zuckert (New Haven: Yale University Press).

Seth L. Schein. 1984. *The Mortal Hero: An Introduction to Homer's* Iliad (Berkeley: University of California Press).

Dennis J. Schmidt. 2001. *On Germans and Other Greeks: Tragedy and Ethical Life* (Bloomington: Indiana University Press).

Robert Schmiel. 1987. "Achilles in Hades." 82 *Classical Philology* 1 (January).

Carl Schmitt. 1996. *The Concept of the Political*. Translated by George Schwab (Chicago: University of Chicago Press).

John Evan Seery. 1988. "Politics as Ironic Community: On the Themes of Descent and Return in Plato's *Republic*." 16 *Political Theory* 2 (May).

Eliot Sefton. 2011. "Nuremberg Prosecutor: Bin Laden Killing Was Wrong." *First Post*, May 8. http://www.thefirstpost.co.uk/78634,news-comment,news-politics,nuremberg-prosecutor-bin-laden-killing-was-wrong-video.

Liliana Segura. 2008. "Michael Moore Dares to Ask: What's So Heroic about Being Shot Down While Bombing Innocent Civilians?" *AlterNet*, August 21. http://www.alternet.org/blogs/waroniraq/95906.

William Shakespeare. 1967. *Coriolanus*. Edited by G. R. Hibbard (London: Penguin Books).

———. 1992. *Macbeth*. Edited by Barbara A. Mowat and Paul Werstine (New York: Washington Square Press).

———. 1994. *Henry IV, Part 1*. Edited by Barbara A. Mowat and Paul Werstine (New York: Washington Square Press).

Michael D. Shear. 2008. "Bloggers Find Something Fishy in McCain Site's 'Family Recipes.'" *Washington Post*, April 16. http://www.washingtonpost.com/wp-dyn/content/article/2008/04/15/AR2008041502881.html.

———. 2010. "McCain Appears to Shift on 'Don't Ask, Don't Tell.'" *Washington Post*, February 3. http://www.washingtonpost.com/wp-dyn/content/article/2010/02/02/AR2010020202588.html.

Amy Silverman. 1999. "Is John McCain a War Hero?" *Phoenix New Times*, March 25. http://www.phoenixnewtimes.com/1999-03-25/news/is-john-mccain-a-war-hero/.

W. B. Stanford. 1993. *The Ulysses Theme* (Dallas: Spring).

Paul Stern. 1993. *Socratic Rationalism and Political Philosophy: An Interpretation of Plato's* Phaedo (Albany: State University of New York Press).

Leo Strauss. 1966. *Socrates and Aristophanes* (Chicago: University of Chicago Press).

———. 1983. *Studies in Platonic Political Philosophy* (Chicago: University of Chicago Press).

Chris Suellentrop. 2000. "Is John McCain a Crook?" *Slate Magazine*, February 18. http://www.slate.com/id/1004633/.

H. S. Thayer. 1988. "The Myth of Er." 5 *History of Philosophy Quarterly* 4 (October).

Robert Timberg. 1996. *The Nightingale's Song* (New York: Touchstone).

Alexis de Tocqueville. 2002. *Democracy in America*. Edited and translated by Harvey C. Mansfield and Delba Winthrop (Chicago: University of Chicago Press).

U.S. Army Center of Military History. 2010a. "Medal of Honor Recipients: Afghanistan." December 3. http://www.history.army.mil/html/moh/afghanistan.html.

U.S. Army Center of Military History. 2010b. "Medal of Honor Recipients: Iraq." December 3. http://www.history.army.mil/html/moh/iraq.html.

Ralph Vartabedian and Richard A. Serrano. 2008. "McCain's Mishaps in the Cockpit." *Los Angeles Times*, October 6. http://articles.latimes.com/2008/oct/06/nation/na-aviator6.

Jean-Pierre Vernant. 1999. "Odysseus in Person." Translated by James Ker. 67 *Representations* (Summer).

Gregory Vlastos. 1991. *Socrates: Ironist and Moral Philosopher* (Ithaca: Cornell University Press).

Eric Voegelin. 1952. *The New Science of Politics: An Introduction* (Chicago: University of Chicago Press).

———. 1953. "The World of Homer." 15 *Review of Politics* 4 (October).

———. 1966. *Order and History: Plato and Aristotle*. Vol. 3 (Baton Rouge: Louisiana State University Press).

H. T. Wade-Gery. 1952. *The Poet of the* Iliad (Cambridge: Cambridge University Press).

Robert Walke. 2004. "Rwanda's Religious Reflections." *BBC News*, April 1. http://news.bbc.co.uk/1/hi/world/africa/3561365.stm.

David Foster Wallace. 2006. "Up Simba: Seven Days on the Trail of an Anticandidate." In *Consider the Lobster and Other Essays* (New York: Little, Brown).

Ernest J. Weinrib. 1982. "Obedience to the Law in Plato's *Crito*." 27 *American Journal of Jurisprudence*.

Roslyn Weiss. 1981. "'Ο Άγαθο΄ς as 'Ο Δυνατο΄ς in the *Hippias Minor*." 31 *Classical Quarterly* 2 (December).

M. L. West. 1985. *The Hesiodic Catalogue of Women: Its Nature, Structure, and Origins* (New York: Oxford University Press).

———. 1999. *The East Face of Helicon: West Asiatic Elements in Greek Poetry and Myth* (New York: Oxford University Press).

Thomas G. West. 1979. *Plato's Apology of Socrates: An Interpretation, with a New Translation* (Ithaca: Cornell University Press).

———. 1984. "Introduction." In *Four Texts on Socrates*, translated by Thomas G. West and Grace Starry West (Ithaca: Cornell University Press).

A. D. Woozley. 1979. *Law and Obedience: The Arguments of Plato's* Crito (Chapel Hill: University of North Carolina Press).

Xenophon. 1990. *Socrates' Defence* in *Conversations of Socrates*. Translated by Hugh Tredennick and Robin Waterfield. Edited by Robin Waterfield (New York: Penguin Books).

Jane S. Zembaty. 1989. "Socrates' Perplexity in Plato's *Hippias Minor*." In *Essays in Ancient Greek Philosophy III: Plato*, edited by John P. Anton and Anthony Preus (Albany: State University of New York Press).

Catherine H. Zuckert. 2009. "Becoming Socrates." In *Reexamining Socrates in the* Apology, edited by Patricia Fagan and John Russon (Evanston: Northwestern University Press).

Michael Zuckert. 1984. "Rationalism & Political Responsibility: Just Speech & Just Deed in the *Clouds* & the *Apology of Socrates*." 17 *Polity* 2 (Winter).

E. R. Zumwalt Jr. 1969. "Silver Star Medal Citation: John Forbes Kerry." http://homepage.mac.com/chinesemac/kerry_medals/PDFs/Silver_Star.pdf.

Index

Made in the USA
Middletown, DE
25 November 2016